P9-DKE-889

DATE DUE

DEC W.P.M.
8 '99

DISCARD

GAYLORD   PRINTED IN U.S.A.

323.042
C246q

BETHANY
COLLEGE
LIBRARY

DISCARD

THE QUIET ATHENIAN

The Quiet Athenian

L. B. CARTER

CLARENDON PRESS · OXFORD

1986

Oxford University Press, Walton Street, Oxford OX2 6DP
Oxford New York Toronto
Delhi Bombay Calcutta Madras Karachi
Kuala Lumpur Singapore Hong Kong Tokyo
Nairobi Dar es Salaam Cape Town
Melbourne Auckland
and associated companies in
Beirut Berlin Ibadan Nicosia

Oxford is a trade mark of Oxford University Press

Published in the United States
by Oxford University Press, New York

©L. B. Carter 1986

All rights reserved. No part of this publication may be reproduced,
stored in a retrieval system, or transmitted, in any form or by any means,
electronic, mechanical, photocopying, recording, or otherwise, without
the prior permission of Oxford University Press

British Library Cataloguing in Publication Data
Carter, L. B.
The quiet Athenian.
1. Democracy — Public opinion   2. Public
opinion — Greece — Athens   3. Athens
(Greece) — Politics and government
I. Title
321.8'0938'5   JC75.D36
ISBN 0-19-814870-4

Library of Congress Cataloging in Publication Data
Carter, L. B.
The quiet Athenian.
Revision of thesis (doctoral) — London University, 1982.
Bibliography: p;
Includes index.
1. Political participation — Greece — Athens.   2. Athens
(Greece) — Politics and government. I. Title.
JC79.A8C35   1986   323'.042'09385   86–3565
ISBN 0-19-814870-4

Set by Dobbie Typesetting Service
Printed in Great Britain at
The University Printing House, Oxford
by David Stanford
Printer to the University

καὶ τοὺς θησαυροὺς τῶν πάλαι σοφῶν ἀνδρῶν,
οὓς ἐκεῖνοι κατέλιπον ἐν βιβλίοις γράψαντες,
ἀνελίττων κοινῇι σὺν τοῖς φίλοις διέρχομαι.

Xenophon, *Memorabilia*, 1. 6. 14

323.042
C2469

Preface

This work first saw the light under the title 'Apragmosyne: A Study in Fifth Century Athenian Society', and was presented to London University as a doctoral thesis in 1982. It was then completely rewritten, substantially reordered, and called 'Political Quietism and the Contemplative Life in Classical Athens'. Finally, as this was felt to be a bit of a mouthful, it took on its present title. These two previous titles will, however, give an idea of what it is about: I wanted to write about all those citizens in classical Athens who, for a variety of reasons — distaste, fear, hatred, inconvenience — were out of tune with the democracy. I also felt that this aspect of life in Athens threw an essential light on the origin of Plato's version of the contemplative life. The book was to be organized through what I intended to be an exhaustive study of the uses of the word *apragmosynē* — quietism — and its cognates during the hundred years after 430 BC.

Despite thorough revision I am aware that the book still bears the hallmarks (and faults) of a doctoral thesis; I have not had the courage to do what I would most have liked, to jettison *all* the footnotes. Rest assured, they are shorter and fewer than they were.

Otherwise, there is nothing else to say except thank you to Dr Oswyn Murray and Professor S. C. Humphreys for their advice and encouragement; to Professor Humphreys in particular, the supervisor of the original thesis, who continued to read and criticize successive versions of it.

L.B.C.

Contents

Abbreviations   x

1. Fame and Honour   1
2. 431: *Apragmones* and the Athenian Empire   26
3. Noble Youths   52
4. The Peasant Farmer   76
5. Rich Quietists   99
6. The Contemplative Life: the Presocratics   131
7. The Contemplative Life: to Plato   155
8. Conclusion   187

Appendix: The Date of Composition of Pericles'
Speeches at Th. 2. 35 and 2. 60   195

Bibliography   197

Index of Passages Quoted or Cited in the Text   205

General Index   208

Abbreviations

BOOKS

APF   *Athenian Propertied Families*, by J. K. Davies (Oxford, 1971).

CAH   *Cambridge Ancient History*.

DK   *Die Fragmente der Vorsokratiker*, by H. Diels, revised by W. Kranz (Berlin, 1952).

EGP   *Early Greek Philosophy*, by J. Burnet (1st edn., London, 1890; 4th edn., 1930).

FGH   *Die Fragmente der griechischen Historiker*, by F. Jacoby (Leiden, 1954).

HCT   *A Historical Commentary on Thucydides*, by A. W. Gomme, A. Andrewes, and K. J. Dover (Oxford, 1959–70).

IG   *Inscriptiones Graecae*.

K   *Comicorum Atticorum Fragmenta*, by T. Kock (Leipzig, 1880).

LCL   Loeb Classical Library.

LSJ   *A Greek Lexicon*, by H. G. Liddell and R. Scott, revised by H. S. Jones (9th edn., Oxford, 1940).

ML   *Greek Historical Inscriptions*, edited by R. Meiggs and D. Lewis (Oxford, 1969).

N   *Tragicorum Graecorum Fragmenta* by A. Nauck, with supplement by B. Snell (Hildesheim, 1964).

PA   *Prosopographica Attica*.

RE   *Real-Encyclopädie*, edited by Pauly–Wissowa.

SGHI   *A Selection of Greek Historical Inscriptions*, edited by M. N. Tod (Oxford, 1948).

JOURNALS

AJAH   *American Journal of Ancient History*.

AJP   *American Journal of Philology*.

BICS   *Bulletin of the Institute of Classical Studies*.

BSA   *Annual of the British School at Athens*.

CJ   *Classical Journal*.

Class. et Med.   *Classica et Mediaevalia*.

CP   *Classical Philology*.

CQ	*Classical Quarterly.*
CRAI	*Comptes rendus de l'Académie des Inscriptions et Belles-Lettres.*
GRBS	*Greek, Roman and Byzantine Studies.*
HSCP	*Harvard Studies in Classical Philology.*
JHS	*Journal of Hellenic Studies.*
TAPhA	*Transactions of the American Philological Association.*
YCS	*Yale Classical Studies.*

1

Fame and Honour

Before beginning a discussion of *apragmosynē*—quietism—in Athens, it is important to be clear about what it was that the *apragmōn*—the quietist—was reacting against. In order to show how odd the *apragmōn* was, how un-Greek, this first chapter will make a brief review of literature from Homer to Aristotle so as to remind the reader of what is, perhaps, almost too obvious to mention, namely that the pursuit of fame and honour was the foremost preoccupation of any Greek who could afford it. Why this should be so is a difficult and obscure question, too big to be attempted here; it must be connected, however, with the fact that Greeks lived in very small communities, and frequently in a state of war with their neighbours. Greek history contains many examples of Greek cities completely annihilated, the male citizens put to death, the women and children sold into slavery. In these circumstances, the individual's sense of personal security was intimately bound up with the security of the city. Again, because of its smallness, the physical reality of the community was present to the individual in a way that is difficult for us to grasp, accustomed as we are to conceiving of the State in abstract terms. Because of the intimate connection between the security of the individual and that of the city, it follows that there was no existence outside the social existence, no reality outside the social reality; hence, the greater one's participation in that social reality, the greater one's sense of self. One was what one was perceived to be; one was measured, and one measured oneself, by one's *timē*—one's social standing, one's public esteem. The pursuit of *timē*, and its companion fame, as understood from Homer to Aristotle, is the subject of this first chapter.

   Fame (*kleos*), honour (*timē*), and glory (*kudos*) are very closely allied in Homer, yet their meanings are quite distinct and I want now to try to distinguish them.

   Fame, first, is often indicated as the highest goal at which a

through space. Thus we are told that it will never die — that is, it will extend indefinitely forward through time; again, it is 'immortal', and it will 'stretch after one'. Menelaus constructs Agamemnon a tomb in Egypt so that he might have 'unquenchable fame' (*Od.* 4. 584), and at the end of the *Odyssey*, in the scene in Hades, the shade of Agamemnon describes to that of Achilles how Achilles' body was cremated and a mound heaped over his remains:

> So that it will be seen from afar off by those now living,
> And by those who come after . . .
> Your name will never die, and evermore among men
> Will you have noble fame, Achilles.

(24. 83)

As well as stretching forward in time, fame also extends in space: it is spread abroad. It frequently reaches up to heaven. Odysseus identifies himself to King Alcinous as 'Odysseus, son of Laertes, known to all men for cunning, and my fame reaches to heaven' (9. 19). Agamemnon enjoys the same distinction, as does Nestor's shield, and anyone who went out to spy on the Trojans by night would gain 'heaven-reaching fame' (*Il.* 10. 212).

An important means of disseminating fame, both in space and time, was the Homeric bard. It was the bard's function to sing the *klea* of men, usually of those who have 'gone before'. *Klea* are the deeds by which men win *kleos* (*Od.* 1. 338).[3]

It is these spatial and temporal aspects which distinguish fame from honour (*timē*): *timē* exists strictly in the here and now. Otherwise they coexist closely, as is made clear in the famous speech of Sarpedon to Glaucus in the *Iliad*. In the midst of the hottest fighting, Sarpedon draws breath to reflect on a hero's lot:

Glaucus, why is it that we are specially honoured in Lycia, with pride of place, the best meats, and well-filled wine cups, and all men look on us as if we were immortal . . . so now it is our duty to take our place among the foremost of the Lycians and to endure the blazing

---

[3] Cf. *Od.* 8. 73 and *Il.* 9. 189. For other uses of *kleos* in the *Iliad*, see 5. 172; 5. 273; 7. 451; 11. 227; 13. 364; 17. 16; 17. 131; 17. 143; 17. 232. There are also thirty-three uses in the *Odyssey*; some of these simply mean 'news' which is the root meaning of the word, e.g. 1. 283; 2. 217; 13. 415; 16. 461; 23. 137. Sometimes the phrase *kleos esthlon* (good report) occurs, a sort of transitional usage. Penelope also has *kleos*, especially by comparison with Clytemnestra (24. 196). The use of *kleos* is almost always formulaic.

of battle, so if any of the thick-armoured Lycians should see us, he would say: 'Not without renown are our kings, ruling in Lycia, eating the fat meat, drinking the sweet wine . . .'

(12. 310)

This speech explains why Achilles does not go home. The King has achieved his position by virtue of his prowess among the *promachoi* — the forefighters — and if he does not set the example in battle he has no authority to demand pride of place among his people. But it is on this point that the dispute arises between Achilles and Agamemnon. Achilles complains that whereas he, Achilles, is the foremost fighter, it is Agamemnon who takes the lion's share of the spoils. This share-out, *geras*, is the material counterpart to *timē*, and without it, *timē* is invalidated. Achilles complains that he takes a greater part in the fighting but never receives a share in the booty commensurate with his achievement:

My hands take the greater part of the painful work of fighting, but when the share-out comes, your portion is far greater, and I return to my ships, weary with fighting, carrying some small thing, my own. But now I am returning to Phthia, since it is far better to go home in my beaked ships than to remain here without *timē*, to pile up wealth for you.

(1. 165)[4]

The significance of this material counterpart is brought out by Phoenix when he urges Achilles to accept the gifts offered by Agamemnon's embassy: 'So go back, on condition that you get the gifts, for the people will honour you like a god. But if you go back into the deadly fighting without the gifts you will no longer have so much honour, however hard you fight.' (9. 602.)

The issue in Book 1 is made acute because there is no spare spoil; everything is shared out, and when Agamemnon has to part with Chryseis in order to save the expedition, he has to take something from one of the other kings in order to restore his

---

[4] Compare Achilles' complaint to the embassy: 'There are shares for those who stay behind and those who fight; thus the base (*kakos*) and the noble (*esthlos*) are held in like esteem.' (9. 318.) These terms are discussed exhaustively by Adkins in the opening chapters of *Merit*.

relative standing, his *timē* (1. 118); thus Achilles is publicly and humiliatingly deprived of his *geras*, Briseis (cf. 9. 111).[5] There is a conflict between the situation which Sarpedon describes and that brought out by the argument between Agamemnon and Achilles. According to Sarpedon, precedence among the people, food, drink, and land, were all to be had at the price of excellence. He who was foremost among the *promachoi* took pride of place at home, took the lion's share of the material wealth. This is what Achilles expected. He was disappointed, and the reason is set forth by Nestor: Achilles should not expect the same *timē* as Agamemnon, because Agamemnon is a sceptre-bearing king to whom Zeus has given *kudos* (glory): 'Neither you, Achilles, should seek to match your strength with the King, since a sceptre-bearing king to whom Zeus has given glory has no equal share of *timē*. If you are stronger you have a goddess for your mother, yet this man is better since he rules over more than you.' (1. 277.)[6] Agamemnon rules over a bigger kingdom than Achilles and thus establishes for himself a superior *timē* and a prior claim on *geras*.

Kudos and *timē* are closely linked in the *Iliad*. They are often coupled together as if they had virtually the same meaning. *Kudos*, however, unlike *timē* and *kleos*, has no extraneous associations: it is glory, pure and simple. An important aspect of both is that they operate within what has been called a 'zero-sum game'. Any given warrior wins *kudos* or *timē* only at another's expense. When Patroclus begs to be allowed to go out and fight, Achilles says:

Now listen carefully to what I say and remember, and you will win me great honour and glory among the Achaeans; I shall get that lovely girl back, and they will give me gleaming gifts. But when you have driven the Trojans back from the ships, even if Zeus gives you glory, do not think of fighting the Trojans, who delight in battle, without me. For you will lessen my *timē*.

(16. 83)

---

[5] On *timē* and *geras*, compare also Achilles' speech to Aeneas at 20. 178: 'Why do you stand so far forward from the crowd? Do you hope to rule over the Trojans and Priam's *timē*? But even if you killed me Priam would give you no *geras* . . .'

Compare too Bellerophon in Book 6, who married the King's daughter and received half his kingdom (6. 193). It would be impossible in this instance to separate *timē* from the material wealth which accompanies it.

[6] Cf. M. Détienne, *Les Maîtres de vérité dans la Grèce archaïque*, 20.

The more glory Patroclus wins, the less honour for Achilles. Likewise, when Agamemnon takes the *geras* from Achilles he increases his own *timē*, and decreases that of Achilles. *Kudos*, however, is not crucial to the plot as *timē* is, for in the quarrel between Agamemnon and Achilles, it is *timē* around which the action revolves. It represents the relative standing of the two men, and Agamemnon is able to overawe Achilles because of his superior resources.

But is it true that *timē* — honour, standing — is only a means of acquiring possessions, as Sarpedon seems at first to suggest? Do the heroes exist only in order to grow rich? Sarpedon's speech continues:

My friend, if you and I could escape this battle, and then live forever, ageless and immortal, I would not fight among the forefighters, neither would I set you in the battle where men win glory. But now, seeing that the spirits of death stand about us in their thousands, and no one can escape or avoid them, let us go forward, either to reap glory or to bestow it.

(12. 322)

Here is a completely different argument: if we could be immortal, ageless, what need would there be to fight — in the fight where men win glory?

Kleos never dies — it is immortal, unquenchable — but men are cruelly bound in by mortality. Achilles, too, in his interview with his mother, knows this melancholy truth: even Heracles himself could not escape death, and when my turn comes, he says, I too shall lie in death, but in the meantime I shall seize noble fame (18. 121).

This urgency to achieve *kleos* has its counterpart in a pessimistic view of man's place in the cosmos and his expectations: 'As the leaves on the tree are the generations of men: the wind blows them to the ground, and others spring in their place' (6. 146). Towards the end of the *Iliad*, Apollo suggests to Poseidon that they should retire from the fight: 'It would be imprudent to continue fighting for the sake of insignificant mortals, who are as the leaves are, and now flourish and grow warm with life and feed on what the ground gives, but then again fade away and are dead.' (21. 462.)

This view of the brevity and insubstantiality of mortal existence is matched by the Homeric view of the afterlife: the heroes are killed, their souls (*psychai*) flee to Hades, but *they themselves* remain to fatten dogs and birds of carrion (*Il.* 1. 3). What flees to Hades is but a breath: the *psychē* was conceived to be that breath which escapes the lips at the moment a man expires—the veriest shadow of a shadow. And in a memorable simile, the souls of the slain suitors in the *Odyssey* are likened to bats twittering in a dark cave (24. 6).

These insubstantial shadows occupy a joyless place, as Tiresias tells Odysseus when they meet (*Od.* 11. 94). The shade of Achilles make the difference clear: 'I would rather be a day-labourer, working for some landless man who had little to exist on, than rule over all the dead.' (*Od.* 11. 489.) So insubstantial are the dead that Odysseus must administer a drink of hot blood before they can even recognize him, and it is Achilles' great boast that *he* will remember his friend though no one in Hades remembers anything (*Il.* 22. 389). *Kleos* is the possession of the living. Through his deeds, his *klea*, a man can live on in the minds and on the lips of the living, though the dead forget.

Kleos, then, springs out of a singularly bleak view of man's place in the cosmos and his expectations in the afterlife. And what makes the heroes so attractive, to my mind, is that, faced with such a hostile environment, they are resolved to leave their imprint on it.

The demand for *timē*, on the other hand, also reflects the transitory nature of heroic times. As far as *timē* is concerned, there is only the present. It is the most striking thing about the dispute between Agamemnon and Achilles in Book 1 of the *Iliad* that after the raid, *all* the spoils had been shared out. There were no spare spoils, No thought was given to the future; no thought for just such a chance as did in fact occur; when Chryseis had to be returned to her father, Agamemnon and Achilles were launched on their deadly quarrel. The transitory, fluctuating, unsettled society that this reflects tallies with the same bleak view of the cosmos that underlies their appreciation of *kleos*.[7]

---

[7] The 'sharing-out' mentality in the *Iliad* is not just a symptom of the fact that the Argives are away from home on an expedition. As late as 482, when an unexpectedly rich vein of silver was struck in the mines at Laureion, and the Athenians had 100 talents at their disposal, they could seriously consider sharing it out among themselves, ten drachmas per man (Hdt. 7. 144; Arist. *Ath. Pol.* 22. 7). See also Adkins, 'Honour and

This embattled, defiant view of the world was to continue among the Greeks until the philosophers with their *Bios Theōrētikos* first rejected worldly acclaim and the accumulation of goods as the criteria of human worth.

Down to the Fourth Century

Let us now take the story rapidly down to the fourth century and review the role of fame and honour, how it changed and how it stayed the same. The discussion covers three fields: those of war, of politics, and of the games, and it will be convenient to consider them in that order.

War also comes first in the chronological order. The first important witness is Tyrtaeus, the seventh-century Athenian poet, who inspired the Spartans in their war with Messene. For him, a man's worth is determined on the field of battle. A man may have other qualities: he may be swift of foot or strong in wrestling; he may be handsome or rich; he may be a great king or persuasive in debate; but if he cannot stand his place in battle and endure the sight of bloody slaughter, he is not truly noble (*agathos*), for this is a man's worth (*aretē*) (fr. 12). Tyrtaeus does not dismiss these other values, of running, wrestling, and so on; he only says that without the essential capacity to stand his place in battle, a man is worthless.[8] The reason comes immediately afterwards: 'For this is a common good to the city and all the people.'[9] This notion of the common good appears for virtually the first time here (virtually, for there are vestigial appearances of it in Homer, especially on the Trojan side).[10] But Tyrtaeus' men are fighting for their city, their *polis*, and this is the difference between them and Homer's heroes. Instead of the hero and his *oikos*, we have the hoplite and his *polis*. The soldier fights for the common good — the city and the people. Homer's influence, though, is still strong. Tyrtaeus describes his soldier fighting among the *promachoi*, just as Homer had done. Yet Tyrtaeus'

Punishment in the Homeric Poems', *BICS* 7, 29: 'The Homeric hero not merely feels insecure, he is insecure'; and 'The warrior knows the world to be insubstantial . . .'

[8] So Werner Jaeger, 'Tyrtaios, Über die wahre *Arete*' (1932) in *Die griechische Elegie*, 119. Cf. Bowra, *Pindar*, 185.

[9] Cf. B. Snell, *Poetry and Society*, 37, on the 'common good'.

[10] Hector appears to be less isolated than Achilles, yet the imperative to stand forward and win glory is just as pressing on him as on his great enemy (e.g. *Il.* 8. 532).

soldier is now a hoplite, arrayed in the phalanx, and there one cannot, like the hero, stand forward to win fame and glory. There, all stand together—for the sake of the common good. If the hoplite falls in battle, he is lamented sorely by the city; his tomb and children are conspicuous (fr. 12. 29); nor will his good name ever die. If the hero survives and comes home, there will be honour for him. The warrior returning from battle is honoured by young and old; no one does him wrong (fr. 12. 31–7). Tyrtaeus' warrior fights on behalf of the city and the people. If he dies, it is they who keep his memory alive; if he returns alive, it is they who honour him.

Tyrtaeus, for all his Homeric reminiscences, lives in a world completely different from Homer's. Instead of the bleak and hostile universe where the hero stood alone and defiant, Tyrtaeus lives in the comparatively cosy *polis*. Homer's hero defied the meaninglessness of death; his tomb would be seen only by passing strangers; Tyrtaeus' memory will be kept alive by those who knew and honoured him. His children will be honoured; Hector's children could expect a rough deal after his death: to be pushed aside by the other children from the dinner-table. Around Tyrtaeus' warrior is a warm, family-like *dēmos* and *polis*, ready to honour him in victory and lament him in defeat. Homer's hero stood alone, taking his life in his hands on his own account only, with no city and people to back him up.[11]

Hence the second significant difference is that whereas Homer's hero measured his honour in terms of his material reward, Tyrtaeus makes no mention of any. His honour, his *timē*, will be the appreciation of his fellow citizens; that will suffice. There will be no prizes.

The pattern for honour and fame that Tyrtaeus sets out here lasts well into the fifth century. Its Homeric language, despite, the great underlying differences of conception, and of social and political structures, lasts too. Simonides, for example, in the first half of the fifth century, laments the fallen at Thermopylae:

---

[11] Hector's position is quite different from that of a hoplite; it is that of a chief among his people as opposed to one who is among equals. The war is eating into his substance without giving him any opportunity to recoup it by raids. His social position and the heroic code combine to make him as lonely as any Argive.

> Far-famed are they whom the earth covers, Leonidas,
> Who fell with you here . . .

(Fr. 122)

And as late as 431 BC, the following inscription was cut in memory of those who fell at Potidaea:

> The city and people of Erechtheus lament the men who fell here
> Among the foremost, before the city of Potidaea.
> Sons of Athenians, they gave forth their life's breath,
> Exchanged it for virtue and the fame of their homeland.[12]

The reiteration of Homeric phrases and formulae, difficult to convey in translation, corresponds, I think, to what was genuinely seen as an affinity with the heroes of old, from whom these warriors claimed descent, either literally or in spirit. It illustrates the all-pervading presence of Homer in their culture.

At almost exactly the same time as this inscription was cut, Pericles was delivering his Funeral Speech over the bodies of those who had fallen in the first year's fighting of the Peloponnesian War: 'Giving their bodies for the common good, each receives praise that never grows old, and a most conspicuous tomb—not that in which men lie, but an imperishable glory among the living . . .' (Thucydides, 2. 43. 2).

A similar sentiment is expressed in the *Erechtheus* of Euripides (423/2 BC): Praxithea is prepared to sacrifice her child for her country; she believes, as Pericles does, that while the country saves its citizens, the citizens cannot save themselves without it, and that they must therefore be prepared to make any sacrifice on its behalf. Their reward will be fame, but here, democratically, it will be *equal* fame:

> Falling with many others in the battle line
> Their lot will be a common tomb and equal fame.

(Fr. 360. 32)

The city has superseded the individual, and it is significant that these examples from works composed in the 420s preserve the attitude already observed in the Archaic period. The hoplite style of fighting continued unchanged; attitudes and vocabulary continued likewise unchanged.

---

[12] Kaibel, *Epigr. Graeca ex Lapid. Conl.* 21, p. 8.

From this time on, however, the Homeric values also emerge in the world of democratic politics, though with certain important modifications: the notion of fighting, appropriate to a battlefield, is replaced by that of 'striving' (*ponos*) and other related terms. In the civic field, in general, fame is henceforth to be had by 'striving'. Already, in the first half of the fifth century, Pindar had said that no earthly fortune was to be had without striving (*P.* 12. 28), and that this was a sign of prowess (*aretē*) (*Ol.* 5. 15).

The connection of toil with achievement and success is a dominant theme in the second half of the fifth century in Athenian politics. Democritus is probably the first to connect exertion explicitly with the political art: 'which is a great art, and he taught that striving brings great things, and fame, for men' (DK 68B157). Exertion brings all that is best and glorious for men; here, for the first time, it is in a political context.

This connection of striving, or effort, with fame is often found in Euripides.[13] In one of his earliest plays, the *Likymnios*, someone remarks that 'striving, so they say, is the father of good fame' (fr. 474N).[14] The subject of the play is Herakles, for whom life and labours are inextricably bound together. Striving is often related to *tolma* (daring) and it is through these two concepts that the Homeric tradition is transformed under the radical democracy, especially in Euripides and Thucydides. 'Only dare,' runs a fragment of Euripides, 'for in good time exertion (*mochthos*) brings forth great good fortune to men.' (*Temenos*, fr. 745N.) *Mochthos* is a more extreme form of *ponos*, and implies hardship and distress on top of labour.[15]

The quality of *tolma*, however, is ambivalent. A fragment from the *Ixion* runs: 'It is daring that brings the greatest things for men. No tyranny, no great house is achieved without effort.' (Fr. 426N.)[16] Daring, as a means to a throne, or a great house such as a Homeric hero might inhabit, implies more than democratic pretensions. Ixion was a noted blasphemer, so that there is a link here between daring too much, aspiring to tyranny

---

[13] See B. Knox, *The Heroic Temper*, for a discussion of these themes in Sophocles, esp. 28–30.

[14] *c.*447 BC. Cf. Goossens, *Euripide et Athènes*, 6.

[15] Compare frs. 237, 238, 240, 242 from *Archelaos* (*c.*408BC). The character of some of these fragments, like that from the *Likymnios*, is highly suggestive of a proverbial origin.

[16] Goossens dates tentatively to 411–410.

for example, and blasphemy, or daring against the divine order. The ambivalence in the meaning of *tolma* is the poetic expression of one of the important tensions in city life at that time: the tension between the traditional regard for prowess, and the need for civic virtues, the balance and moderation that held a democracy together. Thucydides is keenly aware of this, and the daring of the Athenian people, and its transition from a benign and creative quality to a tyrannical and despotic one, is a major theme of his work. At the beginning of his *History* he elaborates the themes I touched on earlier in a war context: the appropriation of Homeric values, originally the property of the hero class, by the *dēmos* as a whole. The ideal of the nobleman (*agathos*) with his prowess (*aretē*) is applied to the Athenian people, not only in war but in general. Thus they 'dare beyond their powers, and run risks beyond reason' (1. 70. 3); they are 'hopeful in the midst of dangers', and they 'go on working away and running risks all their lives, taking least delight in what they've got, since they're always adding to them, preferring unremitting effort to a life of ease' (1. 70. 8).[17]

Clearly these are no mundane labours in the fields or the potteries; they are aristocratic exploits, and refer to the achievements of the Athenians as merchants, explorers, and soldiers, as well as in subduing the greater part of the Aegean to their will. Euripides expresses the same idea in his *Suppliant Women*:

> You see? Is your country so foolish when she
> Turns Gorgons' eyes on those who taunt her?
> It is through striving that she grows great,
> But dull and sluggish cities follow dull policies,
> Peering cautiously about them.

> (321–5)

This play was produced in the 420s, and this passage shows marked similarities of tone and vocabulary to the first two books of Thucydides' *History*. It is characteristic of aggressive, expanding powers such as Athens that they represent themselves as surrounded by enemies.

---

[17] Gomme (*HCT* ad loc.) draws attention to the oracle, quoted by Aristophanes in the *Banqueters*, fr. 230, in *Knights*, 1011–13, and again in *Birds*, 978, 987; and Herodotus explains the Athenians' appetite for *ponos* as due to *isēgoria* (5. 78).

The fruits of *ponoi* are fame and honour, and in the speeches of Book 2 Thucydides makes Pericles emphasize the prestige and glory of Athens: the Athenians inhabit a great and powerful city, he says; it was bequeathed them by their forefathers who made it great by their own efforts. It is therefore fitting that they should uphold its honour; nor should they seek to avoid those same efforts if they wish to share its prestige. Such greatness naturally draws envy but they enjoy fame at the present and will leave an imperishable name behind them.[18]

Pericles' speech elaborates the traditional pattern that stretches back to Homer: the Athenians have performed their exploits, have triumphed over their enemies and become great, have acquired *timē*.

The strength of this tradition, its vitality and the flexibility with which it had adapted to very different circumstances, is shown even in such an unlikely witness as Aristophanes, who refers, in the parabasis to the *Acharnians*, to his boldness (*tolma*) in speaking his mind to the Athenian people, and the fame it has brought him (646-7). Again, in the *Clouds*, Strepsiades confesses his desire to defeat his enemies in debate 'by a hundred stades', and the Clouds promise him 'fame which will rise to heaven' (457 ff.) — a deliberately Homeric reminiscence.[19] In Homer, excellence on the field was matched by excellence in counsel; that parallel held throughout the classical period. Here, Strepsiades is assured of Homeric fame in his dispute with his creditors. The mood, the tone, the attitude to debate, though parodied here, continued through to the debates of Classical Athens. Only the *dēmos* was transformed from a docile and passive body into one which had the vote, and so determined the fate of those who rose to address it. *Tolma* will be displayed and fame won in the debates in the assembly and the lawcourts. Theseus, in the *Suppliant Women*, tells the Argive herald: 'He who wishes to offer useful advice to the city is free to do so. That's the way to achieve prominence [literally, "brightness" — *lamprotēs*]. Who does not wish may keep silent. What could be fairer in a city?' (438-42.) Here, in the civic field, is the same pattern which had been established earlier for the hoplite: service to the city brings

---

[18] Pericles' second speech, Th. 2. 60 ff.
[19] Cf. *Il.* 8. 192 and frequently in the *Odyssey*.

fame. It sheds some interesting light on the Athenian concept of equality too, for here Theseus talks of equality of opportunity: people may not necessarily *be* equal, but they have an equal opportunity to rise to prominence. This is, incidentally, a different formulation of the concept of *isēgoria*—the equality of the right to speak—which was for Herodotus the backbone of democracy (5. 78).

The term *lamprotēs* is a useful one since it brings the discussion back to that tension mentioned earlier, between individual prowess and civic virtue. *Lamprotēs*, in Theseus' speech, is viewed in that benign sense with which Thucydides characterizes the Athenians in his earlier books. One achieves social visibility through socially useful behaviour—offering good advice to the city. It is part of Thucydides' scheme to contrast this Periclean attitude to fame and achievement, which is portrayed in his earlier books, with that in the latter part of the work, summed up in the character of Alcibiades. In Alcibiades' speech to the Athenians before the Sicilian expedition (6. 16 ff.), *lamprotēs*—Alcibiades' own, personal, prominence—is the key theme: Alcibiades is distinguished for his ancestors, his victories in the games, his magnificent choruses. Although Alcibiades emphasizes how much good all this does for the city, it is his own prominence that is important, and which he is defending: those who have *lamprotēs* may be envied by those about them, he says, but after they are dead everyone claims them as kin. *Lamprotēs* in this speech is doing duty for Homeric *kleos* and it brings *timē* in its wake: I have conferred honour on myself and my ancestors, he says, and profit on the city. But through the character of Alcibiades, the idea of *lamprotēs* leads on to that of *tolma*—daring too far. Alcibiades is the principal character through whom the daring of the Athenian people is transformed, as Thucydides interprets it, into a malign and impious quality—from a pious and prudent balance into a dangerous and unstable extreme.

This impious aspect of *tolma* has already been touched on, and Euripides expresses it in another fragment: 'Not through hunting and snatching at all things, by daring too far, and going to extremes, shall men seem reverent.' (Fr. 434N, first *Hippolytus* before 431 BC.) *Tolma* here is the opposite of reverence (*eusebeia*) which is the religious equivalent of the civic virtues of

prudence and justice (*sōphrosynē* and *dikaiosynē*).[20] Another way
of expressing this tension is to say that the contrast between *tolma*
and prudence is the contrast between the aristocratic urge to
dominate (expressed by Thucydides in the person of Alcibiades)
and democratic equality, elaborated by Pericles.

This conflict is represented by Thucydides as sharpening as
the war progressed, and, especially in those passages composed
after the war had ended, he summed up his opinions on the
subject, and expressed the problem in terms of the word
philotimia[21] — the urge to achieve *timē*. Under the pressure of the
war, he says, many cities were torn apart by fractional strife
(*stasis*) and the prime cause of this, as in the exemplary case of
Corcyra, was greed and *philotimia* (3. 82. 8). It is inevitable in
stasis that appetites become sharpened; the normal basis of
civilized society has collapsed, and the prize of ambition becomes
nothing less than the State itself. This was the case also with
Athens in 411 BC when the democracy was overthrown, and it
was proposed that the power of the State should be vested in
the Five Thousand, the moderate, property-owning section of
the population. According to Thucydides, however, this was no
more than a form of words by the Four Hundred oligarchs who
had seized power, since they had in fact no intention of
relinquishing power. They were, he says, motivated by *philotimia*,
and he comments that 'this quality is just as destructive of
oligarchies, when democracies have been overthrown. For, no
sooner is the change made, then everyone regards himself not
as the equal of others, but as greatly superior.' (8. 89. 3.)

Once again, Thucydides' views are corroborated by Euripides,
who discussed *philotimia* in one of his most political plays, the
Phoenician Women, written shortly after the events of 411.[22] The
concept of *philotimia* in the atmosphere of these years is
dramatized in the character of Eteocles. He sets out his creed
in a speech to his mother, who is attempting to adjudicate

---

[20] Nowhere is the true meaning of *sōphrosynē* for the ordinary citizen better brought
out than in Lysias' speech for the cripple, 24. 17.

[21] My attention was drawn to *philotimia* by Dr David Whitehead of Manchester
University, and I am grateful to him for a discussion of it.

[22] The play must be dated within a year of 409 BC; cf. Goossens, op. cit., 628 n.
62. The *Phoenician Women* is valuable as evidence, if any were needed, of the extent to
which Euripides manipulates mythology to suit his ends.

between him and his brother in their conflict over the throne of Thebes:

> If nobility and wisdom were the same for all,
> There would be no strife dividing men.
> There is, however, nothing common among men,
> Except in name. Reality's quite different.
> I must tell you, mother, I'll hide nothing,
> I'd go to the stars, to the threshold of the sun,
> Into the bowels of the earth, had I
> The means, so it would bring me supreme power,
> The greatest of the gods.
>
> (499 ff.)[23]

The tone of the opening lines point forward to Plato's Callicles and Thrasymachus (in his Dialogues *Gorgias* and *The Republic*): there can be no commonly accepted definitions of nobility, wisdom, right or justice. This is a relativist doctrine, asserting individuality and denying any universally understood, universally held, values. It is an anarchist view, appropriate to periods of anarchy such as existed in Athens in 411. The suggestion that concepts are only understood in common by their names, and that in reality everyone attaches his own meaning to them, is, according to Plato, characteristic of sophistic teaching. But if Eteocles appears to be asserting a cynical, modern doctrine, he is in reality only restating the traditional one, which stretches back to Homer. It is that of the heroic individual, for whom civilized society as the fifth century understood it does not yet exist. The hero, or as Eteocles puts it, the tyrant, must be a law unto himself.

Euripides is contrasting a Homeric warrior's attitude with the actual requirements of a contemporary society and finds that it only brings disaster. Jocasta puts the Euripidean alternative. She immediately makes it clear that this attitude of Eteocles is none other than Philotimia — the worst of the gods. Against it she poses Isotes, the force for unity and co-operation. Inequality brings conflict between those with too much and those with not enough. It is equality which produces stability among men (531 ff.).

---

[23] See Goossens op. cit., 602–9 for a discussion of this play in the light of the recent events: the navy in Samos, the oligarchs installed at Athens.

Equality is seen as a form of balance and harmony. The imbalance of wealth or position produces disharmony, and increases the polarization of the oppressors and the oppressed. Tyranny is the logical end of ambition.

It is clear, then, that the Homeric drives to fame and honour were as strong at the end of the fifth century as they had ever been. It is clear, too, that in the view of the most perceptive writers of the time, the democracy was a mechanism, frail and imperfect as it was, by which those drives could be checked and harnessed to socially useful ends; and that when the democracy broke down, the Homeric urge to domination and prowess immediately reasserted itself. The ambiguities and tensions of city life which have been discussed in this chapter, the striving for prominence, and the forces for moderation, were all inherent in the Athenian constitution itself. This is not the place to go into a detailed description of the Athenian constitution,[24] but a few observations will make the point.

Democracy had been established for a hundred years when Euripides wrote the *Phoenician Women*; the citizens had gone to considerable lengths to ensure political equality, and the three distinguishing marks of the democracy were (a) choice of magistrates by lot, (b) responsibility of officers to the people by annual audit and (c) popular control of all measures.[25] Yet strangely, the intricate machinery of democracy disguised what was in many respects still a very aristocratic government. The magistrates, chosen each year by lot, were selected from a short list of only 500, and these were nominated by the parishes (demes) from among their wealthy members.[26] Generals and treasurers, who constituted what might be regarded as an executive, the latter having charge of State finances, were not chosen by lot but elected (a method otherwise regarded by the Athenians as undemocratic), again from a short list of wealthy men. The liturgy, by which all State festivities were financed, was a burden laid upon individual rich men. It was a relic of a pre-democratic past, and was as much concerned with

[24] The standard work is C. Hignett, *A History of the Athenian Constitution*.

[25] So How and Wells, comm. on Herodotus, 3. 80.

[26] Arist. *Ath. Pol.* 22. 5. This would appear to be the case in the fifth century. In his own time Aristotle implies that anyone would stand for office; see *Ath. Pol.* 7. 4 and *Lysias*, 24. 13.

honour, prestige, and social standing as with supposed social levelling.[27]

Democracy was a complicated and ambiguous system of government which, while delivering power into the hands of the mass of the citizens, yet retained for the rich and powerful the opportunity to display prowess and gain prestige. The checks which the democracy laid upon the lust for *timē* constituted the balance of which Euripides speaks. They also created the tension which, when the democracy broke down in moments of crisis, caused that Homeric force to reassert itself with undiminished force.

The Fourth Century

The evidence for the fourth century is of a rather different nature from that of the fifth, coming from philosophers rather than historians and poets. It is clear, however, that *timē* continues to hold its place. Aristotle states the position quite baldly: 'Cultured people (*charientes*) and men of affairs (*praktikoi*) identify the Good with honour (*timē*) because this is, broadly speaking, the goal of political life.' (*EN* 1095b 22.) These 'cultured people' ('men of taste and refinement, educated people' (LSJ)), he goes on, are still men who expect to be honoured for their *aretē*, their prowess, and by men whose opinions they respect (*phronimoi*) (ibid.). Clearly, *aretē* in this context will no longer mean what it did to Homer's heroes, but the underlying significance is unchanged. Whatever prowess means in the fourth century (and it will still include an element of martial valour), if it also includes the capacity to address the assembly — 'to offer good advice to the State', and other factors which we shall come to in a moment, it is still essentially a public quality and is validated by the *dēmos*, even if, in this case, Aristotle prefers the approval of the *phronimoi*. This public quality is underlined by Aristotle when he juxtaposes the political life and those of philosophy and pleasure, both more or less private activities (1095b 17).

Plato discusses the political life and the pursuit of *timē* at greater length, and in his own characteristic way:

Suppose a young man, whose father is a good man (or nobleman — *agathos*) but lives in a city that is not well run, and avoids all the honours

---

and offices and lawsuits, and that sort of meddlesome business (*polypragmosynē*), and is content to be held of no account so long as he doesn't have to be involved—suppose this young man hears his mother complaining that her husband never takes public office, and that she is slighted as a consequence, and she sees that he is not very eager to make money, nor to be involved in the disputing and slanging of politics and the law, but rather prefers to take things easy, and keep his opinions to himself. Oppressed by all this, she complains that her husband is no man at all, too slack, and all the other things women like to complain about in these matters.

. . . going out, the young man sees that those who mind their own business are called silly and held in low esteem, while those who don't are honoured and praised.

(*Rep.* 549 C)

This passage comes from Plato's review of defective constitutions and is a description of a certain kind of wealthy man under the democracy. The term *agathos* is ambiguous here because Plato intends it to contain a note of moral approval, but it still carries its older sense of 'nobleman'. Here is a man who is expected by society to take an important part in politics and yet chooses not to. Why he does not do so is a large question and this book will seek to supply an answer, but for the moment it is important to observe that he represents an *abnormal* position, while his wife upholds the orthodox view. It is normal for a man in his social position to take part in political life and the offices and honours that go with it. The moral disapprobation which he suffers in consequence is not to be taken lightly: not only is he belittled and slighted for shunning public affairs, but his wife too is humiliated in front of her friends. There is no reason to suppose that Plato is exaggerating the wife's significance, and for all his lightness of tone, the central message of this passage is strong enough: there was a heavy social price to pay for not taking part in political life.

The general term for civic and legal affairs (which were often inextricably entwined) was *pragmata*, and the love of this business Plato called *philopragmosynē* (a word probably coined by him). For the man who shuns these *pragmata* there is a phrase which Plato may also have coined (it comes into use in his time): 'to mind one's own business'—*ta hautou prattein*. This phrase is very common in the fourth century.

Plato's three kinds of life differ slightly from those of Aristotle: he places the political life between those of the philosopher and the business man: the pursuit of success between the pursuit of wisdom and money (581 B). And, as he says, the politician's life, the pursuit of success, is devoted to honour and a good reputation.

Xenophon, too, recognizes the place of *timē* in life; he accounts it the distinguishing feature of men as against the brutes:

Love of honour (*philotimia*) is implanted neither in animals, who are incapable of it, nor even in all men. But those in whom a love of honour and praise is implanted, these are those who differ most from animals, and who are reckoned *men*, not merely human beings.

(*Hiero*, 7. 3)

Again, in the *Memorabilia* there is a conversation between Socrates and the young Glaucon, which opens with these words:

'Now Glaucon,' he said, 'you have it in mind to become a leader of the people?'
'I do indeed, Socrates,' he replied.
'Certainly, there can be no more noble ambition . . .'

(3. 6. 2)

Socrates goes on to explain that if you want to win honour, you must benefit your city, and that the man who aspires to be a leader, and hence acquire *timē*, must have an expert knowledge of many fields of activity: revenues, military strength, the mines, food supplies, and so on. Such a man would be what Aristotle called *praktikos*. He would contrast with the man described in a parallel discussion in Plato's *Protagoras* (319 B ff.) where Socrates argues that there is a business of government which stands somehow above all these particular concerns. This would be the province of the Guardians in the *Republic*, Plato's idealized aristocrats who have finally risen above such worldly considerations as *timē*. Plato, however, had a very complicated attitude towards worldly honour, which is discussed in Chapter 7.

It is clear that, in general terms, there is no diminution in the fourth century in the value accorded to *timē*, especially, as one would expect, among the upper class; Aristotle accepts it, and, as in other respects, only Plato is capable of conceiving a society constructed on other principles.

hero can aim.[1] Thus, in the *Iliad*, Athene gives strength and valour to Diomedes 'that he might stand out among the Argives and gain good report (*kleos esthlon*)' (5./3). Again, someone has shot Menelaus with an arrow: sorrow for Menelaus, but fame for the shooter (4. 195). Achilles' choice, as his mother told him, had been simple: go home and grow old in obscurity, or stay fighting the Trojans and gain fame:

> If I stay here, in the fighting round Troy,
> My return is cut off, but I shall have immortal fame;
> If I return home, to my own native land,
> My fame is cut off, but a long life awaits me.

(9. 412)

The implication is that if he does not go home, Achilles must die at Troy; but it is not yet explicitly stated. In the event, Achilles chooses to remain, not to fight immediately, it is true, but to await the inevitable moment when the Trojans shall reach the Argive ships, as they must once he is out of the fighting. Without fame there is no life for a hero.

And there is no fame to be had without involvement in the fighting: as Ajax tells the Argives at the critical moment when the Trojans overrun the ships, 'those who flee get no fame' (15. 564). Earlier, Hector had stepped forward between the ranks of Trojan and Argive and issued a challenge to single combat: let the winner, says he, after stripping the body, return it to his comrades for cremation; if I am fortunate, he goes on, the burial mound of my victim will stand by the side of the sea, and so my fame will never die (7. 91). Conversely, if Agamemnon had returned home *without* taking Troy, and having lost so many men, it would bring him *ill fame* (9. 22).[2] And even away from the field of battle, Odysseus, though exhausted by his travails, is urged to participate in the Phaeacian games: 'There is no greater fame for a man than what he can achieve with his hands or his feet.' (*Od.* 8. 147.)

Fame has two characteristics: it extends through time, and

---

[1] So too E. R. Dodds, *The Greeks and the Irrational*, 29. Cf. Redfield, 30 ff.

[2] *Kleos* is part of a 'shame culture'. Hector, too, fights among the *promachoi* out of shame, in order to increase the *kleos* of himself and of his father (6. 445). There is a sizeable literature on 'shame culture'. See, among others, Dodds, op. cit., and Adkins, *Merit and Responsibility*.

In their history since Homeric times, the functions of fame and honour had been modified. The Homeric hero acquired them solely on his own account; he heaped up treasure as a mark of his standing; he was virtually a lawless figure, answerable only to himself, tyrant in his own domain. In the early *polis* this situation became modified: the hoplite was not alone as the hero had been; the city and people were there to cherish him, to honour him in victory, and to keep his memory warm if he died. No longer did he heap up spoils as a token of his prestige.

In the democratic city there seems to be a fundamental tension: the Homeric urge to fame and honour is still there, and for the most part the leading roles in war and peace are filled by the literal and metaphorical descendants of Ajax, Diomedes, and the rest. But their aggrandizement of honour now encounters the envy of those who believe they live in a State based on equality. The State must take precedence over the individual; then let every man work for the fame and glory of the State, or let a man win fame and glory for himself while bestowing it on the State. This is Alcibiades' boast and Xenophon's advice.

But if aristocratic individualism was constrained within the bounds of the city, if it was compelled to express itself within the concept of service to the city, there was one sphere of activity where it remained entirely untrammelled. This was in the games.

The games were the aristocratic milieu par excellence.[28] The intensely competitive nature of the games is indicated by the great glory of the victor and the humiliation of the loser. Success was total, defeat equally so. There was no shaking hands, no comradeship among the competitors; to win was all. Here the Homeric spirit shines through clearest of all. No wonder, then, that the games were the one aspect of society that changed least in the centuries down to Pindar. Pindar himself is the foremost witness to the victor's glory,[29] and success is signified by the strongest words at his disposal: *aretē*, elsewhere referring to worth or prowess in general, is here exclusively athletic or agonistic.[30]

---

[28] So Finley and and Pleket, *The Olympic Games*, 77, and cf. J. Swaddling, *The Ancient Olympic Games*, 35; B. Bilinski, *L'agonistica sportiva nella Grecia antica*, 49.

[29] Cf. Bowra, *Pindar*, 177–91.

[30] e.g. *I*. 5. 17; *N*. 8. 40. Cf. H. Buhmann, *Der Sieg in Olympia und in den anderen panhellenischen Spielen*, 24.

It seems important that down to the end of the fifty century at least, financial reward played no significant role; in token of this, the prize at Olympia was no more than a laurel wreath. And the rewards which the victor received in his native city smack more of prestige than of gain. There were money prizes, it is true, from Athens at least, for Solon was compelled to lay down a table of prizes, which seems to have been the maximum amounts payable.[31] But as well as money there was a State banquet, the right to eat in the town hall, and a front seat in the theatre side by side with generals, priests, and visiting ambassadors. This is the clue to the real nature of the reward: not merely money, but glory, eminence, and prestige.

The adulation of victorious athletes was not quite universal, however, and a valuable light is shed on the relation between the athlete and the city by the rebuke administered by two disgruntled intellectuals. Xenophanes, the philosopher of Colophon (*c*.500 BC), in an elegiac fragment, describes the fame of athletes, the seat of honour in the theatre, the meals at public expense, and the money prizes. Nevertheless, says he, not even the winner of the chariot race is so worthy as he, 'for my wisdom is better than the strength of men or horses', and however many outstanding athletes a city may produce, it will not on this account be any better governed (DK 21B2).

This is the essence too of a fragment from Euripides' satyr play *Autolycus* (284N): 'Of all the myriad evils there are in Greece, there is nothing worse than this tribe of athletes . . .', the speech begins. Their training does not help them to live well, he says, and they are the slaves of their bellies. In their youth they are an adornment to the city, 'but when harsh age presses upon them, they are gone, casting aside their saffron cloaks'. It is the custom of the Greeks that is to blame, he goes on, for they honour such men with feasts and assemblies. Athletic training is of no use when it comes to defending the city, and cities would do better to honour men who are wise and just.

The polemical tone of these two speeches indicates, I think, how far their authors stood from the stream of ordinary opinion. The frustrated intellectual, feeling he is being neglected by his

---

[31] Cf. Bowra, op. cit., 185; Buhmann, op. cit., 55; E. N. Gardiner, *Athletics in the Ancient World*, 100.

fellow citizens in favour of a succession of wooden-headed athletes, is venting his spleen, though he can have no hope of carrying his audience with him.[32]

The city honoured its athletes, but then the athletes also conferred honour on their cities, and such was the glory that cities were capable of bribing athletes to enter under their name, as in the case of Astylos of Croton, winner in two successive Olympiads, who allowed himself to be proclaimed a Syracusan 'to please Hieron, tyrant of Syracuse'.[33]

The excessive concentration on success had certain strange effects. For example, while athletes, boxers, and wrestlers entered in their own person,[34] men of wealth who entered teams in the chariot races took all the glory while not actually competing themselves. The Sicilian tyrants are notable examples, but perhaps the outstanding evidence of the glory involved is the story of Cimon, banished by Peisistratus (Hdt. 103. 1–3). In exile he won the Olympic chariot race twice running; he caused the second victory to be announced in Peisistratus' name, and the tyrant, in gratitude, recalled him from exile.

The glory implies *aretē* and it is clear from this story that the *aretē* is not simply held to reside in the athletes' capacity to perform well. It must be that the *aretē* was part of their 'nature', as Pindar puts it; the noble family, the ownership of wealth, and everything that goes with it, all imply this 'nature' and therefore partake of *aretē*.

Even Pindar, however, is ready to criticize what he considers to be excessive fame. Hippocleas, for example, had triumphed through *aretē*, through *tolma* and *sthenos* (strength), but even he could not reach the brazen heavens (*P.* 10. 27). The image of the Pillars of Hercules is used, too, to represent that which mortal ambition can reach, provided it goes no further (*O.* 3. 43; *N.* 3. 31; *I.* 4. 12). Hieron, tyrant of Syracuse, is warned against 'peering too far' (*O.* 1. 114); Xenophon of Corinth against insolence and excess (*O.* 13. 9); and Diagoras of Rhodes also against insolence (*O.* 7. 90).

---

[32] Euripides' dislike of athletes may have something to do with the training in boxing he underwent as a lad, as a consequence of a misunderstood oracle. Cf. Gardiner, *Greek Athletic Sports and Festivals*, 131 ff.

[33] Athenaeus, 522. Cf. Gardiner, *Athletics in the Ancient World*, 100.

[34] Later Roman writers found it strange that 'men of great station accounted it an honour to contend in the games' (G. Grote, *History of Greece*, iii. 296).

Excessive fame brings envy with it, and Pindar knew it well. Envy is inevitable, but still it is better to be envied than pitied (*P*. 1. 85), and often the envious defeat their own ends (*P*. 11. 54; *N*. 4. 39).[35]

Envy is also connected with defeat, and just as success meant everything, so defeat was correspondingly bitter and humiliating: 'A most hostile return through obscure streets, amid dishonouring tongues . . .' (*O*. 8. 67); 'Nor did they arouse sweet laughter as they returned to their mothers, but they slunk through byways, out of sight of their enemies, gnawed by misfortune'. (*P*. 8. 85).

This study of fame and honour has helped to show how little, in certain respects, life changed for the Greeks from Homer to Aristotle. The Homeric hero's pursuit of fame was connected with a singularly bleak view of man's place in the cosmos and his expectations in the afterlife; but for the fifth-century citizen, life was still fairly bleak too: the *polis* was there as his security, but how secure was the *polis*? In time of war, and that was most of the time, the Greek city faced a chance of complete annihilation, of death and enslavement. The greatest, most prosperous, most powerful city of them all, Athens, in her moment of defeat, could seriously expect such a fate (X. *Hell.* 2. 2. 3). If one's whole security was bound up with a small number of fellow citizens, visible, countable, it follows that one's personal security, and with it one's very sense of self, was closely dependent on social standing, honour, *timē*. If *timē* seemed at first to reflect the transitory, unsettled nature of Homeric times, it soon becomes clear that later centuries were little more secure, if at all. The Homeric hero had seemed to live in the present only, giving no thought for the future. Yet, in the fifth century itself, we find the Athenians seriously considering sharing out the windfall of silver found at Laureion; and Themistocles was the first leader ever to suggest laying up capital for the future.

It follows also that those with the greatest stake in society should be most zealous to take charge in it. Within the mechanism of democracy, the nobleman is found in all commanding positions. His pretensions to honour and prestige were mostly channelled

---

[35] Cf. Bowra, op. cit., 187.

into socially useful ends, yet there was always a tension between that urge to dominate and the democratic demand for equality, and when democratic control broke down in moments of crisis, it showed itself as strong as ever.

If this striving towards honour and fame is as strong as has been suggested, it follows that any reaction, or contrary movement, must have great significance. It will be the object of this book to examine the origins, so far as possible, and the various manifestations of this counter-movement, this *apragmosynē*: quietism, or 'minding one's own business'.

2

431: *Apragmones* and the Athenian Empire

In the year 431, Pericles made his famous Funeral Speech over the graves of those who had fallen in the first season's fighting. In it, as Thucydides reports him,[1] he describes Athens as the 'school of Hellas'. The speech is a eulogy and a defence of the Athenian way of life — of what Athens is, and what she has achieved. It is a war-time speech intended to draw the people together and to reinforce their common identity, to unite them against the common enemy. Their unity is brought out especially in the passage where Pericles declares that service to the city is open to all, regardless of their financial circumstance:

In their private disputes everyone is equal before the law, but in questions of public standing men are not chosen for their social class, but are honoured for their ability (*aretē*), and no one, if he has any good to do the city, is kept in obscurity by poverty.

(2. 37. 1)

Pericles here makes a novel departure from Greek tradition: he is suggesting that a man might be possessed of *aretē* whatever his background, and that he might be able to perform some *agathon* — some useful political service — and receive *timē* in return. This is in contrast, not only to tradition, but also to conditions throughout the fifth and fourth centuries, where, as Aristotle put it, politics is the sphere of the *charientes* — the educated élite. It is, in fact, the ideal of the radical democracy: henceforth all men share the rights and duties hitherto the prerogative of the upper classes. In an ideal society, differences are made to disappear, and that means that in Athens *aretē* has become the

[1] The date of composition of Pericles' speeches is discussed in the Appendix, p.195.

property of all.[2] The whole people has become the ruling élite.[3] In traditional thought, *aretē* was a quality reserved pretty exclusively to the upper class. It was the wealthy few who were bred up to be leaders of men, to display their prowess on the field of battle and in counsel. This is clear from the kind of words they use to describe themselves—*chrēstoi*, useful ones; *dynatoi*, powerful ones. Now Pericles has taken away their distinguishing attribute and made it available to the whole *dēmos*. This is the ideal of the radical democracy; where does it leave the *chrēstoi*?

In an ideal city, the ideal citizen is one who, while attending to his own affairs, can also find time to attend to those of the city. Pericles is harsh on those who will not co-operate:

Here, men are concerned no less with the city's affairs than with their own, and even those engrossed in their own work are by no means ignorant of politics. We alone regard the man who takes no part in politics not as minding his own business (*apragmōn*), but as useless (*achreios*).

(2. 40. 2)

Pericles' ideal democracy requires the participation of all, but here, Thucydides tells us, for the first time, there are those who will not co-operate, will not participate in their democratic duty.

The speech is a more sophisticated elaboration of themes set forth in Book 1 (1. 70 ff.); there Thucydides pictured the Athenians as active, vigorous, confident, and expansive, and that is how Pericles sees them in this speech. Yet here he is forced to admit that there are men in the city who do not share these admirable qualities. Is Pericles referring to some group or class known to his audience, or is he talking in general, rebuking anyone who might be inclined to backsliding? This second possibility will not be ruled out, for I shall discuss other kinds of political apathy in succeeding chapters; however, I suggest that in this passage Pericles is referring to a particular group, and the clue lies in the Greek word *achreios*—useless. The upper class, the class accustomed to a prominent role in politics, styled itself the 'useful' ones. Can it be coincidence that Pericles is

[2] Is the funeral speech an idealization? Cf. Burnet, *EGP* (1st edn.) 277; Gomme, *HCT* ad loc. 2. 37. 3.

[3] Just the accusation made by their enemies. Cf. Ps.-Xen. *Ath. Pol.* 1. 8.

talking about those who are backing out of politics and calls them 'useless' (*achreios* is the opposite of *chrēstos*)? Is it possible that the 'useful' people, or some of them, are not being as useful as they might be? If such an impulse were felt at all in noble breasts it is given unequivocal expression in a speech of Euripides, written, by coincidence, in 431. This is the prologue to the lost *Philoctetes*, spoken by Odysseus. The speech survives in three fragments and two paraphrases by Dio Chrysostom. Here are the fragments:

What should I think? If I stayed quietly (*apragmonōs*) in the ranks I would fare no worse than the wisest.

(Fr. 787N)

Thus Odysseus poses the problem to himself, and answers as follows:

There is nothing so vain as man, for it is those who achieve something special whom we honour and regard as men indeed.

(Fr. 788N)

I am loath to waste the good will (*charis*) I have earned by my exertions (*mochthoi*) and I don't shrink from those labours which face me.

(Fr. 789N)

And here is one of the paraphrases:

I fear that my reputation among the Greeks as the best and wisest of them all may one day be shown up by my allies as futile, for, after all, what is this wisdom and intelligence which compels us to exert ourselves more than the others for victory and our common safety when, all the time, I could be just one of the crowd and fare no worse than the best? Yet it would be difficult to find anything more conceited than man. Those who openly reach after more [than the others do] — these are the men we admire, and think them men indeed. So it is through this lust for honour that I go on, shouldering the burden of public affairs, wearing myself out, always ready to confront new dangers. I am afraid to destroy the good name I have established in the past.

(*Orations*, 59)

We encounter in this play the first datable use of the word *apragmōn*.[4] This is one of only two surviving instances in

---

[4] In the adverbial form *apragmonōs*. The occurrence in Antiphon's *Second Tetralogy* is earlier if we accept the conjectured dating of that work to the 440s. See Chapter 5, note 23.

Euripides (the other being in the *Antiope*). It is not a poetic word. Odysseus' role as a *chrēstos* is recognizable: he is a leader of men, a chief, honoured by the many, and driven by the familiar urge to honour and fame, even at the cost of exertion and danger. 'Nothing is more vainglorious than a man' he says. Odysseus was, for Plato, the very type of such a man.[5] Pericles too would have recognized these norms as self-evident. What, then, is this truly extraordinary admission that Odysseus makes: 'If I stayed quietly in the ranks I should fare no worse than the wisest'? This is the point at which the Homeric world of daring, of prowess, of exertion, honour, and fame, comes up abruptly against the world of the radical democracy.

It does not really matter if Odysseus, as a character of fiction, or Euripides himself, is biased in his opinion. The important point is not so much whether the upper classes were worse off under the radical democracy as whether they *thought* they were. It is their own perception of their position *vis-à-vis* the masses which will determine their behaviour. At the same time it must be remembered that this play is not a private reflection by the poet, but was presented for approval to a mass audience. It is unlikely that Euripides would have expressed these thoughts if he expected them to be drowned by jeers of derision, especially as they occur not during the main action of the play where they might have been answered by an antagonist, but in the prologue where they may be allowed to stand as a generalized reflection on current practice. Parallel instances abound in Euripides' plays.[6]

Odysseus asks himself why he goes on striving, labouring, risking, when it is possible to remain anonymous in the ranks, and fare no worse than the wise man (or nobleman; it is clear from Dio's paraphrase, as elsewhere, that these are the same). His answer is that he is afraid of losing his reputation for intelligence and hence his status among the Greeks. But status (*timē*) in the *Philoctetes* is no longer accompanied by substantial material rewards as in Homer, and this is the burden of his meaning. The captains and chiefs may perform their deeds, they

---

[5] Plato, *Rep.* 620 c. The shade of Odysseus rests at last from his toils.
[6] Euripides' perceptions on political matters have been discussed exhaustively by R. Goossens, *Euripide et Athènes*; and di Benedetto, *Euripide: Teatro e società*.

may strive and run risks. The city will honour them but they will not, at the end of the day, be any better off than the ordinary citizen.

The speech, if it has any relevance at all, and judging by Euripides' other plays I think it must have, is saying that there was for the Athenian upper class a considerable disincentive to entering public service, in particular the generalship. Is there any other evidence that this might be so?

The Athenians still elected their generals from among the rich, and continued to so so throughout the classical period. Lamachus stands out because he is the only documented example of a general who was not rich.[7] Yet though rich men undertook the generalship largely at their own expense, the *dēmos* would come down very hard on them if they failed in the discharge of their duty. For the general, there was the not inconsiderable risk of prosecution if a campaign failed; we know of six generals in the ten years of the Archidamian War who were fined or exiled, and one who stayed away to avoid the danger of it.[8] Ten generals were elected each year, but we know that generals sometimes served more than one year. If we suppose that only seventy generals served in those ten years, it would appear that they stood a one in ten chance of prosecution. I suggest that this is a high probability. Even if there had been more than seventy generals, the risk would still have been high.

Again, the character of the *euthynai*—the audit at the end of the year of service—was such as to give a general, or prospective general, pause for thought. It was not merely an opportunity for anyone who had a grievance against him arising from his conduct in office to seek redress, or even for a public-spirited 'watch-dog of the people' to call him to book; more than these, it was an opportunity for his enemies to get at him, to make mischief, to besmirch his reputation, and if possible to ruin his career.

[7] J. K. Davies suggests Lamachus had been rich and become poor (*Wealth and the Power of Wealth in Classical Athens*, 62). During the course of the war there are isolated references in the comic poets to generals being elected from among those not of good family: Eup. fr. 117; Ar. *Frogs*, 718).

[8] Pericles, Paches, Eurymedon, Sophocles, Pythodorus, Thucydides son of Olorus. Demosthenes stayed away. See Fornara, 'The Athenian Board of Generals', *Historia Einzelschrift*, 1971, and W. K. Pritchett, *The Greek State at War*, ii. 4 for a catalogue of all known trials of generals down to 338.

The story of Paches' death by his own hand at his *euthynai* is most instructive. During his campaign in Lesbos he had got possession of two free women by force, after killing their husbands. They afterwards complained, or caused a complaint to be made, at his *euthynai*, and such was the scandal that he slew himself in open court.[9]

The significance of this story is considerable because it shows that citizens of subject cities were able to bring their complaints against Athenian generals or governors to the popular courts at Athens. Some idea of the conduct of these courts comes across in the accounts of the trial of the generals after Arginousai by Xenophon, and of the fantasy trial of Labes the dog in Aristophanes' *Wasps*. What strikes us most about these trials is their, by modern standards, irrational and illogical character. There appear to have been no rules of evidence, and accordingly plaintiffs, accusers, and 'watch-dogs of the people' were free to introduce any scurrilous material they chose. By the same token, defendants were free to defend themselves as best they might, introducing no matter what extraneous matter; parading their children on the platform in a plea for mercy was probably only the most colourful element.

Aristophanes' Paphlagonian boasts of his power to 'trim the generals' (*Knights*, 166),[10] and there need be no doubt that the real Cleon, who as Thucydides tells us, was noted for his loud voice and threatening manner, could pose a considerable threat to any general at his *euthynai* if he chose, regardless of the facts of a particular case.

The generalship, like other official posts, was, in some respects, a survival from the past. In a sense, the general is still the 'shepherd of the people' from Homer — the man to whom the people naturally look for leadership. The Homeric captains and chiefs could expect substantial rewards for their pains, as I showed in Chapter 1; they were entitled to the first choice of booty, tripods, oxen, slavegirls; they expected lands, a place of honour at the dinner-table, the choice meats, and wine cups. It is clear, however, that by the fifth century this was no longer the case

---

[9] *Anth. Pal.* 614. This story was written down nearly a thousand years after the event. *CAH* (v. 218 n.) merely records the story; Grote accepts it (v. 178).

[10] See Chapter 5, note 41.

because, although the *dēmos* still looked to the generals to provide leadership in time of war and in the conduct of the Empire, the *dēmos* itself had slowly usurped the ultimate authority. If the captains and chiefs now attempted to lay hands on the booty, as in the case of Labes/Laches, there would be a public watchdog to bring them to justice.

The attitude of the democracy towards the choice of its leaders at this time is preserved by the author of the Ps.-Xenophon *Constitution of the Athenians*:

Then there are those offices which bring safety to the whole people if they are in the hands of the *chrēstoi* and danger if they are not. The people want no share in these; they do not think they should cast lots for the post of general or cavalry commander, for they know they are better off if they have no part in these offices but leave them to the most capable (*dynatoi*). They are only interested in those offices which bring pay and profit to themselves.

(1. 3)

It is clear from this passage, as from elsewhere (Arist. *Pol.* 1282ᵃ 31), that generals were elected from among the wealthy only, and that there was no money to be made from the post, at least officially. The fact that it often involved expense may also be significant, and it cannot be coincidence that other public offices put their holders to sometimes considerable outlay: the trierarchy cost a talent in a year; going on an embassy was an expensive business; and there were the liturgies.[11]

Evidence of a general's expenses comes from the fourth century: when Aristophanes went on an expedition to Cyprus in 390, Lysias tells us 'it was Aristophanes who personally supplied most of the funds', and this included hiring sailors and mercenary soldiers, and buying weapons (Lys. 19. 22); then there are Timotheos' expenditures (Dem. 49. 6-8) in 373; and those of Nausicles, Diotimos, and Charidemos (Dem. 18. 114). Xenophon tells the story of Nicomachides, an experienced soldier who was beaten in the election for general by a business man, Antisthenes, who appeared to know nothing of warfare (*Mem.* 3. 4). Socrates makes the point that Antisthenes, being rich, will

---

[11] On ambassadors' expenses, see D. J. Mosley, 'Envoys and Diplomacy in Ancient Greece', *Historia Einzelschrift*, 22 (1973).

be able to supply the soldiers' needs.[12] It is impossible to know whether this anecdote is historical, that is, of the fifth century, or reflects conditions at the time when Xenophon was writing; in other words, were these expenses by generals a consequence of the loss of imperial revenue, or had they always been the case? I suspect the latter.

It has been argued, however, that if generals were put to expense, there would also have been opportunities for them to recoup themselves while on expedition.[13] Evidence for the fifth century is confined to one oblique reference in Thucydides, and otherwise one is compelled to argue by analogy, or backwards from the fourth century. At the time when the oligarchs were planning their coup in 411, Thucydides reports Phrynichus, one of the oligarch leaders, as saying that he doubted whether the subject cities would support them, since they (the subject cities)

wanted to be slaves under the oligarchs no more than under the democracy; they would prefer to be free, no matter what the system. They did not think the so-called upper classes would give them less trouble than the democracy, for it was they who were the proposers and contrivers of the crimes which the democracy committed, and they mainly profited from them too.

(8. 48. 5)

It is not clear whether Phrynichus is talking in general—is the whole of the Empire to be construed as a crime? After all, Pericles had referred to it as a tyranny. Or does Phrynichus refer to individual, isolated, actions? Are we to think of the sacking of cities, or perhaps of straightforward extortion by force of arms? Members of the Athenian upper class went out as generals and governors to administer, oversee, and control subject cities. Perhaps they had the sort of opportunities which were offered to Cicero when he went out to serve a term as proconsul of Cappadocia? In his *Letters to Atticus*, (5. 16, 5. 18, and especially 5. 21), he tells how he is showered with honours because he has

---

[12] Cf. Davies, op. cit., 128.

[13] Discussed by Pritchett, op. cit., 126–32; See also Perlman, 'The Political Implications of Proxenia in the Fourth Century', *CQ*, NS 8 (1958), 190 ff.; de Ste Croix, *The Class Struggles in the Ancient World*, 604–5; Lactor, *The Athenian Empire*, 21 and 146; M. I. Finley denies it ('Empire in the Greco-Roman World', *Greece and Rome*[2], 25 (1978), 8).

not extorted money from the natives: 'In return for these benefits, which amazed the natives, I allow them to confer on me none but verbal honours; I forbid statues, temples, and chariots, nor am I a burden to them in any other way.'

A parallel example comes from the fourth century in the case of Androtion (Tod, *SGHI* II. 152), who is awarded the privilege of becoming hereditary *proxenos* (representative) of Arcesine on the island of Amorgos. Amorgos had been in the Delian League and is known to have paid tribute in the years 434/3 to 429/8 BC. In 373 it had been enrolled in the Second Athenian Confederacy and Athens stationed a governor and garrison there in contravention of an express promise. In the decree, which probably dates from around 357, Androtion is honoured for his kindness as governor, his loans free of interest, and his advance of wages to the garrison. In addition to becoming *proxenos*, Androtion is awarded a gold crown to the value of fifty drachmas. The implication is that Androtion's kindness to the citizens of Arcesine, like that of Cicero to the Cappadocians, is in contrast to the normal practice of provincial governors, and hence that provincial governors normally regarded the Empire as a source of profit.

There is another and more explicit testimony from the fourth century. Demosthenes, in a speech, tells the Athenians:

Every general who has ever sailed from Athens — I will stake anything on this — has extracted money from Chios and Erythrae and from any city in Asia he can. Those with only one or two ships take less, those with a larger fleet more. And those who give, either more or less, are not so insane as to do so for nothing; they buy protection for their traders, safe passage, convoy, that sort of thing. This kind of extortion goes under the heading 'good will'.

(Dem. 8. 24)[14]

On the face of it, this would appear to be just the kind of thing we are looking for: Athenian generals extorting money from provincial cities. However, Demosthenes goes on: 'Where else do you think they would find the means to pay their soldiers, since you give them nothing, and they don't have it themselves?' (Ibid., 26.)

---

[14] Cf. Dem. 4. 24, 45, 47; 2. 28. Cf. Grote, IX. 217.

What might have been an excuse for a general to enrich himself in the fourth century will not really hold for the fifth. Even if payment was sometimes irregular, Athens certainly had the means to pay its sailors in the earlier period. Generals could not use this as an excuse. Again, despite much to the contrary from fourth-century orators, there is some evidence from inscriptions that offices which might have been thought to be a source of profit—such as steward of public moneys and general—were not always filled;[15] a post such as steward (*tamias*) was in fact regarded as a liturgy—an expense to its holder rather than the opposite (And. *On the Mysteries*, 132).

It might be thought too that generals engaged in collecting arrears of tribute from subject cities would have opportunities to enrich themselves, yet there is evidence throughout the fifth century of increasingly tight financial control. The decree of Kleinias (ML 46) for example, dated approximately to 446, provided for a system of *symbolae* to seal money-bags and hence prevent embezzlement of tribute money; on other occasions, stewards were sent out to accompany generals and oversee collection of the tribute.

We know that in many cases democracies had been set up in subject cities by Athens, and that in others the local *dēmos* was more friendly towards Athens than towards its own local oligarchy. The case of Mytilene springs to mind: during the siege of Mytilene by the Athenians in 427, the *dēmos*, given arms at last by their masters, turned immediately against them and demanded that the food stores be shared out (Th. 3. 27). Both Thucydides and Ps.-Xenophon make the point that the *dēmos* in Athens naturally sided with the *dēmos* in other cities, while oligarch sided with oligarch (Th. 3. 82; Ps.-Xen. 1. 14). Where did the Athenian general, member of a naturally oligarchic class, stand, caught between the *dēmos* of Athens, and that of some subject city? From this consideration alone, any comparison with Roman conditions is absolutely out of order.[16]

The point is not whether Athenian generals were more or less eager than anyone else to embezzle funds or otherwise grow rich in the execution of their duty when they could find an

---

[15] M. H. Hansen, 'Perquisites for Magistrates', *Class. et Med.* 32 (1980), 122.

[16] de Ste Croix, *Origins of the Peloponnesian War*, 44.

opportunity, but rather that they were kept in check by a *dēmos* which was suspicious of its upper class anyway, and particularly watchful for any kind of irregularity among its generals. Nothing we know of Athenian juries inclines us to believe that they would be lenient towards a general accused of malversation; it was, after all, *their* money in question.[17]

There were, however, two other possibilities for generals: (*a*) to lend money to a city; (*b*) to acquire property in a subject city as a source of income. There is definite evidence under both these headings, and it would seem likely that a wealthy general or governor visiting a subject city would be well placed either to lend money at favourable rates of interest, or to invest in property. We know that Athenians were lending money and investing in property. For example, the treaty between Athens and Selymbria (ML 87)[18] speaks of the restitution of land or houses owned by Athenians or their allies and lost in the recent war between Athens and Selymbria (410–408) but not of the restitution of debts or money on deposit. It appears from this that, before 410, Athenians had owned houses and land in Selymbria, had had money deposited, and had been owed money, presumably by the Selymbrians, singly or together.

Another inscription is the decree of Aristoteles (Tod, *SGHI* II. 123, dated before 377) which contains two important clauses: in one, Athens promises to restore all property possessed by Athenians in allied territories; in the other, Athenians are henceforth forbidden to own property in allied territory. It has been plausibly suggested that the first clause refers to land owned by Athenians before 404.[19]

The most direct evidence, however, comes from the Hermokopid inscriptions. The largest fortune known in ancient Athens consisted of property in Euboea, in the Lelantine plain, in Geraistos, and in Diros; this was the property of Oionias,[20] convicted of defacing the Herms in 415. When it was sold, it

---

[17] Most trials seemed to have involved money. See references in note 8, above.

[18] Property of Athenians outside Attica is discussed by P. Gauthier, 'A propos des clérouquies athéniennes du vᵉ siècle' in *Problèmes de la terre en Grèce ancienne*, ed. M. I. Finley.

[19] By Ed. Meyer. Cf. Gauthier, op. cit., 170.

[20] The Hermokopid inscriptions were published by K. W. Pritchett in *Hesperia* 22 (1953), 225–99. For Oionias, see Stele II, 177–9, 311–14.

realized the staggering sum of 81⅓ talents. The extent of this amount may be gauged from the fact that the threshold for liability to liturgy service—which defines what the Athenians considered rich—was a property of three talents, and that no more than 400 qualified, out of a total of 30,000 citizens.[21] Other men named in the inscription as owning property outside Attica are Adeimantos son of Leukolophides, who was back in favour, and office, by 408, and Nikides son of Phoenix. There are records of land held in Abydos, Thasos, and Naxos (Plat. *Euthyphro*, 4), and Andocides in 392 speaks of the desire of the Athenians to recover 'the Chersonese, our colonies, our landed property abroad, and the debts owed us' (3. 15). Since 'our landed property' is distinguished from 'our colonies' which were State ventures, it is fairly certain that Andocides is referring to private property.

The property of Oionias was so enormous that it is difficult to believe it was typical of overseas possessions. Most other large fortunes known to us were far smaller than this: Conon was worth about forty talents, and Callias left fourteen talents. Only Nicias is thought to have been worth more: perhaps as much as 100 talents.

However, I doubt whether Oinias acquired his property in Euboea in the manner described above: that is, through visits in some official capacity. For one thing, he is not known to have held any offical post. It is possible he had acquired the land through marriage; it seems likely that the Euboeans had a 'special relationship' with Athens and that an Athenian might marry a Euboean without endangering the civic rights of his children.[22] Even if that were not the case, it may have come into his family through marriage in an earlier generation, before Pericles' marriage laws, as Thucydides is thought to have acquired his mineral rights in Thrace.

The question, therefore, is this: if opportunities abounded for generals and other officials to grow rich in the service of the Empire, what does Odysseus mean in his speech, and why should the generalship and other official posts have continued, in the headiest days of democracy, to be reserved to a wealthy few?

---

[21] See J. K. Davies, op.cit., 16.
[22] Lysias, 34. 3 See *RE* s.v. *epigamia*: 'jedenfalls vor 413'.

The significance of Odysseus' speech must be that although opportunities were there for wealthy men to grow rich by the Empire, this is not to say that the *chrēstoi*, the traditional governing class, were necessarily doing so. It is possible, for example, that during the war, investment in the Empire would have been regarded as a high risk, since in the event of a change in the fortunes of the war the investor stood to lose everything, as did, in fact, happen. (A high-risk, speculative investment would have attracted a proportionately high rate of interest and if allied cities were forced to borrow money, for instance to pay tribute, at high rates of interest, this extortionate element could be what Phrynichus referred to as 'crimes'.)

The idea that Athenians of all classes were indiscriminately making money from the Empire is in any case contradicted by Thucydides himself in his second speech attributed to Pericles in 430. The city had been assailed, not only by a second Peloponnesian invasion, but also by the terrible and unexpected blow of the plague. In their demoralized state, the people attack Pericles for having led them into war, and the speech he makes in his defence (2. 60 ff.) is a justification for the Empire—how the Athenians acquired it and why they are keeping it. In particular, he must justify himself against the arguments of those who would give it up, the *apragmones*. Pericles justifies the Athenians very much in the terms I explored in Chapter 1: aggression is dignified as 'striving' (*ponos*)—'Your fathers achieved all this through their exertions'; yet in the end he cannot deny that the Empire was achieved through aggression, which may be wrong. The justification for that aggression was *timē*: like a Homeric warrior the city has struggled, taken risks, endured labours, and as a result has achieved honour and fame. The *apragmōn* in this context is one who would give it all up, who would rather the Athenians had never acquired the Empire:

It is no longer possible for you to give it up, in case anyone here in the present circumstances is panicking and wants to play the fine gentleman in political obscurity. You rule your Empire like a tyrant; it may have been wrong to take it, it is certainly dangerous to let it go. If these sort of people were to persuade others they would quickly bring the city to destruction, even if they lived somewhere by themselves on their own. Men who are politically apathetic will not be safe unless they co-operate with people who are active, and they

are useless in a city that rules an Empire, though they would make
safe slaves in a city ruled by others.

You must not be led astray by people like these, nor should you
be angry with me, with whom you yourselves decided to go to war.

(2. 63. 2)

It is clear that the term *apragmōn* is being used here in a different
sense from that in the previous passage (2. 40. 2). There it
signified one who withdrew or abstained from political life. Here
it refers to men who are talking of giving up the Empire and
persuading others to do so. Clearly these men are not literally
apragmones because then we should not expect to find them at
the assembly, attempting to persuade others of their point of view.
These men are in politics, and they are endeavouring to shape
policy, but they are opposed to Pericles and the aggressive
imperial policy of Athens. Thucydides is using the word in two
slightly different senses: (*a*) simply to refrain altogether from
political activity; (*b*) to be involved, but to endeavour to shape
foreign policy towards a low-key, non-aggressive, quietist
approach. This duality of meaning will be encountered again
in later contexts.

Some writers have suggested that Pericles is not referring in
this passage to any specific group, but generally to those who
were reacting in a momentary panic under the double blow of
the invasion and the plague. Thus A. W. Gomme, in his *Historical
Commentary to Thucydides* (2. 177): 'Pericles has not here, I think,
any specific group in mind, but those who, to whichever group
they traditionally belonged, were at this moment in a nervous
state and said: "We are all for *apragmosyne*, let us make peace
for peace is much better than war." '

There was a momentary panic, it is true, because the
Athenians made overtures of peace to Sparta at this time, but
the opposition to the Empire referred to by Pericles in this speech
was of a more settled and long-term character. This is made clear
a little later; after going on to praise the Athenians for their
achievements in subduing the greater part of the Aegean to their
will, and in raising their city to be the greatest in Hellas, he says:
'although this may be disparaged by those who are politically
apathetic, it will be praised by those who also want to achieve
something.' (2. 64. 4.) The meaning of this passage is clear: there

were men in Athens, and men whose opinions had to be reckoned with whether in politics or not, who were, and had long been, opposed to the creation of the Empire. Their existence must be acknowledged, I think, even in the face of the evidence reviewed above. It is the men referred to here on whom previous discussions have centred. In the first article to discuss *apragmosynē*,[23] Nestle expressed the belief that these speeches were written by Thucydides after 404, and that, in addition to reporting more or less what Pericles said, he was also composing a defence of Pericles' policies against those who blamed him for the outcome of the war. The *apragmones*, according to Nestle, were the philosophers and 'internationalists' found in the company of Protagoras and Hippias, as Plato depicts them, but the speech should also be read as a defence against the accusations of Socrates and his friends as reported, for example, in the *Gorgias*.

This interpretation was contested by Dienelt,[24] who adduced evidence to show that Socrates was no *apragmōn*. Both were partial in their use of evidence, and Ehrenberg[25] correctly pointed out that Socrates stands outside any such classification. For Ehrenberg the *apragmones* were in favour of a quiet time and against war: '*Apragmosynē* involved anti-imperialism, non-aggressive policy, quiet attitude, and therefore peace' (p. 52).

The most interesting suggestion, to my mind, comes in an article by H. T. Wade-Gery on the career of Thucydides son of Melesias,[26] in which Wade-Gery notes Nestle's article and offers Thucydides and his followers as the men referred to by Pericles (app. D). Some of the points made in the article have since been contested, and I think rightly, by A. Andrewes,[27] but important though these criticisms are, I do not think they undermine the basic idea that it was Thucydides, or at least men like him, whom Pericles was attacking.

[23] W. Nestle, 'Apragmosyne', *Philologus*, 81 (1926), 129–40.

[24] K. Dienelt, 'Apragmosyne', *Wiener Studien* 66 (1953), 94–104, reprinted with an addition in *Die Friedenspolitik des Perikles*, 1958.

[25] V. Ehrenberg, 'Polypragmosyne: A Study in Greek Politics', *JHS* 67 (1947), 46–67. Other articles which refer to *apragmosynē* are by G. Meautis, K. Kleve, W. R. Connor, E. Levy, A. W. H. Adkins, J. W. Allison. See Bibliography.

[26] H. T. Wade-Gery, 'Thucydides Son of Melesias', *JHS* 52 (1932), reprinted in *Essays in Greek History*, 239–70.

[27] A. Andrewes, 'The Opposition to Pericles', *JHS* 98 (1978), 1–8.

Thucydides was born around 500 and died about 426.[28] His father had been a great Olympic champion, and the friend of Pindar.[29] His international style of life and the friendships, struck at the games which transcended local boundaries, constituted a non-intellectual cosmopolitanism. This was the real opposition to Athenian imperialism and the war with Sparta, which was its logical outcome. It was this Thucydides who led the opposition to Pericles in the mid-440s and who had opposed the central act of imperialism by Pericles — the appropriation for the Athenians' private use of the surplus of the League funds — and its tangible result: the temples which arose in Athens and the consequent growth of an urban population. It was he too, according to Wade-Gery, who had been behind the series of prosecutions aimed at weakening Pericles in the late 430s.

Thucydides had been about twenty at the time of Salamis, nearly forty when Ephialtes was assassinated, and lived to see the city embark on its war with Sparta. His life, in other words, spans the *Pentecontaeteia*; he saw the whole of the rise of the Empire and the transformation of Athens. The Empire, and the enormous increase in trade and wealth it brought, increased substantially the amount of business transacted by the State: *pragmata*, civil and legal, grew out of all proportion to what they had been in his young days. It follows that the performance of civic duties had grown from something more casual, even amateur, to something highly professional and full-time.[30] In this context, an elderly *apragmōn* is one who looks back nostalgically to a time when politics was a slower and less complicated business. Thucydides and those like him, according to this thesis, were fighting a rearguard action.

As far as Thucydides himself is concerned, however, it must be remarked that Thucydides the historian makes no mention of his namesake, and that, only a few years after the legal actions which, according to Wade-Gery, he is supposed to have instigated against Pericles, the son of Melesias is represented by Aristophanes as an old man 'bowed with age' and broken by

---

[28] See Davies, *APF* 7268. II.

[29] This identification is the most important achievement of Wade-Gery's article.

[30] J. K. Davies, *Democracy and Classical Greece*, 111.

misfortune, no match for the fluent and glib young orators who are persecuting him.[31]

The burden of Andrewes's argument on this score is that there is nothing we know about Thucydides the son of Melesias which requires him to be opposed to the Empire as such, and it has been suggested, as I have outlined above, that men of his class could in fact do very well out of it.[32]

I do not necessarily subscribe to Wade-Gery's suggestion that it is specifically Thucydides to whom Pericles is referring, but I should like to offer some, shall we say, ideological reasons why men like him would have been opposed to the creation of the Empire and to its continuance, and in particular to the war with Sparta, which was the logical outcome.

First, I think Wade-Gery draws very pertinent attention to Melesias' friendship with Pindar. Pindar is thought to have been born about 520, and hence would have been a slightly younger contemporary of Melesias. His work took him throughout the Greek world and he could truly be called Panhellenic or an 'internationalist'; in the games especially he would have been in the company of the well-born from every part of the Greek world. His verse is imbued with the outlook of this international nobility, who were his patrons. Among the many themes which run through his poetry, one in particular is significant and Pindar becomes especially eloquent when he sings of *hēsychia*: peace, tranquillity, order and stability; almost any good which can befall a city may be summed up in it. *Hēsychia*, 'that is dear to cities . . .' (O. 4. 16); 'Let him that gives tranquillity to the community seek the bright light of manly peace (*hēsychia*)' (fr. 109); again, Hieron of Syracuse is exhorted to establish *hēsychia* in the city of Aetna which he is founding for his son (*P*. 1. 70).

Pindar is perhaps at his most sublime in the eighth Pythian ode: 'Kind hearted Peace, daughter of Justice, who makes cities great'. *Hesychia* is represented by Pindar, and by other archaic poets such as Theognis and Aeschylus,[33] as the opposite of

---

[31] Ar. *Ach.* 703; *Wasps*, 947 with schol. Cf. W. R. Connor, *Theopompus and Fifth Century Athens*, 38.

[32] See also P. Harding, 'In Search of a Polypragmatist', in *Classical Contributions*, eds. G. S. Shrimpton and D. J. McCargar. He draws attention to Kimon, a leading *chrēstos*, who actively promoted the Empire (Plut. *Kim.* 11. 2).

[33] e.g. Theognis, 43–7; Aeschylus, *Persians*, 820–2, 840–2; *Agamemnon*, 750 ff.

hybris, unbridled ambition, and its concomitant *koros*, excess. Hybris is the mother of *koros* (*O.* 13. 10); *hēsychia* herself punishes *hybris* (*P.* 8. 1); the tyrant who can manage to choose *hēsychia* avoids baneful *hybris* (*P.* 11. 53). The city (Corinth) in which dwells Justice and Peace (*eirēnē* standing in for *hēsychia*) shall expel *hybris* (*O.* 13. 1).

These thoughts are often expressed in mythological stories, and in the story of Bellerophon, as Pindar tells it,[34] the poet specifically contrasts his own wish for a modest portion with the *hybris* of Bellerophon who sought to fly up to the threshold of heaven itself:

Let me not incur the envy of the immortals as I pursue whatever pleasure the day brings, passing calmly to old age and time's allotted span. We are all mortal, though our fates are different.

(I. 7. 39).

The ode containing the story of Bellerophon was dedicated to Hieron. So were two others, both containing a similar warning: the story of Tantalus who was unable to cope with his good fortune, but through surfeit (*koros*) was seized by an overpowering madness (*atē*) and was punished in the underworld with the eternal fear of the rock about to fall and crush him (*O.* 1. 54); and Ixion who could not cope with his great good fortune and was visited with a 'madness of spirit' and an equally famous punishment (*P.* 2. 21). Pindar, who can seem elsewhere to flatter, is here not afraid to deliver a direct message to his patron, then tyrant of Syracuse.

Together with the warning against *hybris* there are, as in *Isthmian* 7 (above), also the homilies on the quiet life, the unambitious daily round, the exhortation to pursue 'due measure', to remember that one is only mortal: 'In our quest of gain it is right to pursue the due measure; but far too keen are the pangs of madness that come from unattainable longings' (*N.* 11. 48).

In his appeals to oligarchs and tyrants alike, Pindar always implies a norm of good behaviour which in his eyes is aristocratic and goes under the name of *eunomia*; it is characterized by moderation:

---

[34] This part of Bellerophon's story is not found in Homer, which may indicate that it is a creation of the Archaic period.

Of all those in the city I find the middle estate flourishes with greater prosperity, and I condemn the fate of tyrants. I would encourage those deeds of prowess (*aretai*) that serve the city; envious ruin is avoided if that man who has seized the highest place shuns baneful pride and dispenses peace.

(*P*. 11. 53)

Here, *atē* (envious ruin) represents those rivals and enemies who will see to it that the tyrant comes to no good. The way to succeed is to hold the highest place in a peaceful manner. Pindar characterizes rule in the cities by the best people not only as the best form of government, but also as a moderate form of government. It seems likely too that Thucydides the historian, though he had admired Pericles and his achievements, came to regard the downfall of Athens in these terms—baneful pride laid low by envious ruin.

Eunomia is found by Pindar in several cities: Thebes (*Pae*. 1. 10); Opous (*O*. 9. 16); Corinth (*O*. 13. 6); Cyrene (*P*. 5. 67); and Aegina (*I*. 5. 22). Two of these cities, Cyrene and Aegina, were actually under kings or tyrants; *eunomia* is used with a poet's licence, or perhaps a flatterer's art, in these cases. Still, *eunomia* stood as an ideal, even if it rarely existed in reality.

There was, however, one state where it was said to exist, and that was Sparta. Both Herodotus (1. 65) and Thucydides (1. 18) thought that Sparta enjoyed *eunomia*. Thucydides links Sparta's *eunomia* with the absence of tyranny. He also characterizes the Spartan attitude, especially in foreign relations, as one of *hēsychia*. This is especially important since it shows that the Pindaric world-view was by no means obsolete at the outbreak of the Peloponnesian War. It becomes apparent in the comparison of Sparta and Athens in the first book of Thucydides' history; there the two opposing principles—the urge to honour and fame, to striving, daring, reward, discussed in Chapter 1, on the one hand, and that towards moderation, calm, and quiet on the other—are represented by Thucydides as the dominant characteristics of the Athenians and Spartans respectively.

In the conference of the Spartans and their allies (Th. 1. 67 ff.) the Corinthians come forward and castigate the Spartans for their tardiness in countering the aggressive expansion of the Athenians. They do so in terms of an analysis and comparison of the national characters. This is natural, since Thucydides regards the city as being the aggregate of its citizens (Plato takes a similar attitude in his comparison of imperfect societies and their corresponding character types).[35]

I have already discussed the Athenian character (as Thucydides sees it) in Chapter 1: the central characteristic of the Athenians is their daring (*tolma*). They are also called *neoteropoioi*(1. 70. 2). Intellectual restlessness, commercial and artistic inventiveness, as well as military aggressiveness, are all blended in this word. As Euripides puts it in his *Suppliant Women* (321–5), it is through her efforts (*ponoi*) that Athens grows great; other states, eager to avoid trouble (*hēsychoi*) keep their policies dark and look cautiously about them. Euripides' speech is important because it shows that Thucydides' analysis, which might otherwise be attributed in part to his passion for antithesis, was shared by at least one other Athenian.

The whole of Sparta's attitude to foreign relations is summed up as *hēsychia*: 'Alone among the Greeks, you Spartans deliberately avoid trouble, and defend yourselves not by force, but through delay . . .' (1. 69. 4). The Corinthians then go on to define what they mean by the Spartans' *hēsychia*:

You will not realize that for the most part men preserve peace if they use their power justly, but make it clear that they will resist if they are wronged; on the contrary your idea of justice is not to harm others and to avoid being harmed yourselves.

(1. 71. 1)

I have translated *hēsychia* as 'peace', and it is clear from the context that it has the same meaning which *apragmosynē* had for the Corcyreans (1. 32. 5)—to maintain peace by avoiding conflict, by leading a quiet, almost passive existence, as opposed to the dynamic and expansive policy of the Athenians. By comparison with what appears to us to be the positive mentality of the Athenians, *hēsychia* inevitably takes on a negative quality: it is 'sitting tight'. How close *hēsychia* can be to *apragmosynē* appears at 1. 70. 8: the *ascholia epiponos*—restless striving—of the Athenians is opposed to *hēsychia apragmōn*. These last two terms simply reinforce one another; one could not be said to qualify the other.

---

[35] There is no sign here of the idea of the State as something external to and in opposition to the body of the citizens.

The Spartan attitude is defended by King Archidamus (1. 80 ff.). The central point of his advice to his allies is not to rush into any decision but to think things out at their leisure (*hēsychia*). This slowness to act is specifically connected with *sōphrosynē*, which King Archidamus identifies as their central attribute, with modesty, sage counsel, and a lack of *hybris*: 'We alone, through this (our slowness to act) do not become arrogant when we are successful' (1. 84. 2).

The point of this digression into Pindaric and Spartan values is obvious: there was throughout Classical times, through the Peloponnesian War and into the fourth century, a section of the upper class in Athens, well represented in the field of literature, to whom these values were particularly congenial. The earliest extant writings to indicate this may be those of Critias, discussed in the next chapter, but all the themes I have touched on are well canvassed by Aristophanes, Euripides, and above all by Plato.

There is, for example, the speech by Right in the contest of speeches in the *Clouds*; the speech is in general a farrago of fact and fantasy, whose principal object is to extract as many laughs as possible from the audience. Nevertheless, we can see that Aristophanes has been drawing on a body of opinion close to that outlined above. In the speech, the poet deplores the passing of a kind of education that sought to instil the virtues of moderation and justice (961 ff.). He praises boys' hardiness in all kinds of weather, their modesty, silence, and obedience. The speech exhibits characteristics recognizably 'Spartan', and quite unlike the 'education' which, according to Pericles, Athens afforded to all Hellas.

Again, Euripides, when he espouses the cause of the small farmer (see below, Chapter 4) paints his virtues in these colours. The farmer is, according to Euripides, modest and prudent, slow to make up his mind. He is noble, hard-working, peace-loving, *apragmōn* and *hēsychos*. He is especially contrasted with that symbol of the Athenian democracy, the shameless mob-orator (*Orestes*, 902 ff.).

It is Plato, however, in whom this tradition flows most copiously, and it is clear from his work that, though he usually likes to set the scene of his dialogues during the Peloponnesian War, and goes to some trouble to strike an authentic note, nevertheless the manners and style of life, the values and morality expressed here continued to be significant and worthwhile to him well into the fourth century. The tradition was a valid and vigorous one.

All this is set out clearly in the *Charmides*, discussed at length in the next chapter. This dialogue purports to take place in 431, and is a discussion of the nature of *sōphrosynē*, in which Critias suggests that it may be synonymous with *apragmosynē*. Critias is shown in the dialogue, and is known independently from his writings, to have had strong pro-Spartan sympathies. In fact, the very character of Socrates himself, throughout Plato's work, is made to exhibit these characteristics and moral values. Socrates is hardy, frugal, moderate, innately noble. He is strictly upright in his life, prudent in his dealings, the very embodiment of *sōphrosynē*; and in his abstention from public life, *hēsychos*.

It is clear that there was in Athens a section of opinion at the time of the outbreak of the Peloponnesian War which, whatever formal allegiance it might feel to its own city, was aligned *ideologically* with Sparta, and whose world-view was broadly that of Pindar. To such people the aggressive imperialism of Athens was the striving of overweening ambition, of baneful *hybris*. Even Pericles was aware of this attitude when he advised the Athenians not to seek to gain more, but to hold on to what they had already got. He was conscious of the danger of going too far, and Thucydides sees the later part of the war in these terms: Athens overreaching and being struck down in her pride. It is a matter of degree: Pericles may advise not going any further; to others, Athens had already gone too far.

These were the men who opposed the Peace of Callias in 449, for once peace descended between Persia and Athens, it was inevitable that hostility would sharpen between Athens and Sparta. Neither is it far-fetched to suggest they would oppose, as Plutarch says they did, the construction of the temples on the acropolis, if they were of that frugal, not to say parsimonious, character thought to be typically Spartan (cf. Plat. *Gorg.* 518 E and below, Chapter 7).

The element of internationalism should also be stressed. The implication is that the loyalty of a powerful and wealthy man to his friends and relations in other states could conflict with his loyalty to his own country. In this context, the significance of

Pericles' marriage-laws cannot be over-emphasized.[36] They were aimed directly at those who sought to strengthen their connections with the rich and powerful in other states through the bond of marriage. The consequences of this may be traced through the history of city-states. In a contest for power within a city, party friendship can count for more than loyalty to the city itself, and rival factions may call on their kin in neighbouring cities to help them. Hence, as often happened, an internal struggle developed into war between cities. In their desire to dominate the State, men were sometimes prepared to destroy the State. This was the case in Athens in 411 when, as Thucydides tells us, the oligarchs 'had no intention of being the first to be destroyed by the democracy when it was restored, but would rather call in the enemy . . .' (8. 91. 3), and there are no less than twenty-seven documented cases of cities betrayed by treachery during the Peloponnesian war.[37] When Pericles surrendered his lands to public ownership at the outbreak of that war for fear that he might be favoured by Archidamus as he ravaged Attica, he was responding to a suspicion clearly in the minds of the Athenian people: Archidamus' friendship with Pericles will be stronger than his enmity to Athens.

Internationalism, then, represents a conflict of loyalties: men such as the son of Melesias would be unwilling to be dragged into a war in which they would be ranged alongside those they despised (the masses) and against those friends and relations they might have in foreign cities. But is this kind of internationalism, the internationalism of the games, the same as that other, intellectual, brand, of Hippias and Protagoras, of which Nestle spoke in his article? According to Hippias, in a celebrated phrase, men were brothers not by custom (*nomos*) but by nature (*physis*). This must have been what his audience, which was composed of men from Thucydides' class, wanted to hear. Hippias abolished their obligations to their fellow citizens (according to *nomos* — the traditional laws of the city) and underlined their ties with their friends and relations in other cities — those like

---

[36] See Jacoby, comm. on Philochorus, 119 (*FGH* IIIb, suppl. 1) with the appendix on the law, pp. 471–82. Most recently, C. Patterson, *Pericles' Citizenship Law of 451–450,* 1981. She denies that the law was aimed at weakening these connections, and points out that such connections were valuable, e.g. with ambassadors, *proxenoi*, etc. (100 ff.).

[37] A. L. Losada, *The Fifth Column in the Peloponnesian War,* 15 ff.

themselves in their true nature (*physis*). Hippias provided an ideological basis for a loyalty felt instinctively.

It must be pointed out, however, that neither Hippias nor Protagoras was advocating a life of *apragmosynē* within the city. They drew their income from the fees of those young men like Socrates' friend Hippocrates (see next chapter) who wanted to learn the art of dominating events; for them, a man's innate worth, his *aretē*, was expressed by his capacity to control the *dēmos* (Plat. *Prot.* 316 B). The *apragmosynē* of men like Thucydides lay in their desire to steer the city back to a more modest and less aggressive foreign policy, one which would enable them to reach an accommodation with Sparta. It should be clear from this that such men, the 'Internationalists', are not to be confused with other *apragmones* who simply wanted to avoid politics altogether. *Apragmosynē*, as I said, has these two distinct meanings in Thucydides, and the failure to see this is, I think, a weakness of Nestle's article.

I come back to the central question: if opportunities abounded for members of the upper classes to profit by the Empire, possibly through official posts like the generalship, what are we to make of Odysseus' speech? And why did all the important official posts continue to be in the hands of a wealthy few? In other words, what was the incentive to *apragmosynē* for a wealthy Athenian?

The heart of the matter, it seems to me, lies in the contradiction in the position of the *chrēstoi*. Expected, on the one hand, to perform a leading role, to lead the *dēmos* into battle, to offer up prayers on its behalf to the gods, to negotiate on its behalf with foreign powers, and in large measure to underwrite its expenses, they were nevertheless answerable to a popular tribunal which, by all accounts, was short tempered, short-sighted, and had a short memory. This is the picture which Euripides presents in the very year of the Funeral Speech; for his Odysseus a public career offers the prospect of fame and honour, but, as Odysseus makes clear, nothing else: 'If I were to remain anonymous in the ranks I would fare no worse than the wisest'.

The fact is that the evidence I have reviewed so far is inconclusive: we know that generals on active service might be expected to contribute to the expenses of the expedition; we also hear of opportunities for them to extract money from subject cities. Yet we have no idea whether one outweighed the other, or whether they roughly balanced out. Euripides' Odysseus inclines me to think that generalship was not an automatic opportunity for aggrandizement.

I also hinted that investment in allied cities might have been regarded as a speculation—a high-risk speculation, since in the event the investors lost all their money. It seems to me reasonable to suppose that there existed a wide gulf between the *chrēstoi*, men like Thucydides son of Melesias, bred to a high social position yet out of tune with the radical democracy, and other kinds of rich men; as I pointed out in Chapter 1, both Plato and Aristotle, in the three kinds of life they describe, distinguished between those who pursued a public career and those only interested in making money.

In other words, because some men were investing in the Empire, we should not therefore assume that all *chrēstoi* were, or necessarily wanted to. I have sketched what I regard as the ideological outline, framed according to Pindaric and Spartan values, of the kind of man I believe would not.

The position of the *chrēstoi* is critical around this time, and in the next chapter I shall examine their position with regard to the radical democracy further, in the phenomenon of 'noble youths'. Later on I shall show how, after the fiasco of the oligarchic revolutions, their ideology was transmuted by Plato into the philosophic concept of the Contemplative Life.

I have in this chapter been discussing a section of the Athenian upper class, the *chrēstoi*, but Thucydides' references to *apragmones* are in fact vague; as I said earlier, he could have been talking about other sections of Athenian life which I have not yet mentioned. In subsequent chapters I shall attempt to examine the whole phenomenon of *apragmosynē* in the late fifth century. I have mentioned the position of the *chrēstoi*; there are two other areas of Athenian life to which it is possible Thucydides was referring—the Attic peasant, and the 'rich quietist': it will be seen that the meetings of the assembly never constituted more than a sample of the citizenship and that a large part, possibly even a majority, of the peasantry came seldom if ever to the assembly. This was the fact which endeared them to oligarchic theorists, so that it was on the *apragmosynē* of the peasants, the backbone of the hoplite census, that the oligarchs relied in 411. There was also a section of the Athenian wealthy classes which endeavoured to avoid politics and public life—the 'rich quietists'. In the developed democracy they felt, or thought they felt, the animosity of the poor and dreaded confronting them on the benches of the popular jury courts. This led to a peculiar life of generous contributions to public festivals and other expenses combined with a timid and respectful attitude toward the jury if and when they became involved in litigation.

Through these three broad categories I hope, in the subsequent chapters, to clarify the kind of men Thucydides could have been referring to—the *apragmones*.

3

Noble Youths

The noble youth was, of course, a phenomenon of every generation of Athenian life, but during the 420s he takes on a particular interest in the context of this discussion. And it is, paradoxically, not so much for what he does, as for what he does not do, that he attracts attention. In every age, noble youths were groomed for an important social role, yet, in the 420s, there is evidence to suggest that some at least were rejecting their traditional place in society and choosing a private life instead. Consider first the character of Euripides' Hippolytus.

Hippolytus

Hippolytus was a figure of legend and cult, and in this particular context, of fiction. But such is Euripides' approach that we can consider some aspects of Hippolytus' character as reflecting real life in 428 BC, the year in which the play was produced. Hippolytus is a young prince who has devoted himself exclusively to the hunt, and to the worship of Artemis. He constantly justifies himself in his way of life, using two terms especially: *sōphrōn*[1] and *semnos*. His *sōphrosynē* is usually, though not always, associated with his virginity, on which he lays great stress. It is made clear at the beginning of the play that Hippolytus is of an age to marry, yet deliberately chooses not to. Whereas *sōphrosynē* was normally considered self-control, with him it has become exaggerated in the sexual sphere into abnegation. It has become transformed into its opposite: a quality which symbolizes

---

[1] Hippolytus describes himself as *sōphrōn* at 995, 1007, 1034–5, 1100, 1364–5. H. North (*Sōphrosynē*) identifies Hippolytus' *sōphrosynē* exclusively with his chastity. This is not the whole story: cf. 995 ff. Barrett comments on lines 79–81: 'Hippolytus' requirement of *moral* purity is alien to the ordinary Greek until Hellenistic times.' See also D. W. Lucas, 'Hippolytus' *CO* 39 (1946), 19–33; and H. North, 'A Period of Opposition to Sophrosyne', *TAPhA* 78 (1947), 1–17. None of these commentators notices the political significance of his words at 986 ff: his fastidiousness towards women is matched by that towards the common people.

moderation and balance has become a dangerous and unstable extreme.

A similar transformation is visible in Euripides' use of *semnos*.[2] Its root meaning is 'august, holy' and as such it is applied in the play to Artemis and Aphrodite, the two goddesses who represent opposite poles of conduct, as well as being used as an epithet for any kind of divine manifestation: the Corybantes, Diktynna, the Mysteries. It is a delicate piece of dramatic irony to take this epithet and apply it, in a reversed sense, to Artemis' devotee, Hippolytus. While she is revered as *semnos*, he is *accused* of it, accused of being 'haughty and reserved'. This ironic use of *semnos* parallels the distortion of Hippolytus' *sōphrosynē*.

His physical chastity is mirrored by a kind of psychological chastity, a refusal or incapacity to confront his own nature. Perhaps he was just immature: this immaturity, a kind of ignorance or blindness, is brought out in the discussion with the slave at the beginning of the play when he says, quite sincerely, 'What proud man (*semnos*) is not odious?' Even after he has been broken by the power of a god, his blindness is intact: 'Ah, Zeus, Zeus, do you see? I was reverend (*semnos*), god-fearing, before all men in prudence (*sōphrosynē*) (1364). Whether Euripides regards these excesses in his character as merely immaturity, something he will grow out of, or as some freakish distortion of personality, is difficult to determine. The Greeks were conscious of the various ages of man, and would criticize those they considered to be not acting their age.[3] The important point is that Hippolytus is an abnormal character when measured against the normality of Theseus.

---

[2] Kypris is *semnos* at 99, 103; Artemis at 61, 713; the Mysteries at 24; the Corybantes at 143, Diktynna at 1130. Hippolytus describes himself as *semnos* at 1364; his hands are 'pure' at 83. Theseus *accuses* Hippolytus of being *semnos* at 957, 1064, 1080. *Semnos* is 'stuck-up' in Aristophanes' *Frogs* (178), and *Wealth* (275), and it can mean 'elegant, gentlemanly' (*Wasps*, 1174). Plutarch says that Pericles' enemies accused him of adopting a *semnos* manner to win popularity (*Per.* 5.3); usually, as with Cleon, the opposite is alleged.

[3] Cf. Hippocrates' seven ages of man (Pollux, 2. 4) (cf. Chapter 5, note 44) and a recently discovered inscription from Bactria (L. Robert, 'De Delphes à l'Oxus. Inscriptions grecques nouvelles de la Bactriane' *CRAI* (1968), 416–57), where the virtue of a young man is 'self-control' (*enkratēs*). The disparaging use of terms like *neanias* and *meirakion* implies that the young men in question were not acting their age (cf. Chapter 5). Hippolytus, however, refers to himself as a man (994, 1031).

Hippolytus has been accused of raping his stepmother. He opens his speech as follows:

> I am not clever (*kompsos*) at speaking before a crowd.
> I am more accomplished before a few of my own age.
> This is as it should be, for those who can sway
> The mob are of no account among the wise.
>
> (986–9)

Theseus has accused him of hungering after the throne. He replies:

> But is it sweet to hold sway?[4] To the wise man
> Not at all, since sole power corrupts the minds of those
> To whom it gives pleasure. I would rather win
> First place in the Hellenic games and be second in
> The city, living a prosperous life with noble friends.
> Thus it is possible to do well in life[5]
> And the absence of danger is a greater pleasure (*charis*)
> Than any tyranny could give.
>
> (1013–20)

Given Hippolytus' own description of his life, his opening remarks, though reminiscent of a rhetorical commonplace,[6] go much further; they are a genuine description of himself. Hippolytus prefers a life apart from power and responsibility: his political virginity is as complete as that of his sexual nature. The force of *kompsos* is particularly relevant, and ties up with the later references to the corrupting influence of power. *Kompsos* here represents everything that is devious, cynical, manipulative, everything that is not straightforward and honest; everything that to a young and ardent mind is distasteful and repellent in democratic politics.[7] To him, all that is valuable is associated

---

[4] I have put the question mark after *hēdu* in 1013 with Murray. Barrett follows the MSS and places it at the end of the line. I have preferred to read *prassein gar eu paresti* in 1019 against Murray and Barrett. Freed from the dangers attendant on kingship, Hippolytus is able to thrive, prosper, 'do well', especially in the games (cf. schol.).

[5] Barrett interprets *prassein* to mean 'exercise political power' (LSJ iii. 5) and compares the position of Creon in *Oedipus Tyrannus*. Creon's position, however, is one of power without responsibility; Hippolytus, by contrast, wants no contact with power.

[6] Cf. Barrett on this line.

[7] *Kompsos* started as 'neat, intelligent, attractive' and slides through meanings like 'witty', 'clever', to 'clever-clever', 'slippery', and to 'untrustworthy', like Theramenes (*Frogs*, 967) and the Unjust Argument's muse (*Clouds*, 1030). Euripides is *kompsos* three times in Aristophanes. Already in Sophocles' *Antigone* (440) the word is pejorative (line 324). The chorus of flatterers in Eupolis' *Kolakes* proclaim themselves *kompsos* (fr. 159), and in Euripides' *Aiolos*, *kompsa* contrast with the big issues that concern the city (fr. 16).

with a few select friends: 'I speak more fluently among a few of my own age', while the crowd, and with it political power, in whatever form, represents that which is corrupt, dangerous, and unbalanced. The *charis*—charm, grace—of Hippolytus' life is to live out of danger. It is not merely that the people are an enemy to members of his class, but that, in the extremely competitive world of democratic politics, to compete is to invite attacks from one's rivals. That the people were considered an enemy became apparent in the previous chapter in the discussion of the plight of generals, and will emerge again later in this chapter. It is not unusual, either, for Euripides to discuss democratic politics in a mythological context; his plays offer many examples.[8]

Hippolytus is the type in many ways of a young Athenian nobleman,[9] educated in the old-fashioned way, who finds the democracy unattractive and is not prepared to adjust to it. Those who *are* accomplished at pleasing the mob were a well-known phenomenon in 428, attested in many sources; they are 'beneath' the attention of Hippolytus and his friends.

Hippolytus prefers to turn his attention to the Hellenic games; he would rather be first in the games and second in the State. But to be second in the State, as in the games, is to be nowhere: to win is all.[10]

The connection of sport with a distaste for democratic politics occurs elsewhere, notably in the *Gorgias* of Plato, where we hear of the 'lads with the cauliflower ears' who maintain that Pericles had 'made the Athenians lazy and cowardly and garrulous and covetous by his introduction of payment for service to the State'.[11]

The parallel with the situation in the *Gorgias* is continued in the references by Hippolytus to the few *sophoi* in contrast to the many. Hippolytus prefers 'living a prosperous life, with a few friends. Scope for action is assured, and freedom from danger brings gladness greater than a throne's.'

---

[8] e.g. *Philoctetes, Erechtheus, Heracleidae, Suppliants*, and later *Ion, Orestes, Electra, Antiope*.

[9] Not in every way, *pace* Connor (*The New Politicians in Fifth Century Athens*, 185), but Euripides has taken recognizable types as his models.

[10] See above Chapter 1.

[11] Plato, *Gorgias*, 515 E. Cf. Dodds ad loc. The dramatic date of this dialogue is confused: there are various dates, running from 429 to 405 BC. This particular passage refers to Pericles, who died the year before the *Hippolytus* was presented.

The reference to Hippolytus' noble friends reminds us of the political clubs in Athens—the *hetaeriae*—through which much political energy was channelled by the rich and prominent. But in 428, exactly half-way between 444 and 412, their power appears to have been at a low ebb. In 444, Thucydides had been ostracized and, according to Plutarch, all opposition to Pericles, and with him to the radical democracy, ceased. The upper class either retired passively into the background like Hippolytus, or began to plot against the democracy, as the Paphlagonian insists in the *Knights*,[12] or they were forced to come to terms with the political situation pandering, like Nicias, to the crowd.

The qualities associated with Hippolytus—his claim to *sōphrosynē*; his devotion to a close circle of noble friends; his enthusiasm for the hunt;[13] his dislike for democratic politics; his awareness of the dangers lying in wait for such as himself who dare to meddle in politics—these are qualities found in other young men during the 420s.

Charmides

In the first line of Plato's *Charmides*, Socrates says that he has just returned from active service in Potideia. Plato, as is his custom in the early dialogues, sets a historical date to his scene. It is late summer, 432.[14] It is important in discussing this dialogue to test its historicity. Are these the views of young men in 432, or are they ideas which were in the air in the 390s, when Plato wrote the work? The dialogue is a useful starting point to search for parallels to Hippolytus. Hippolytus is a fictional character but in drawing him Euripides looked to real-life figures to supply him with a model. Plato too, I submit, has taken some trouble to think himself back into a world four years before he was born.

Socrates returns from Potideia in 432. He goes immediately to the *palaestra* of Taureas in search of old friends, and as he enters, recognizes most of those he sees. He is brought into the presence of Critias and, after greetings have been exchanged

---

[12] Much evidence is collected by M. Calhoun in *Athenian Clubs*. That the clubs were in the doldrums in 428 is the opinion of F. Sartori (*Le eterie nella vita politica Ateniese*, 64).

[13] On the upper-class, character-forming properties of hunting, cf. Xenophon's treatise, 1. 5.

[14] This is the general opinion. It could conceivably be spring 429; cf. Grote, v.104.

and news imparted, Critias introduces his cousin Charmides, a beautiful and noble young man (and, incidentally, Plato's uncle).[15] Such is his beauty that the others are jostling round for a chance to sit beside him. He is descended from two of the noblest families in Athens: his father is descended from Critias the son of Dropides, whose family had been commemorated in the panegyrics of Anacreon, Solon, and many other poets as 'famous for beauty and prowess and all other high fortune' (157 E). His mother's family is equally distinguished, for his maternal uncle Pyrilampes is reputed never to have found his equal for beauty and stature in Persia at the court of the Great King, or anywhere else in Asia in all the places to which he was sent as ambassador (158 A).

Plato's mother Perictione was Charmides' sister; Critias was a cousin, on his mother's side, of Andocides, another of the richest men in Athens (And. 1. 47). Between them, Critias and Charmides represent the pinnacle of *noblesse*, and at this date, of *jeunesse*. They are the gilded youth of 432.[16]

Plato is writing a dialogue on *sōphrosynē*, the very quality which Hippolytus claimed as his own. Charmides is described as excelling in it (157 D), so Socrates asks him what he thinks it means. Here is his first answer:

Sōphrosynē, he said, he thought meant doing everything in an orderly and quiet fashion, walking in the street, or conversing, or anything else. And in fact, he said, 'I think it is a kind of quietness (*hēsychiotēs*).'

(159 B)

This passage helps to date the intellectual climate of the dialogue to around the year 430, for it is reminiscent of the right argument in Aristophanes' *Clouds* of 423, who, in talking of the old style of education, says: 'When people still kept to traditional

---

[15] Again, like Hippolytus, not a boy; Socrates: 'He wasn't unremarkable even then when he was a *pais* (boy), but now I imagine he must be a *meirakion*.' When Charmides appears, Critias says 'what do you think of the *neaniskos*?' (154 D.) He is surrounded by amorous friends, which could put him in the late teens. Cf. Dover, *Greek Homosexuality*, 85 ff. A *neaniskos*, like a *meirakion*, is old enough to enter politics: Glaucon is not yet twenty; Alcibiades was around twenty-three when he is first mentioned as a well-known public speaker. Alcibiades at twenty was still a *meirakion* (Plut. *Alc.* 7). In Menander's *Dyskolos*, Gorgias is a *meirakyllion* (line 27); at line 39 he is a *neaniskos*, yet he is of marriageable age.

[16] Critias is older than Charmides and is his guardian.

ways, justice flourished, and *sōphrosynē* was the custom' (961).[17]

Again, in the discussion of the national characters of the Athenians and Spartans in Thucydides' first book, there is a close identification of *Sōphrosynē* with *hēsychia* on the Spartan side. This book would have been written almost certainly during the 420s. The identification of these characteristics as Spartan is one that will recur, but in this context it carries no overt political or anti-democratic connotation as yet. In any case, Socrates takes no notice of the cultural aspects of *hēsychiotēs*, for he takes Charmides' words in a very literal sense: it is slowness and quietness, and he is easily able to show that there are many occasions where quietness and slowness are inappropriate — writing and reading, playing the lyre, boxing and the pankration, running, leaping, and bodily exercises. In every case, speed and agility are most attractive, while slowness and quietness are ugly and wrong (159 D).

His first attempt at a definition being demolished, Charmides tries another: 'That *sōphrosynē* means minding your own business (*ta hautou prattein*)' (161 B). This phrase has already been encountered (above, p. 19) in a quotation from the *Republic*; there it meant *apragmosynē*, the deliberate withholding from public affairs. The phrase occurs often in Plato and other fourth-century writers, and whether or not the phrase was in use before them,[18] the identification of *sōphrosynē* with *apragmosynē* had been made by Aristophanes soon after 420 (*Peace*, 1297; *Birds*, 1432 ff.).

Socrates, as before, chooses to misunderstand the sense of this definition. He points out that a schoolmaster does not mind his own business when he is teaching others, nor a physician when he is healing the sick; nor a weaver or builder when they are engaged in their trades. But he avoids the real point of the definition which becomes apparent in another source, Xenophon's *Memorabilia* (3. 7). Here, too, Socrates is having a conversation with Charmides, though the fictional date of the dialogue is much later (*c*.408).[19] Charmides is a respectable man, far more capable than the politicians of the day, but he

---

[17] Cf. Dover comm. on this passage.
[18] There is a phrase in Sophocles' *Electra* which is reminiscent of it. Clytemnestra says to Electra: 'Mind your own business!' (678.)
[19] See Davies, *APF* 8792X, for details of this dating.

nevertheless shrinks from addressing the assembly and taking part in politics. In other words, just as twenty years earlier, Charmides prefers to 'mind his own business', but this time Xenophon's Socrates goes straight to the point:

'Tell me, Charmides, if someone was capable of winning prizes in the Panhellenic games, to bring honour on himself and make his country more famous throughout Greece, and yet did not wish to compete, what kind of a man would you think him?'

'I should think him a coward and a weakling.'

The question goes to the heart of the cultural environment which Charmides inhabits, a world of honour and reputation; the games stand as a metaphor for the political world which custom, breeding, and education have prepared Charmides to enter.

In the ensuing dialogue, Socrates shows that Charmides is fluent and able in private discussions, yet is afraid to address the assembly. But, says Charmides, bashfulness and timidity are natural to a man, and affect him more powerfully in a crowd than in a private meeting. Socrates is of a very different opinion:

You are ashamed to address the feeblest and most foolish of men: the fullers, the shoe-makers, builders, smiths, farmers, business men . . . for these are the men who make up the assembly. You are like a man who can beat trained athletes, and yet is afraid of amateurs. You can converse easily with the leading men of the city, some of whom despise you, and you are a far better speaker than those who are involved in city affairs, yet you are afraid to go before those who never give a thought to politics and have never learnt to despise you, for fear you may be laughed at.

Undoubtedly, Socrates is speaking on behalf of Xenophon here. Throughout his works, Xenophon makes it clear that it is a gentleman's duty to take a prominent position in public life. Plato's Socrates was concerned to elucidate ethical terms: it is his Socrates who was prosecuted for corrupting young men. Xenophon's Socrates could hardly be accused of corrupting Charmides in urging him on a path of public duty.

But Charmides is the same man in both dialogues. In his metaphor of the games, Socrates could have been addressing Hippolytus: 'You'd be glad to be first in the games — well, why not in the assembly too?' But for Hippolytus as for other young men of the time, the games are not a metaphor for politics, but rather a refuge from them.

Plato gives other examples in his early dialogues of young men who have failed to make a mark in public life. In the *Meno*, Socrates enquires into the nature of *aretē*. At the beginning, his interlocutor Meno gives him the definition of a man's *aretē*: 'The virtue (*aretē*) of a man consists in managing the city's affairs capably, and so that he will help his friends and injure his enemies while taking care to come to no harm himself.' (71 E.) This definition or something like it occurs elsewhere in Plato and, given that it has been propounded for Socrates to analyse, may well represent a normal attitude. It embodies a positive, aggressive, attitude to life: it sets the tone of the political world in which *apragmosynē* has appeared — it is a dangerous world; it is the competitive world for which the games provide the appropriate metaphor. Further on in the dialogue (93 B ff.) Socrates tells how Themistocles, Aristeides, Pericles, and Thucydides, all of whom were, by general consent, paragons of *aretē*, were none of them able to impart the quality to their sons. Yet all the sons received what was considered a first-rate education: Cleophantus, son of Themistocles, could stand upright on a horse's back and throw a javelin from that position, and had many other accomplishments. Aristeides gave his son Lysimachus the best education in Athens. Pericles taught his sons riding, music, athletics, and all the other skilled pursuits. Thucydides gave his sons Melesias and Stephanos an excellent education — among other things, they were the best wrestlers in Athens.[20]

The education they have received is like that given to Charmides, or that described by the Right Argument in the *Clouds* as being the 'good old way'. Yet none of these men has made any mark in the city. Why should this traditional education have failed them all? In the *Memorabilia*, Socrates has a conversation with another young man, Glaucon, which provides part of the answer. Glaucon, Plato's brother, was probably born around 428, and is about twenty at the fictional date of the dialogue. Despite his youth, he is eager to enter public life;[21]

---

[20] Cf. Plato, *Laches*, 179 C.

[21] On Glaucon's age, see note 15 above. Such an early start in politics would also allow Charmides to be *kalos* yet eligible for a public career.

unfortunately, he finds himself being dragged from the platform as a laughing stock. Socrates finds the reason: Glaucon knows nothing of the running of the city, its revenues, expenditure, military strength, naval strength (and that of its enemy), its garrison, its silver mines (3. 6). Compared with the knowledge and expertise implied here, the old-fashioned accomplishments mentioned above — the lyre-playing and wrestling in which the generation of Charmides has been trained — will have been less than useful. Circumstances have changed and a new approach is needed. If *aretē* cannot be passed down from father to son, perhaps it can be taught by professional instructors — sophists. Another young man, Hippocrates, sets about acquiring *aretē* under these changed conditions. He asks Socrates to introduce him to Protagoras, the famous sophist:

> This is Hippocrates, a fellow-countryman, the son of Apollodorus; he is of a great and prosperous family and I should say the equal of any of his contemporaries in natural gifts. He is very eager to make a name for himself in the city, and he thinks he can best achieve this by spending some time with you.
>
> (Plat. *Prot.* 316 B)[22]

And Protagoras promises to teach the young man the political art, and how to be a good citizen, that is, how to succeed in civic affairs, and become a real power in the city, both as speaker and man of action. (319 A).

If the traditional education had become insufficient, then Hippocrates, who is of the highest birth, is not above taking lessons in the political art. The unwillingness of Charmides to face the crowd fits into this picture. The democracy is more demanding of its ministers than it used to be, and in the face of this those who wish to get on in public life must equip themselves more thoroughly than before.

But was the *apragmosynē* of noble youths merely a question of nerves, as in the case of Charmides? Let us consider his cousin, Critias. Although it was Charmides who had offered the definition of *sōphrosynē* as *apragmosynē* — 'minding one's own business' — Socrates says later that he is pretty certain that this definition came from Critias, and this would seem to be Plato's

---

[22] The *Protagoras* has two dramatic dates: 432 and 419.

opinion too.[23] We know that both Plato and Aristotle considered Critias to have an undeserved bad reputation,[24] and, in this dialogue, Plato seeks to show the young Critias before he developed into the tyrant. He is a young man, a little older than Charmides, and he too, like Hippocrates, has been studying with a famous sophist, Prodicus of Ceos. But whereas Hippocrates was in pursuit of political skill, Critias shows no interest in politics and instead has been studying the meaning of words, for which Prodicus was famous (163 D). The distinction which Critias attempts to draw between the meanings of 'do' and 'make' is not unlike Socrates' own quibbles. Socrates and Critias seem to have much in common, and there is no doubt that it was this friendship that played a large part in Socrates' condemnation in 399. However, in 432 Critias showed no appetite for a political career. His formulation of *sōphrosynē* points the other way, and the picture which Plato draws of him in this dialogue accords well with the remaining fragments of his own writing:

> Chilon of Lacedaemon, the wise, it was who first said this:
> Nothing too much, for all good things come in time.
>
> (DK 88B7).[25]

Plato, too, puts this famous saying into Critias' mouth (164 D). It is interesting too that Critias attributes the thought to a Spartan because elsewhere he shows a marked sympathy for Spartan values and tastes. In the fragment of his *Spartan Constitution*, Critias praises their moderation and *sōphrosynē*, amongst other things in their drinking parties (DK 88B6). The tone of his writing fits a young man who is a 'layman among philosophers, a philosopher among laymen' (DK 88A3); a young man who admires old-fashioned dignity and restraint and finds it in Sparta,[26] and one who is opposed to those, as Xenophon describes them (*Smp.* 1. 4), like generals, cavalry commanders, and others who are 'hungry for office' (DK 88B47).

---

[23] So Tuckey (*Plato's Charmides*, 20).

[24] Arist. *Rhet.* 1416b 26 (DK 88A14).

[25] Cf. Tuckey, op. cit., 15.

[26] The interesting fragment of *Rhadamanthus* (B15) need not represent Critias' own views. It would seem to be spoken by one of those characters well known in Greek tragedy — Ixion, Pirithous, Salmoneus, Tantalus — who rebel against the divine order and are punished accordingly.

Critias has a long way to go before he becomes the violent and depraved man of Xenophon's *Hellenica* (1. 2. 12), but it was Plato's intention to show him as he had been at an earlier period.

Rich young men; Spartan sympathies; the homosexual atmosphere of the gymnasium; a distaste for democratic politics; are these characteristics, in this combination, confined to the 420s? In order to broaden the discussion and to provide a closer check on the authenticity of Plato's picture, let us examine another set of aristocratic young men of this same period. Let us look at Aristophanes' *Wasps*, produced in 422.

Wasps

The two principal characters in the play are a young man, Bdelycleon (the name signifies 'loathes Cleon'), and his father, Philocleon ('loves Cleon'). It is part of Aristophanes' comic fantasy that while Bdelycleon mixes in the best society, is fluent in all the latest fashions, wears the most expensive clothes, and despises the excesses of the democracy, (symbolized in the play be the lawcourts), his father is dressed in rags, subsists on lentil soup, and ekes out an existence on his jury pay of three obols.

Bdelycleon is close in spirit to the young Knights, presented on the comic stage only two years previously by Aristophanes. The first words used to describe him are: 'Bdelycleon, a man of pomposnortical manners' (134), and the adjective, typically Aristophanic, implies both a horsy connection, and the same haughty manner (*semnos*) of which Hippolytus had been accused.

Bdelycleon's dramatic function is to wean his father off the lawcourts which are his passion (as well as his livelihood); he shuts him up indoors, and when the chorus, composed of old jurymen like Philocleon, try to rescue him, Bdelycleon beats them off. They shower him with curses, and in doing so they reveal the kind of characteristics the democracy hated and feared in upper-class youth: he is a conspirator, they say, he is aiming at tyranny, he is a long haired Amynias, a lover of monarchy, a friend of Brasidas, tassel-fringed (473 ff.).

This farrago of insults gives us an idea of how Bdelycleon (and Critias and Charmides) appeared to the man in the street during the 420s. The qualities described here correspond, in fact, to those which in Plato's dialogue characterized Critias and Charmides. The young men have homosexual leanings (Amynias was ridiculed for his effeminacy); they are unsympathetic to the democracy (Bdelycleon is accused of conspiring against it); they admire Sparta (Brasidas was a famous Spartan general, while tassel-fringed cloaks were regarded as a Spartan style).[27]

Bdelycleon is accused of aiming at the tyranny, but he strenuously denies the charge.[28] 'Lord, no one's heard the word tyranny these fifty years, and now I hear it on all sides in the market-place. If I buy a perch instead of sprats, the fishmonger will mutter: "He's aiming at the tyranny!"' [29] Bdelycleon is represented in the play as being against the democracy, but that does not mean that he is aiming to overthrow it. His father's passion for the lawcourts is presented as a childish fad, and appropriately Bdelycleon encourages him instead to stay at home and make do with a toy lawcourt. Bdelycleon is against lawcourts, but he has nothing to offer in their place, except a toy replica. The lawcourts are the most important institution of the democracy, excepting only the assembly itself. In rejecting them, Bdelycleon, like Critias and Charmides, is simply turning his back on the democracy.

If Bdelycleon cannot offer his father any alternative to the democracy, he can, in Aristophanes' fantasy, at any rate take him to an elegant party. He insists on his father discarding his tattered old clothes, and dressing in sumptuous but unpatriotic ones: a rich, fleecy cloak from Persia, and luxurious Laconian slippers.[30] The old man must then be taught to parade up and down in a mincing, effeminate way (1168), and he is told suitable subjects for conversation, because there will be learned and clever men present, and the proceedings will have an educated and elegant tone. Philocleon ought to be able, for instance, to talk about some sacred embassy he had been on. A sacred embassy was an office distributed as a liturgy amongst only the very wealthiest citizens. Or, Bdelycleon goes on, he could mention

---

[27] Cf. Macdowell on this passage. See also lines 1069–70 on the 'ringlets' of modern youth.

[28] See *Knights*, 624 ff.

[29] Does the suspicion of tyranny come from his outrageous behaviour (*hybris*) towards his father? R. Seager ('Alcibiades and the charge of aiming at the tyranny' *Historia*, 16 (1967), 6–18) reaches such a conclusion about Alcibiades.

[30] Laconian slippers were common in Athens. Aristophanes introduces them solely for the name.

the pankration (one of the events at the games), or a boar hunt, hare-coursing,[31] or a torch race: all upper-class pastimes. Then Philocleon must learn how to comport himself, how to 'pour himself on to the cushions in a supple, athletic way'; he must praise some piece of plate, admire the ceiling, or the hangings on the wall. For all this, says Bdelycleon, is how the *sophoi*, the elegant and educated young men, behave (1196).

Later in the story, Philocleon is introduced to some of these young men, and they are named as Hipyllus, Antiphon, Lycon, Lysistratus, Theophrastus, and Phrynichus. Since they were all real people, and active at the time, it will help this discussion to examine what is known of them.

Of Hipyllus, nothing is known.

Antiphon must be the same as the oligarch of 411, since there is no further identification.[32] He wrote speeches for delivery in the lawcourts, and at his own trial in 410 gave what Thucydides described as the finest speech he had ever heard (8. 68. 2). After that speech, he is reported to have told the playwright Agathon that he would rather have pleased one man of refinement (*spoudaios*) than any number of the common people (Arist. *EE* 1232[b] 7). Thucydides says of Antiphon that he was

> one of the most capable Athenians of his time; he had great power, both to think things out and to put them into words but he never went before the *dēmos*, nor willingly before any other assembly for he was regarded with suspicion by the people on account of his reputation for cleverness. However, he was the one most able to give advice and assistance to those who had to appear before the assembly or the lawcourts
>
> (8. 68. 1)[33]

The democratic view of this practice is expressed in a fragment from Plato the comic dramatist: Antiphon is ridiculed as a lawyer who 'preferred to sell dishonest speeches for high prices to litigants with a bad case' (fr. 103 K). Antiphon acknowledges

[31] Cf. note 13 above, and Macdowell, op. cit., on this passage.

[32] So Macdowell on 1270.

[33] Plato, *Euthydemus*, 305 B on men like Antiphon: 'Was he one of those skilled in contesting cases in court, an orator, or one of those who sends such people in, who compose the speech which the orators deliver? These are the men, my dear Crito, whom Prodicus calls the frontiermen between philosophy and politics. They think themselves the wisest of men . . .'

his work in the speech he made in his own defence after the oligarchic coup of 411: 'My accusers say that I used to write speeches for others to deliver in the courts, and that the Four Hundred profited by this. But this would never have been permitted me under the oligarchy, while under the democracy it is I who have the power . . .'. The argument is somewhat disingenuous, since Antiphon was the leader of the oligarchs in 411, but we have only this fragment from his speech and cannot know what else he might have said.

Antiphon's *apragmosynē*—his enforced political idleness—is of a different colour to Charmides', but is an excellent illustration of the suspicion which educated and fluent members of the upper class drew from the common people. That such men could be attacked by their rivals for being too clever and convincing is also evident from a speech of Cleon's at the time of the Mytilene debate (Th. 3. 37. 3). To be educated and have polished manners had become a liability under the radical democracy.

Lycon of Thoricus was a wealthy man. Xenophon depicts him, in the year after the *Wasps* was presented, celebrating the victory of his son Autolycus at the pankration with a dinner at the expense of the fabulously rich Callias (who was enamoured of the victor). Callias meets Socrates and a group of his friends, including Charmides, and invites them to the banquet: 'I think my banquet would be more splendid if it were adorned by men such as yourselves, pure in soul, rather than by generals and cavalry commanders and men hungry for office' (*Smp*. 1. 4.). If Xenophon is not biased here (and we do not know who else was invited to the banquet), Lycon appears to be moving in *apragmōn* circles, with men like Socrates and Charmides, in 421. Twenty-two years later he was one of the prosecutors at Socrates' trial.[34]

The references to Lysistratus in contemporary literature are sometimes thought to refer to two different men, though the likelihood is that there was only one. He is well known in Athens from 428 onwards and is ridiculed by Aristophanes on several occasions as a public speaker. He was one of those accused of mutilating the Herms, and was forced to flee the country. He

---

[34] Socrates' companions include Antisthenes, who later became known as a cynic philosopher and prided himself on his ostentatious poverty.

named as a friend of Andocides (And. 1. 122). He was back in
Athens by 399.[35]

Nothing is known of Theophrastus, though Aristophanes
describes him as a 'most superior person'.

The name Phrynichus occurs as fourteen separate entries in
the *Prosopographica Attica* (the *Who's Who* of ancient Athens); it
was therefore a fairly common name, and must be dealt with
carefully. It seems that there could be possibly as many as three
separate men of this name in the period under review: the
Phrynichus who is the 'dancer' in Andocides' speech *On the
Mysteries* (1. 47); the Phrynichus mentioned by Aristophanes here;
and the tyrant of 411. Both the *PA* and Macdowell (comm.
Wasps, 1302) identify the last two. Lysias (20. 11) alleges that
Phrynichus had been a shepherd boy in his youth but had come
to Athens to be a sycophant — to make a living out of malicious
prosecutions. At some point he had had to pay a fine to the
treasury. This latter part of Lysias' account rings more true than
the former: if, as a rising politician, he had brought an action
at law that had failed to win a minimum of votes, he would have
been liable to a fine.

The probability is that all three men are the same person, for
the reason that they are not further distinguished. It is likely
that the words 'the dancer' which refer to the Phrynichus
mentioned by Andocides in his speech *On the Mysteries* (1. 47)
is a gloss which has crept into the text, because this Phrynichus
had been confused with the dramatist, contemporary with
Aeschylus, who was especially associated with dancing. The
Phrynichus mentioned by Andocides was a cousin, either of
Andocides himself or of Callias son of Telocles, who was brother-
in-law both to Andocides and to a brother of Nicias.[36]

Clearly, this Phrynichus moves in the highest circles, but so
does Aristophanes' Phrynichus, and so, we can be sure, does
the oligarch of 411. Lysias' reference to a humble origin may

---

[35] *RE* makes him two men. The difficulty is as follows: Lysistratus fled from Athens
after the affair of the Herms and returned in 399. But Aristophanes refers to a Lysistratus
in *Lysistrata* (1105). The best solution is to assume that Aristophanes is not referring
to a person at all, but to one who brings peace, who disbands the army. So Ehrenberg,
who explains this passage convincingly (*People of Aristophanes'* 180).

[36] See Macdowell, op. cit., on And. 1. 47, and the family tree on p. 206 of that
edition.

be no more than a common type of slander, familiar from
Aristophanes, according to which the majority of Athenian
politicians were the offspring of barbarian slaves.

The party, then, is composed of political and non-political
figures. This is probably natural. It also seems to be in the highest
social stratum. Whether Phrynichus is cousin to Andocides or
to Callias, we must choose between two of the wealthiest families
in Athens. Lycon, too, was rich. Of Antiphon and the others
we cannot be sure, though judging by Aristophanes' description
and the preparations of Bdelycleon and his father, the whole affair
is obviously most elegant and sophisticated. Macdowell
comments on this group:

> To conclude that Phrynichus' set was an oligarchic *hetaereia* is to go
> too far. It is not clear that any oligarchic revolution was being planned
> as early as 422, nor that the members of the group held oligarchic
> views . . . Phrynichus' set should be regarded simply as a group of
> men with similar tastes and interests, whose purpose in meeting was
> more social than political . . . Aristophanes regards them as snobs who
> treat contemptuously those whom they regard as their inferiors.

(comm. Wasps, 1302)

Some deductions may be drawn about this group from what
Bdelycleon had said beforehand. He gets his father into exotic
and unpatriotic clothing, teaches him to parade in a homosexual
way, to talk of hunting, the pankration; these had been
characteristics of the young men previously mentioned — Critias,
with his admiration of Sparta, the homosexual youths at the
gymnasium, the 'lads with the cauliflower ears' — they all inhabit
the same milieu. It is a fair inference that Phrynichus' guests
belong there too. They are oligarchic in all but revolutionary
intent, and this for no other reason than that no opportunity
existed.[37] Within a few years the situation would change. The
prospect of the Sicilian expedition was to provoke the affair of
the Herms, and, with the collapse of that expedition, the oligarchs
would begin to feel their strength.

Out of the eight figures discussed (Critias, Charmides, the
guests in the *Wasps*), three are mentioned in Andocides' *On the*

---

[37] Ehrenberg compares Bdelycleon's friends with Hippolytus. Cf. *People of
Aristophanes*, 110–11.

Mysteries as being implicated in the affair of the Herms: Critias, Phrynichus, and Lysistratus (1. 47). In addition, the figures of Andocides himself and his father Leogoras are of interest. Andocides is thought to have been born around 440.[38] His father, then, was born probably between 470 and 460. Andocides' grandfather, also called Andocides (I) was a prominent supporter of Pericles around the middle of the century; he was general in 446/5, and one of the ten Athenian envoys who made peace with Sparta. He was general with Pericles at the revolt of Samos in 441/0.[39] His son, Leogoras, married a sister-in-law of Pericles' son Xanthippus, but did not, so far as we know, hold any office. The family was extremely rich, and during his exile after 415, Andocides the younger endeavoured to win back the Athenians' favour by supplies of timber and bronze to the democrats in Samos, and later promised a large number of corn-ships from Cyprus.[40] The family was friendly with the King of Macedonia, and in his wanderings, Andocides visited Sicily, Italy, the Hellespont, and Ionia, as well as Cyprus, where he evidently had good friends, since he was offered an estate there as a present.[41]

Leogoras and his son conform, as far as we can see, to the pattern established by the sons of Themistocles, Aristeides, Pericles, and others: Andocides the elder, the contemporary of Pericles, was prominent in public affairs as general and ambassador in important negotiations. His son, however, shows no sign of having performed any public duties. Leogoras would have been rather older than Critias, while his son was younger than Charmides. They fit into the pattern of *apragmosynē* that appears after the middle of the 440s. Yet suddenly they are at the middle of a major public scandal, accused of seeking to overthrow the democracy. They are symptomatic of an upheaval in the whole upper-class oligarchic social scene. Men like Nicias were accepted in public only because they very carefully

---

[38] He was young in 415 (And. 2. 7). At the time of his trial he was over forty (*Against Andocides*, 46) yet still young enough to have children (148). Cf. Macdowell's introduction to his edition of *On the Mysteries*, 2 n. 8.

[39] *IGi²* 1085 (*ML* 51); And. 3. 6; Aeschines 2. 174; Androtion, F38. Cf. Macdowell's introduction to his *On the Mysteries*, 1.

[40] And. 2. 11; 2. 21.

[41] Lys. *Against Andoc.* 6; Plut. *Life of Andoc.* 11; Andoc. 1. 1.

cultivated the popular taste (see Chapter 5); many of these men, however, had seldom, if ever, been before the people. Their generation had either despaired of, or despised, an appeal to the people, and at length resorted to extreme lengths to turn the national purpose.

Their opportunity came after the disaster in Sicily, and the creation of the *Probouloi* at Athens—a 'Council of Elders'—a throwback to an older, more primitive kind of government, sign of a general faltering of purpose. Among the oligarchs who seized power in Athens in 411 appear not a few of the men discussed in this chapter. Critias, though foremost among the tyrants in 403, seems to have played a more moderate part in 411.[42] Thucydides never mentions him in this context, and it is conceivable that he was, like Plato and Aristotle later, trying to protect his reputation. Phrynichus was 'most enthusiastic for the oligarchy' (Th. 8. 68. 3); Andron was one of the Four Hundred, though he turned against Antiphon and was one of the prosecutors at his trial, and so survived himself (Plut. *Lives of 10 Orators*, 833 E). Charmides was one of the ten in the Piraeus in 404 (X. *Hell.* 2. 4. 19); Antiphon was, as Thucydides says, 'the man who planned the whole thing' (the oligarchy of 411) (8. 68. 1).

The aim of this chapter has been to examine an identifiable social group as it appeared in the years around 430, and then to note how that group behaved in the succeeding years down to the end of the century.

Plutarch said that after the ostracism of Thucydides in 443/3 the opposition to Pericles, and with him, to the radical democracy, collapsed; Plato said many of the sons of prominent contemporaries of Pericles failed to make any mark in public life.

Looking at evidence for the period around 430, and first at the *Hippolytus*, we find the picture of a young nobleman, the centre of a group of close friends, fond of the hunt and with a distaste for the world of democratic politics. He makes a strong contrast between the crowd, the rabble whom the Athenian politician must address, and the select and cultured circle of his

---

[42] Wade-Gery defends Critias' part in the coup of 411 ('Critias and Herodes' in *Essays in Greek History*).

friends. He regards the assembly as dangerous for men like himself. In the period when the *Hippolytus* was written, those in high office were particularly susceptible to attacks from popular leaders: any mistake, failure, or peccadillo was liable to attract the spite of a 'watch-dog of the people', and prosecution could ruin a man. The Athenian nobility at this time seemed to carry all the responsibility without gaining any corresponding respect.

Hippolytus prided himself particularly on the quality of *sōphrosynē*; Euripides, in creating a dramatic character, caused this quality to be warped: Hippolytus' *sōphrosynē*, instead of representing steadiness and sobriety, is a dangerous and unstable extreme: a form of *hybris* against a god, and subject to the appropriate punishment. The destruction of Hippolytus shows how far his view of *sōphrosynē* was from the real thing.

But men of his class in the reality of Euripides' Athens did value this quality, and it is fitting that in his dialogue *Charmides*, Plato makes it the point of discussion. The young Charmides is credited with the quality, and the replies he gives under cross-questioning reveal what were traditional views at the time. These views receive some corroboration from other contemporary sources. Charmides associates *sōphrosynē* with quiet and orderly behaviour—*hēsychiotēs*. In Thucydides' Book I this was a quality regarded as especially Spartan, and the historian contrasts it in the Spartans with the restlessness and inventiveness of the Athenians. It had been praised by thinkers in the previous century as the opposite of factional violence in aristocratic societies, and had come to be regarded as an aristocratic virtue.

From a historical point of view, then, we can place Charmides' education in a tradition which is aristocratic and pro-Spartan. This tradition is expressed in other ways: the scene is laid in a gymnasium, haunt of noble youth,[43] and, at this time, activity is divided into the athletic and the intellectual. The purely athletic aspect is represented by the 'lads with the cauliflower ears' who, like Hippolytus, live only for success in the games. Athletics, boxing, and wrestling had not traditionally been considered antithetical to a public career; on the contrary, Xenophon's Socrates uses the games as a metaphor for public life, and hitherto

---

[43] Other Platonic dialogues laid in gymnasiums are the *Lysis, Euthydemus, Theaetetus* (144 c), *Phaedrus* (227). Cf. Bilinski, *L'agonistica sportiva nella Grecia antica*, 59 ff.

a success at the games had afforded an excellent start to a public career. Yet in our particular evidence, we find Hippolytus contrasting the games and democratic politics, and the young noblemen, who are enthusiastic sportsmen, appear to flaunt openly a taste for Spartan fashions and styles, at a time when Sparta was the national enemy and differed from Athens across a wide cultural spectrum.

This taste for Spartan things was a kind of nostalgia, a looking backwards to a time when members of their class enjoyed the respect still paid to their friends in other, more backward, states. Sparta represented the 'good old days'. This is the impression that Aristophanes gives in his *Clouds* when the Right Argument defends himself; the boys who sit around under the plane tree in the gymnasium are, like Charmides, characterized by *sōphrosynē* and *apragmosynē* (961 ff.). Like him, they walk in a modest fashion through the streets and comport themselves in a respectful manner to their elders. The portrait is augmented by Bdelycleon and Pheidippides before his transformation. Bdelycleon too dislikes the democracy, because everything he dislikes about the lawcourts is what, in fact, he dislikes about the democracy itself; it is concentrated in the demagogues, who, he claims, are cheating the people out of what is rightfully theirs. Although he does not say so, the implication is that the better sort, such as himself, have been ejected from their rightful and traditional place in the public scene, usurped by upstarts.[44] Perhaps the most important thing about Bdelycleon is that he can formulate no alternative to democracy — apart from the probably farcical one of dividing out the revenues among the householders.[45] At this stage there seemed to be no alternative.

One other feature which most of these young men have in common is their homosexuality. This too has a nostalgic, reactionary quality; in the *Clouds* it is associated with the 'good

---

[44] There is a comic disproportion between the lives of Bdelycleon and his father. How could the one be the father of the other? But to Aristophanes such things are no problem at all. The alternative would be to make Bdelycleon a parasite, a hanger-on to the upper class. Such parasites, *kolakes*, were, in fact, well known to the comic playwrights and have nothing in common with Bdelycleon. Cf. especially Eupolis, fr. 159 (*Kolakes*) where a chorus of them describe a typical day (*c.* 421 BC).

[45] Perhaps not so very farcical; cf. Chapter 1, note 7; Chapter 4, p. 95 on a similar proposal by Aristotle.

old days', and in the debate between Right and Wrong it proves the farcical undoing of Right (1087 ff.). To Plato in his *Charmides*, it is a normal state; the young man is subject to the amorous attention of his friends. Writers in the earlier part of the century had been freer in their allusions to homosexual love: the Achilles of Aeschylus' *Myrmidons* had spoken very frankly of his love for Patroclus; Pindar had also changed or adapted mythology to a homosexual theme.[46] Just as homosexuality was associated with traditional or reactionary qualities, so it was associated with Sparta, which, in the eyes of upper-class Athenians, enshrined the 'good old ways'. Plato regarded it as a specifically Spartan attribute.[47] Hippolytus, though a special, fictional, case, a possible example of sublimation, is reminiscent of Charmides and his friends. Callicles is portrayed in a group of homosexual friends. Critias praises the *sōphrosynē* of Sparta. *Sōphrosynē*, homosexuality, *apragmosynē*, are three of the central characteristics of the young men discussed here.[48]

Under Socrates' cross-questioning, Charmides had given a second definition of *sōphrosynē*, afterwards attributed to Critias: *sōphrosynē* is 'to mind your own business'. This phrase is so common later, at the time when Plato wrote the dialogue, that it is difficult to decide whether it had currency at the fictional date of the dialogue, 432. Yet the phrase was widely understood as an expansion of the term *apragmosynē*, which had been the reformulation of the idea of *hēsychia*, so common in the literature of the previous hundred years as the rejection of aristocratic strife in Greek cities; a reformulation in the face of Athenian democratic *polypragmosynē*. In his first book, Thucydides had contrasted *hēsychia* in Sparta with the expansionism, the restlessness and the inventiveness of the Athenians.

In the discussion of the gymnasiums we saw that they were the scene not only of athletic but also of intellectual activity. This seems also to have been of two kinds. There is Socrates analysing the word

---

[46] Dover, *Greek Homosexuality*, 196 ff. The Greeks of the fifth and fourth centuries knew there was no homosexual love affair between Achilles and Patroclus. Pindar uses a similar license in *Olympian Ode* I, in which Pelops is carried off to Olympus to serve Zeus as Ganymede later will. Cf. O. Murray (*Archaic Greece*), for whom homosexuality was a phenomenon of Archaic Greece, rather going out of fashion under the democracy.

[47] Dover (op. cit. 185 ff.) quotes Plato's *Laws*, 636 AB.

[48] See Chapter 5, note 47 for further on homosexuality.

sōphrosynē; there is Critias studying words with Prodicus and Aristophanes giving a long list of subjects in his *Clouds* (meteorology, astronomy, geography, biology, physics, as well as grammar, morphology, and literary criticism). But alongside these there is the other branch of sophistic studies, the province, notably, of Protagoras and Gorgias: the art of statesmanship. In the same context as Charmides we find Glaucon, keen to enter public life while not yet twenty, and Hippocrates who is seeking to enrol with Protagoras in a course of study in the political art. I shall return to these young men in Chapter 5, and have introduced them here only to point out that *apragmōn* young noblemen did not constitute the whole of their generation. What proportion they did, in fact, constitute is impossible to know, but without doubt when they did move into action they were able to rock the State to its foundations.

From 424 onwards, a series of changes or signs of change may be detected in the position of the young nobles *vis-à-vis* the State. In the *Knights*, they are accused of plotting against the State; in the *Wasps*, Bdelycleon is forced to rebut the same charge. The democracy seems extraordinarily sensitive to treason from its upper class.[49] Why should one hear talk of conspiracy and tyranny so often and after so many years? The enemies of democracy hated and distrusted its expansionist policy. The decision on Sicily prompted an organized demonstration; the affair of the Herms and the speech of Andocides indicate that the *apragmōn* youth of the 420s was coming round more and more to an active attitude, and that the social club, the *hetaereia*, formed the perfect means for organizing action. In 411, Peisander set about counter-revolution by 'organizing the clubs'.

I have been concerned to trace names through the thirty years until the end of the century; half a dozen can be more or less traced from an *apragmōn* existence in the 420s to an active part in counter-revolution in the last decade, and of these Critias and Antiphon are the two most interesting examples. Plato's portrait of Critias seems to harmonize with the fragments of his writing: a young man of noble family, scholarly and eager to learn, an admirer of Sparta and an intellectual. Antiphon is the public

---

[49] With good reason. See L. Whibley, *Political Parties at Athens*, 82; J. Isaac, *Les oligarques*, 25.

speaker who does not dare to address the assembly, out of a reputation for cleverness; this is a phenomenon which goes right to the heart of the position of young men of good family in democratic Athens. It would seem fair to conclude that two such powerful figures as these would have drawn along with them many others of a similar background and persuasion who have gone unrecorded. The portrait we have studied, the noble youth, with his mind on *sōphrosynē*, this is a figure which, with a few exceptions, seems confined to the 420s.[50]

---

[50] Exceptions are Amphion (Eur. *Antiope*, *c*.409 BC) and Ion (*c*.413). See Chapter 7.

4

The Peasant Farmer

It is as well to emphasize at the outset that the small farmer—the peasant proprietor—shared many of the characteristics which I shall identify with other kinds of small proprietor—tradesmen, craftsmen, and small businessmen—who were all known as *banausoi*. Xenophon, for example, criticizes the *banausos* as being 'held in utter disdain in our cities', for his work spoils his body, forcing him to sit still indoors, sometimes by a fire, all day. In particular, such trades leave no time to devote to one's friends or the city (*Oec.* 4. 3). Xenophon's view of civic duty is one proper to a *kalokagathos*—a gentleman—far removed from the craftsman working on his own, or with a few slaves. Such a craftsman would be the cripple who, in a speech of Lysias, is defending his right to a State pension of one obol a day. In his defence he enumerates many of the qualities which, as will be seen, go to make up the *apragmosynē* of the peasant farmer. He dismisses such hypothetical charges as being a sycophant: 'Has anyone ever been brought to trial at my instance and lost a fortune?'; or of being a busybody, a hot-head, a seeker of quarrels; or of being grossly insolent or violent. No, he is a man who has committed no offence, who is neither rendering an account of State monies placed in his charge, nor undergoing an examination into his conduct in office, but rather defending his right to one obol (Lys. 24. 24).

Nevertheless, theorists do distinguish the farmer from the tradesman: Aristotle classifies the farmer, the tradesman, and the craftsman (*Pol.* 1289^b 33), as the three component parts of the common people (*dēmos*). Plato also makes a theoretical tripartite division, but this time of the whole population, in which the *dēmos* is one part. First there are the 'drones' (kēphēnes), a class of thriftless idlers, who dominate proceedings in the assembly most of the time, and from whom the popular leaders are drawn; a second part is the class of money-makers, among whom are to be found the wealthiest men; and the third part is the *dēmos*. 'The *dēmos* is the third group; they till their own soil, own little property and give no offence to anyone. But whenever they are gathered together they are the most numerous and carry most weight in the assembly.' (*Rep.* 565A.)

It is interesting to note that, whereas for Aristotle the *dēmos* included city-dwellers like the tradesmen and artisans (as it does for Ps.-Xenophon), Plato restricts the term to the rural proprietor—the *autourgos*—who owns little, and lives quietly (*apragmōn*). He is the man with whom this chapter is concerned.

The *autourgos* is the man who tills his own soil by himself; Xenophon contrasts him with the overseer of slaves on a large farm (*Oec.* 5. 4), and Thucydides, in Pericles' first speech (1. 141. 3) describes the Peloponnesians as *autourgoi*, who have no money, either privately or in common. Thucydides is describing the Peloponnesians at the outbreak of the war; their lack of resources, which compels them to undertake only short campaigns, is in contrast to the Athenians' wealth, amassed from the Empire. But though Athens as a state may be rich, the individual *autourgos* is no richer than his Peloponnesian counterpart.

An ancient commentary (scholion) to this passage defines *autourgos* as 'one who tills his own land on his own without the help of slaves'; another (on Eur. *Or.* 920) as 'one who works his own land' (these scholia may, of course, be no more than scholarly deductions from the word itself).[1] In practice, the term could include the man who owned one or two slaves; the essence of it is that *he himself* must also work on the land.

Plutarch imagined the *autourgos* as the independent and uncorrupted peasant, before Pericles set about winning him with offers of overseas settlements (cleruchies), pay for jury service, and theatre seats (*Per.* 9). But if the peasant was modest and prudent (*sōphrōn*) in the 'good old days', he continued so perforce. As Lysias' cripple says: 'A poor man has no choice but to be *sōphrōn*.' (24. 17.)

The few testimonies considered so far already show certain clear characteristics of the Attic peasant (and craftsman): he is poor, or at any rate can amass no capital; his work leaves him no time to attend to the affairs of the city; he is no meddling

---

[1] Cf. Gomme, *HCT*, on 1. 141. 3: '*Autourgoi* almost the same as *georgoi*'.

busybody, rather his poverty keeps him temperate and well behaved; and he is seldom in the assembly. But if the *dēmos*, the greater part of the citizen body, thus found it so difficult to attend to their civic duties, one wonders how the democracy actually functioned at all. The fact is that the authorities did have trouble getting the citizens together. Even during the earlier part of the Archidamian War, when many country-dwellers were cramped together in the city, they still had to resort to the red-paint-tipped rope to herd citizens up to the Pnyx (Ar. *Ach.* 22). At some point, around 400 BC, pay was introduced for attendance, at first one obol, then two, then three. But they still had to use the rope (Ar. *Eccl.* 379).[2] And this applied only to those actually in the *agora*. There could be no taking the paint-tipped rope around the towns and villages of Attica. Gomme estimated that not more than a third of the citizen body was living in Athens in 430, and still less than a half a hundred years later.[3]

This is in accordance with Thucydides' statement (2. 14 ff.) that at the outbreak of the Peloponnesian War the country-dwellers of Attica still constituted a majority of the citizen population. They had, he says, lived from time immemorial in the countryside, in independent towns, each with its own town hall and Government. And even after Theseus had unified Attica, the old habits were retained and most Athenians were born and bred in the country. Theseus had compelled them to have one political centre, but otherwise they looked after their own affairs. Consequently, they were most reluctant to move with their entire households, especially since they had only recently resettled

[2] Cf. Arist. *Ath. Pol.* 41. 3 on the introduction of pay because of the difficulty in getting good attendances at the assembly. Cf. Hignett, *Hist. Ath. Const.* 396. Ussher and others conclude that the red rope mentioned at *Eccl.* 378 was used to keep late comers out, on the assumption that there would be no shortage of comers once the three-obol payment had been introduced. Yet no ancient commentator notices this, and the mention of the *symbolon* at *Eccl.* 297 seems conclusive: using the analogy of the lawcourts (e.g. Arist. *Ath. Pol.* 68. 2) those present at the assembly received a ticket (*symbolon*) which they afterwards handed back in return for three obols. The fact that Chremylus did not get a *symbolon* means either that there was only a limited number available, or that they ceased to be distributed once proceedings had begun. The passage is also discussed, though with slightly different conclusions, by M. H. Hansen, 'The Athenian Ecclesia and the Assembly place on the Pnyx', *GRBS* 23 (1982), reprinted in *The Athenian Ecclesia*.
[3] Gomme, *The Population of Athens*, 47: 'Rather over a third of the population, say 60,000, seem to have been living in the town by 430; nearly a half, say 80,000, a hundred years later.'

themselves after the Persian Wars. It made them most miserable to leave their homes and the temples bequeathed them by ancestral tradition, and to have to change completely their way of life, abandoning what each man regarded as his own city. The references to the temples and 'what each man regarded as his own city' signify the strength of the attachment of the country-dwellers to their native towns and villages. After, or indeed alongside, political institutions, it was religious sites, holy places, and the ceremonies associated with them which most strongly identified the citizen with his city, and Thucydides implies that these country-dwellers felt stronger ties with their towns and villages than they did with Athens, the seat of Government.

The country-dwellers lived in towns and villages which were thought once to have been autonomous,[4] and although Athens had usurped control, the communities continued in many respects to function as before. Here were the numerous shrines and holy places mentioned by Pausanias in his guidebook to Attica. What evidence there is suggests that the small- and medium-sized proprietor continued to predominate.[5]

Later in Thucydides' *History*, the oligarchs, when they have usurped power, send delegates to Samos to try to win the goodwill of the army. They claim that they are not in fact 400 but 5,000, and that, in any case, no assembly had ever mustered more than 5,000, due to expeditions and other employments which took the citizens abroad (8. 72. 2). The reason given by Thucydides cannot possibly account for the missing 25,000 (assuming, for this argument, a male citizen population of 30,000). The costliest expedition ever mounted by the Athenians numbered about 8,300 men, composed of 4,000 hoplites, 300 cavalry, and 4,000 sailors in 200 triremes (though these would not all have been citizens) (6. 31. 2). Even allowing for losses the Athenians suffered in the years up to 411 BC, this still leaves us a long way short of 30,000. In fact, the reason why the oligarchs had never seen more than 5,000 at the assembly was quite simple: the Pnyx

---

[4] See C. W. J. Eliot, *Coastal Demes of Attica*, 44; Jan Pecirka, 'Homestead Farms in Classical and Hellenistic Hellas' in *Problèmes de la terre en Grèce ancienne*, 134.

[5] V. N. Andreev, 'Some Aspects of Agrarian Conditions in Attica in the Fifth to Third Centuries', *Eirene*, 12, p. 10; Claude Mossé, 'Le Statut des paysans en Attique en ive siècle' in *Problèmes de la terre en Grèce ancienne*, 181.

could not hold any more. Excavations of the Pnyx have shown that in the period down to 400 BC it could have held about 6,000 men, and even in Plato's time, between 6,500 and 8,000. It is remarkable, too, that the figure 6,000 crops up several times in legal documents as a quorum. Whatever estimate we take of the size of the Athenian population around 400 BC, we must accept that a meeting of the assembly never constituted more than a sample of the citizenship.[6]

Apart from the political issue, the question of how much the countryman came into Athens is dominated by the question of money. The extent to which the peasant was self-sufficient was the extent to which he could do without money. And this question, though complicated, can be reduced to one of whether he produced his own cereals. The farmer who grows only olives and grapes is clearly growing them for sale; the man who grows corn (barley, most likely) may be doing so for his own consumption only. He is aiming at self-sufficiency.

Although self-sufficiency (*autarkeia*) was always the aim of the Attic peasant, and his household economy was constructed in terms of consumption, not production, there seems to have been a move away from literal self-sufficiency from at least Solon's time. According to Plutarch, Solon realized that the soil of Attica could yield no more than a bare subsistence to those who tilled it (*Solon*, 22). The fact that he allowed olive oil, alone among foodstuffs, to be exported, indicates that olives were already being cultivated, if not as a cash crop, at least in a sufficient surplus

---

[6] Even if the oligarchs are not to be trusted, it is remarkable that the figure of 6,000 crops up several times as a quorum: And. 1. 87; Dem. 24. 45; [Dem.] 59. 89. *IG* 1²
114 declares that decisions on capital punishment and the declaration of war can only be made by the 'full *dēmos*'. What this full *dēmos* was has been clarified by excavations of the Pnyx carried out in 1930–1. Three phases of the Pnyx were established:

Pnyx 1 (*c*.500–400)	*c*.2,400m²
Pnyx 2 (*c*.400–330)	*c*.2,600m²
Pnyx 3 (*c*.330–)	*c*.5,550m²

The numbers these areas might hold were calculated as follows:

Pnyx 1	6,000 citizens maximum
Pnyx 2	6,500–8,000 maximum
Pnyx 3	13,400 maximum

It would appear that the 'full *dēmos*' was the same as the 6,000 quorum. Cf. M. H. Hansen, 'How many Athenians attended the Ecclesia?', *GRBS* (1979), 115, reprinted in *The Athenian Ecclesia*.

to be available for barter (ibid., 24). The olive was the product *par excellence* of the Attic soil and some early Athenian coins bear the olive-oil amphora as a design. Again, the fact that during the 150 years after 600 BC Athenian black-figure vases 'effectively won the markets of the Greek world'[7] indicates the extent to which a section of the Athenian population was engaged in non-agricultural employment.

Corn production did continue throughout the Classical period, but as a subsidiary crop intended, for the most part, for consumption by the farmer and his family.[8] In Aristophanes' *Peace*, Trygaeus celebrates his home-coming to the 'good old ways' (i.e. pre-war conditions) which gave 'fruit cakes, figs, and myrtle-wreaths, and sweet new wine and olive groves . . .' (572 ff.). Corn is not mentioned.[9] In the *Ecclesiazousai*, Chremes, a town-dweller, has brought his grapes to market to sell, and with the proceeds is going to buy barley meal (817 ff.). The fact that he is paid in obols indicates that the amount was modest — a surplus over his own needs rather than a cash crop.

Dikaiopolis, marooned in the city, gazes wistfully out at the country, 'loathing the town, sick for my village home, which never cried "come buy my charcoal, or my vinegar, or my oil, or my anything else", but freely gave all . . .' (Ar. *Ach.* 32 ff.). This, like all Aristophanes' descriptions of country life probably contains an element of sentimental idealization, but it points nevertheless to a comparison with the town: the town-dweller lives entirely within a money economy; the countryman largely outside it.[10]

If one reflects how long it would actually take for a country-dweller to get into Athens — a day's walk in the case of the outlying districts — and how often the poor farmer or artisan

---

[7] Boardman, *Athenian Black Figure Vases*, 9.

[8] Gomme, *Population of Athens*, 45 n. 1; M. K. Langdon, 'A Sanctuary of Zeus on Mount Hymmetus', *Hesperia*, suppl. 16. 1976. Archaeological excavation in Attica in connection with dwellings has been mainly concerned with large and prosperous houses rather than the dwellings of *autourgoi*: e.g., J. E. Jones, L. H. Sackett, A. J. Graham, 'The Dema House in Attica', *BSA* 57 (1962), 105; and the same authors' 'An Attic Country House below the Cave of Pan at Vari', *BSA* 68 (1973), 418.

[9] Cf. lines 557, 596, 1159, 1248, and cf. Ehrenberg, *People of Aristophanes*, 74.

[10] Cf. Claude Mossé, *The Ancient World at Work* 54: 'The peasant of Attica was really a vine grower and gardener rather than a farmer.'

could afford to take a day off work,[11] one concludes that in all probability the larger part of the country population came only seldom into Athens, perhaps for the principal festivals, which were held in the early part of the year when work on the land was lighter. More commonly the country-dwellers celebrated their own rural festivals, as Aristophanes' protagonists do.

Every one of Aristophanes' protagonists (with the exception of Dionysus, Cremes, and the heroines of the women's plays) is a rustic *autourgos*: Dikaiopolis, Demos, the chorus of the *Georgoi*, Trygaeus, Peisthetairos, Euelpides, Chremylus, and Strepsiades, though he may be a little richer than the others.[12] Several of Aristophanes' early plays were written during the Archidamian War and the distaste which his heroes express for city life is often mixed up with their hatred for the war. But as we examine them, we shall see that this preference for a quiet country life is a constant preoccupation with Aristophanes and is as vigorously expressed in his latest surviving play as in his first.

The *Acharnians* was produced in 426, when, because of the war, many of the country-dwellers were crowded into the town. From the beginning, the protagonist Dikaiopolis expresses his hatred for the town as well as for the war. Dikaiopolis sees the contrast between town and country partly, at least, in terms of money, and the lack of need for it, and the private market which he sets up later in the play is conducted by barter. The chorus compares all its advantages with the market square in Athens. This is the first of a series of lists in Aristophanes' comedies of those things in city life and the city square (*agora*) which the countryman dislikes so much. First there are the sycophants— informers and malicious prosecutors; one of them comes to Dikaipolis' private market and threatens to denounce him. Sycophants were a kind of unproductive, parasitic growth on the body politic, which, to the countryman (or to Aristophanes) symbolized the corruption of city life. He goes on to attack other well-known figures to be seen in the town square: effeminate young fops, politicians, social climbers; Aristophanes makes the

---

[11] Cf. N. G. L. Hammond, *A History of Greece to 322 BC*, 216 n. 2. Professor Hammond walked from Athens to Marathon in six hours and returned the same day in seven. How many Greeks could have equalled this feat? *Per contra*, see P. Harding, 'In search of a Polypragmatist', in *Classical Contributions*, 46.

[12] The *Georgoi* and *Islands* also seem to have been about, or featured, *autourgoi*.

same contrast which Plato will make between the peasant on the one hand, and the 'drones' lounging about in the square, who dominate proceedings in the assembly, on the other.[13]

With this sordid picture of city life, Aristophanes juxtaposes the rural Dionysia, the festival celebrated by Dikaiopolis on his return from the war and all the business involved in the city. This festival is a celebration of jovial licence: feasting, drinking, tumbling a Thracian slave girl.

The *Knights* was presented at a time when the Spartans had only just ceased ravaging Attica (spring, 424 BC). We may therefore imagine the protagonist Demos in the same situation as Dikaiopolis, confined in the city against his will. He is described as *agroikos*: a 'countryman'; but the word also means 'crusty', 'rough tempered', the soul of rugged, peasant, independence. In the story, he has come under the influence of the 'Paphlagonian', whose chief weapon is the fear of conspiracy, with which Demos is obsessed.[14] In his efforts to distract Demos he is forced to make ever more extravagant promises: Demos will sit in judgement in Arcadia, he will rule over all Greece, he will receive five obols a day — enough to live on comfortably. Yet his opponent, the Sausage-seller, realizes intuitively that Demos will never be really happy until he is restored to his native haunts, to a diet of porridge and olives, and his *apragmōn* country ways (805 ff.). Like Plato, Aristophanes identifies the people (*dēmos*) with the rural peasantry.

In the same year as the *Knights*, Aristophanes brought out his *Georgoi* (Farmers); here is part of fragment 100:

Farmer: I want to get back to my farm.
B (Sycophant?): Who's stopping you?
Farmer: You. If I give you a thousand drachmas will you get me out of serving in office?
B: Hand it over.

The farmer wants to escape having to serve in one of the magistracies chosen by lot. The sycophant, if that is what he is, claims to be able to mislay or lose his name when the lists are drawn up. It tells us something about civic corruption, about

---

[13] Lysias also makes this distinction (20. 12).
[14] *Knights*, 624 ff.: the Paphlagonian accuses the Knights of being conspirators and the council 'wore mustard looks and puckered up their brows . . .'

unscrupulous officials, and that there were countrymen prepared to buy their way out of their civic duties. This farmer, incidentally, if he could spare a thousand drachmas for a bribe, was not particularly poor.

Strepsiades, in the *Clouds* (423 BC), is another countryman who loathes the town. He is not poor, for he has several slaves, yet his way of life is described in terms reminiscent of Aristophanes' other rustic protagonists. He describes the comfortable life he led before he got married: 'I had the sweetest country life: unwashed, unswept, living at ease, teeming with bees and sheep and olive-cakes . . . smelling of new wine, drying figs, and wool in abundance.' (43 ff.) Strepsiades' country life may be crude and simple, but it is full of good things, it is easy, and it is straightforward. The wife with whom he has contracted such a disastrous marriage is a 'fine town lady, sophisticated, with a lot of style, rank with scent and saffron, and tongue-kisses, living a life of eating, spending, sex' (51 ff.).

For Strepsiades, as for Dikaiopolis, the town signifies expense; his frugality and careful husbandry, which have produced an abundance of figs and fleeces, go for nothing when his wife is interested only in keeping up a style of living in town which he cannot afford, and which has plunged him into debt. 'Uncle Megacles' (the name carries overtones of illustrious rank) is held up to him as a pattern of behaviour, and his wife, in addition to her own expense, has encouraged their son to lead an aristocratic existence, to mix with the 'knights', and to aspire to ride in the Panathenaic procession. Strepsiades' hopes of seeing his son out on the hills herding goats are firmly squashed.

It does not matter that there is a comic, even fantastic, disproportion between Strepsiades' life and that of his wife and son. This is not unusual with Aristophanes, as we saw in the *Wasps*. It underlines an antithesis which is one of Aristophanes' most enduring preoccupations: between the town and the country; between money and frugality; between pleasure and hard work; between variety and simplicity; between *polypragmosynē* and *apragmosynē*.

The theme is taken up again in the *Peace* (421 BC): Trygaeus, arriving in heaven, introduces himself as:

Trygaeus, of the deme Athmonon,[15] an expert vine-dresser,
No sycophant, nor lover of meddlesome business.

(190)

The play is a heartfelt protest against the war, but even when
the chorus, farmers like Trygaeus, are expressing their joy at
the thought of being able to return to their farms, it is in these
same terms—to escape from 'meddlesome business' (*pragmata*).
The second half of the play is taken up with preparations for
and the celebration of Trygaeus' wedding with Opora, the
goddess of fruits. The blessings of peace are recited in terms
reminiscent of Dikaiopolis and Strepsiades: 'Fruit cakes, figs,
and myrtle-wreaths and sweet new wine, olive groves . . .'
(572 ff.).

In addition, Trygaeus leads back Theoria to the council (871).
His slave is amazed: 'What do you say? Theoria? Is this the
Theoria we used to celebrate at Brauron?' In his comic fantasy,
Aristophanes has impersonated on the stage one of the most
famous festivals of the Attic countryside, long unable to be
celebrated because of the war and the occupation of Attica.
Although the festival had been assimilated into the Athenian
State, it retained its rustic character: Artemis Brauronia was
patroness of crops; sickles, viticultural implements, bridles, and
trappings were presented to her.[16]

Again, when he goes on to describe the celebrations that will
follow his return, Trygaeus is in fact describing the *Apatouria*,
the festival at which young men were admitted to manhood and
inscribed in the phratry list; this was another festival frequently
celebrated in the countryside.

---

[15] Athmonon lay some five or six miles north-east of Athens, and is generally
identified with the modern village of Marousi. Unfortunately, nothing much can be
made of the demes mentioned by Aristophanes, since they seem to have been chosen
for comic reasons. Thus Kikynna, Strepsiades' deme, also means 'ringlet, lock of hair'.
Phlya, mentioned in *Wasps*, was about five miles from Athens; however, Phlya may
also mean *phlyaria*, 'idle nonsense'. And the deme Anaphlystos, mentioned in *Eccl.* 979,
can be translated 'Wankingham'. For positions of demes see Traill's map in 'The Political
Organisation of Attica', *Hesperia*, suppl. 14.

[16] Brauron is the modern Vravrona, near Marathon. The sanctuary of Artemis
contained an ancient wooden statue. Four sanctuaries claimed to have the original statue,
which testifies to its importance. See Pausanias, 1. 23. 9 and 1. 33. 1. with Levi's notes.
See also Ar. *Lys.* 836 ff. on the social chic of serving as 'little bear' in the ceremony
at Brauron. Cf. R. A. Tomlinson, *Greek Sanctuaries*, 110 ff.

The description of these festivals is testimony of the extent to which life in Attica went on independently of Athens. Almost the whole of the second half of the play is given over to the description of the good things peace provides in the country.[17] These good things are summarized again in a fragment from Aristophanes' *Islands*:[18]

> To live in the fields on a small farm,
> Far from the business of the city square,
> With a yoke of your own oxen,
> To hear the bleating of your sheep,
> And the sound of the new wine trickling into the vat,
> To enjoy a supply of wild birds for the table,
> And not to be kept waiting in
> The town square by an insolent fishmonger
> To buy fish that is two days old,
> Overpriced, and with his thumb-print on it.

In his *Birds* (414 BC), Aristophanes takes this theme a stage further: not content with escaping from city life into the Attic countryside, his two protagonists Euelpides and Peisthetairos are seeking a spot even more secluded, even more *apragmon* (44). Like other Aristophanic protagonists, they are countrymen, and call themselves 'anti-jurymen' (110), a term which, as is clear from the *Wasps*, signifies a disapproval of the frenetic, corrupt, and false side of democratic life.

The town/country antithesis is presented as vividly in Aristophanes' last extant play as it was in the first. In the *Wealth* (388 BC) Chremylus is an older, more subdued version of the *autourgos* encountered in the earlier comedies, and much of their swagger and vitality is bequeathed rather to his slave Carion. The destruction wrought in Attica during the Decelian War had been severe (Th. 7. 27. 3.); there was much devastation of property (which must have included olive trees and vines) and all sheep and farm animals were lost. In addition, Athens no longer enjoyed the revenues of Empire in the years after

---

[17] 999 ff.; 1126 ff.; 1140 ff.; 1159 ff.

[18] Fr. 368. Edmonds dates to around 415 BC; Bergk to around 406 BC. Bergk supposes Aristophanes to have been advising the Athenians to take a more lenient attitude to the islands after their defection of c.412 BC. On the good things the countryside provides, cf. also fr. 294 from a postulated second *Peace* or, more likely, *Georgoi*.

400 BC. Chremylus' poverty, then, is the poverty of most Attic peasants.[19]

Aristophanes' view of the contrast between the countryman's life and the evils of city life is unchanged nearly forty years after the production of *Acharnians*. Consider this exchange between Carion and a sycophant:

Sycophant: And don't you think, you idiot, it's my duty to do all I can to aid the State?
Carion: Do all you can — isn't that just busybodying (*polypragmosynē*)?
Sycophant: It means to uphold the established laws, and punish anyone who breaks 'em.
Carion: Doesn't the State appoint jurymen for the job?
Sycophant: And who's to prosecute?
Carion: Whoever likes.
Sycophant: And that's me. So the State's business devolves on me.
Carion: Goodness, it's got a rotten leader. Wouldn't you rather just lead a quiet and peaceful life?
Sycophant: That's a sheep's life.

(911–22)[20]

For the city-dweller, the farmer's *apragmon* existence is a sheep's life; for the countryman, city life involves *polypragmosynē*: busybodying, meddling and prying, litigation.

For Aristophanes, then, *pragmata* signify a nexus of activities clustering around the assembly, the lawcourts, and the market square. In the rural mind they all seem to be lumped together: sycophants, beardless youths, scheming politicians, eager lawyers, overcharging fishmongers, city slickers with the gift of the gab (Eur. *Bacch.* 717), long-haired effeminates. To all this is juxtaposed the *gēdion*, the smallholding, which, viewed through Aristophanes' comic prism, seems a paradise of plenty — figs, olives, new wine, sheep and oxen, feasting and contentment — and which, in fact, provided a life without much excitement, plenty of work, stability, and security. This more realistic side comes out in a passage from Xenophon's *Cyropaedia*. Pheraulas is asked whether he comes from a wealthy family:

---

[19] G. Glotz, *The Ancient World at Work*, 253.

[20] I cannot accept Levy's contention (228 ff.) that there is some sort of development from the sycophants in the *Acharnians* (non-political) to the one here (political). The distinction between political and non-political prosecutions must have been extremely difficult to draw at all periods.

'Wealthy?' Pheraulas exclaimed, 'my family gained a livelihood with their hands. My father worked, and brought us up and educated us as best he could. As soon as I was grown up, since he couldn't afford to keep me idle, he sent me out to work in the fields. And so I kept him in his turn while he lived. I dug, and I sowed; it was a pretty small farm, but it did not cheat me—it was even handed. The seed which it received it very justly returned again, and with a little to spare, though not much. Sometimes, in a fit of generosity, it paid me back twice over.'

(8. 3. 37–8)

This realistic note is found too in Euripides' portraits of the *autourgos*; their more sober quality provides a useful check on Aristophanes' exuberant flights of fantasy.

The autourgos becomes *persona grata* to Euripides from 421 onwards. He is introduced, for the first time, in the *Suppliant Women*, in the guise of the 'middle class'. Speaking in the person of Theseus, Euripides discourses on the body politic, which is divided into three parts: there is a class of wealthy men, only concerned to get richer; then there are the poor, possessed by envy and sedition; and thirdly there is the 'middle class' which is the saviour of the city, for it 'preserves the order which the city ordains' (245). The distinction which Euripides draws between the poor, misled by unscrupulous leaders, and the rich, who think only of themselves, is reminiscent, even in its imagery, of the division which Plato will draw in the *Republic*, and this helps us to identify the 'middle class' with Plato's *dēmos*, seldom in the *agora*, but all-powerful when gathered together. The idea of the 'middle-class', which appears here for the first time, becomes very important after the disaster of the Sicilian expedition, when it becomes the central feature of a number of theoretical, moderate, oligarchic constitutions. The identification of the *dēmos* and the peasant farmers is made later in the *Suppliant Women*, this time from a hostile standpoint:

> Incapable of reasoning well, how could you
> Expect the *dēmos* to run a city well?
> These things cannot be taught quickly; it takes time.
> The poor farmer, even if he is no fool,
> Is too occupied with work to turn his
> Attention to city affairs.

(417–22)

The *autourgos* appears in person in tragedy in the *Electra* (413 BC). He is, however, a special case, and we must be wary of comparing him with examples furnished by Aristophanes. For one thing, he feels his poverty deeply. There is dramatic necessity here, since his means must contrast as severely as possible with those of the family from which Electra is sprung. We are told he has a pair of oxen, which might otherwise denote a certain measure of prosperity. Euripides may not be setting out to give us sociological exactitude, but this serves to remind us that to some extent poverty is a question of comparisons: this *autourgos* is poor compared with Electra's family, but perhaps in reality he is no poorer than Trygaeus or Dikaiopolis. In the same way, Chremylus' poverty may be a question not of absolute need but of comparison with town life, and hence of expectations. The real point of Euripides' *autourgos* is the insistence on his nobility of character in contrast with the poverty of his circumstances.

Again and again, Euripides returns to the theme: the farmer is proud of his ancestry yet in a humble station (37); Electra is the daughter of a king, and though she is his wife he has allowed her to remain a virgin, out of respect for her status. This is his *sōphrosynē* (53). He tries to prevent Electra from working, as the wives of other *autourgoi* do, because she is a princess. She is grateful for his care (67). She recognizes how hard he has to work (73), and he agrees with her, telling how he leads his oxen out to the fields at daybreak (78 ff.). Later, in a conversation with her brother, she emphasizes again her husband's nobility of character: 'He may be poor, but he is noble (*gennaios*) and treats me with reverence (*eusebeia*)' (253 ff.). Left alone, Orestes broods on the implications of all this:

'There's no clear sign to tell the quality of a man. The natures of men are confused: I have seen a worthless man the son of a noble father, and an honourable man born of obscure parents — want of spirit in a wealthy man, high thoughts in a poor one. How can one judge correctly? By wealth? That's a bad sign. By poverty? Poverty's a disease and teaches a man bad ways. Prowess in arms? But who, looking at a troop of soldiers can pick out the man of worth? Better to let such things go.
    This man is not great in Argos, does not boast of his family. He's just one of the crowd, yet, if you test him he's truly noble (*aristos*). Do not despise him, you who are the prisoners of a mass of worthless

prejudices; it is by their conduct and their character that men show their nobility.

Such men as these can run their homes well, and the city too. A man with a beautiful body, if he has no brain, might as well be a statue in the town square. A strong arm can bear the lance's thrust no better than a weak one. It's a man's courage and his nature that make him what he is.

$$(367-90)^{21}$$

The opening statements about the unreliability of a man's antecedents as a clue to his character are a preparation for the idea that in an apparently obscure and humble man, true nobility can reside. Here the divorce of moral nobility from ancestral nobility is complete, perhaps one of the first examples. All manner of terms normally appropriated by the well-born and rich have been heaped on the *autourgos*: he is noble (*gennaios*, *aristos*, *eugenēs*); he is 'equal to the gods'; reverent (*aidos*) and prudent (*sōphrōn*), and not violent (*hybristēs*). This is significant because it was written at a time when, it has been suggested, the aristocracy had virtually ceased to exist.[22] Terminology previously used with reference to the aristocracy was now free to be appropriated for moral use. The idea that innate worth must show itself in action has a Homeric ring, however, and *aretē* always signified the ability to act, to take part in public affairs, throughout the Classical age.[23]

Another quality which had earned Electra's approval was the

---

[21] Adkins (*Merit and Responsibility*, 176 ff.) draws attention to this passage in a discussion of *aretē*. According to him, the *aretē* of the *autourgos* is an early example of the 'quiet' usage: the word ceases to mean 'bold, commanding, noble (of birth)' and takes on a co-operative meaning; 'It seems evident that the new use of *agathos* is directly related to sophistic thought.' The reference to nature (*physis*) is also related to sophistic thought: cf. Hippias (Plat. *Prot.* 337 c) and Antiphon the Sophist. Both these writers, however, emphasize bonds across national frontiers, rather than across social divisions. Compare too Antisthenes the Cynic on moral superiority against that of birth, discussed by S. C. Humphreys in 'The *Nothoi* of Kynosarges', *JHS* (1974), 88–95.

[22] This is Ehrenberg's view (*People of Aristophanes*, 110–11): 'the nobles were moving rapidly towards self-destruction . . .'. Euripides' threefold division of the State includes no aristocracy as such. Neither does Plato in the *Republic*. Aristotle refers to the upper classes as *epieikeis*, *chrēstoi*, etc. Yet, in the *Charmides*, attention is drawn to the young men's distinguished antecedents. The most significant passage, however, is the opening paragraph of the *Laches*, where they discuss the impossibility of transmitting aristocratic *aretē* from generation to generation.

[23] This is the normal view (as opposed to Plato, say); e.g. Plato *Meno*, 71 E and X. *Mem.* 4. 2. 11.

respect her husband had shown her which had preserved her virginity. Euripides makes a good deal of this: 'I would be ashamed to violate the daughter of illustrious parents, unworthy as I am . . .' says the farmer. Electra twice refers to it: 'You did not abuse me in my distress . . .'; and to Orestes 'He did not seek to disgrace my noble name'. In each case, the verb is *hybrizein*; the word was used in Classical Athens to signify criminal assault which was punished particularly severely. Again, the farmer is twice described as *sōphrōn*: prudent and self-controlled. What Euripides is showing us is an attitude of respectfulness towards one's betters. This *autourgos* shows a sturdy independence, yet knows his place; he is, in a word, respectable, and it is this which endears him to the oligarchic and fourth-century theorists.

Euripides brings another *autourgos* into his *Orestes*, acted in 408 BC. The scene is a meeting of the assembly, and the *autourgos* is contrasted with a demagogue. The demagogue is a man with an 'unstoppable mouth', impudent, fluent, persuasive, and bold. Then follows another speaker:

Nothing much to look at, but a courageous man,
Not often seen in the market-place,
A farmer—and it is those who are the saviours of the land—
Intelligent, when he chose to express himself;
Blameless, living a life uncompromised.

(902 ff.)

The *autourgos*, a man seldom in town, one who avoids the taint of the *agora*, this is the man who is the saviour of the State. In the *Suppliant Women*, Euripides had described the 'middle class' as the saviour of the State, and, as will be seen, there is a strong presumption that the two are the same.

The *autourgos* is intelligent, too—when he chooses to express himself—but he is contrasted with the demagogue who expresses himself with insolent ease. The countryman's 'intelligence' is well glossed by Dover: 'The countryman, blunt, and brutal in speech, is honest, upright, a pillar of traditional values, whereas the townsman has the gift of the gab.'[24]

The countryman's proposals, conservative and traditional, do

---

[24] K. J. Dover, *Greek Popular Morality*, 112–14.

not win the assent of the assembly, but there is, among them, one group which does approve of what he says—a group of gentlemen whom Euripides refers to as the *chrēstoi*. We have already met these men in the discussion of Pericles' speeches (Chapter 2), and shall meet them again in Chapter 7. They are men accustomed to being 'useful' to the State, to taking a leading part in affairs. In this scene, however, they seem to be taking a passive role: 'The *chrēstoi* seem immobilised, unwilling to take the initiative, incapable even, of rendering support' (Connor).[25] The ineffectualness of the *chrēstoi* in the face of the popular assembly, and their attraction to the *autourgos*, take on particular significance at this time of upheaval in the Athenian State.

If we try to assemble a composite portrait of Euripides' *autourgos* we find a man who lives in the country, far from town; he is poor and compelled to work long hours to make a modest living; he comes seldom to town and the assembly; he is expressly contrasted with the shameless mob-orator; he is respectful of those wealthier than himself; he is loaded with terms of moral approbation—he is prudent, truly noble, modest; he can run his home well and the city too; finally, he is the 'saviour of the State'.

What is surprising is that a poor and obscure farmer, one who must rise early and work all day, is the 'saviour of the State' and can 'run the city well'. It would seem that Euripides' hero is a good citizen not because he is always busy and zealous in his city's affairs, but just the reverse—because he is in fact unable to come in to the assembly very often. Euripides here seems in agreement with the architects of the various moderate oligarchic constitutions which appear around this time. Aristotle too, much later, approved a moderate, property-based democracy, the main quality of which was infrequent meetings of the assembly (see below).

The oligarchic constitutions which appeared in 411 and again in 404 were all based on the hoplite, the man who could furnish his own arms in time of war. In 411, Thucydides tells us, the assembly voted to transfer power from the Four Hundred oligarchs to the Five Thousand, that is, to all those who could

---

[25] Connor, *The New Politicians in Fifth Century Athens*, 117. *Chrēstoi* are discussed in Chapter 6.

provide their own weapons. And at first, Thucydides goes on, Athens was better governed than ever before in his time, for there was a 'reasonable blend of the few and the many' (8. 97). In Aristotle's version, the franchise was to be restricted to 'those best able to serve the State with their bodies and their property, up to a total of not less than 5,000' (*Ath. Pol.* 29. 5). (There is no necessary conflict between these two accounts. Thucydides does not set the figure of 5,000 as a ceiling; indeed, he says that it must include all the hoplites, and he must therefore have been prepared for a higher figure if necessary. In fact, the true figure may have been nearer 9,000, according to Lysias, *For Polystratus*, 13.)

Then again, at his trial in 404, Theramenes declared that he had wanted a moderate government, one restricted to the cavalry and hoplite classes (X. *Hell.* 2. 3. 48). The anonymous document (Ps.-Herodes Atticus) which may be by Critias, and was written close to this time, also proposes a hoplite census.[26]

It is significant, however, that there was only ever one proposal specifically to restrict the franchise to those who owned land. This was when the democrats were returning to Athens in 403 after the downfall of the Thirty, and Phormisius proposed that of these only those who owned land should be readmitted to citizenship.[27] The proposal was heavily defeated. Elsewhere there is no specific connection between the hoplite and the *autourgos*. The feeling from Euripides, as we have seen, and from Aristotle (see below) is that the oligarchs favoured the farmer, for it seems likely that the hoplite class corresponds to Euripides' 'middle class' which guarded the city's laws, and that the middle class was composed of men like Orestes' farmer who was the 'saviour of the State'. Nevertheless, however close the correspondence appears and however convenient, the oligarchs

[26] Ps.-Herodes Atticus, 30. Albini discusses the date of this work very thoroughly in his introduction. Most scholars have guessed between 410 and 399 BC. Wade-Gery in his article 'Kritias and Herodes' in *Essays in Greek History*, narrows it to between April and September 404, and attributes the work to Critias. Albini settles for no definite date. Most recently, D. Russell denies a date in the fifth (or fourth) century for this work (*Greek Declamation*, 111).

[27] Lysias, 34 (introduction by Dionysus of Halicarnassus). See Goossens, *Euripide et Athènes*, 556; di Benedetto, *Euripide: Teatro e società*, 208. Compare too C. Mossé, *La Fin de la démocratie athénienne*, 250, on the attraction of the peasant for the oligarchic theorist. She identifies the peasant with Euripides' 'middle class'.

never specifically make the connection between hoplite and *autourgos* in their constitutions.

The problem is confused because we are talking here not so much about real peasants, or even comic peasants, but rather about theoretical peasants, who seem to change shape as they are projected in the minds of their creators to fill their necessary roles. On the one hand the peasant is required to be a 'sturdy yeoman', self-sufficient, modestly prosperous, capable of providing his own arms, and of being away from home on campaigns, the complement of the knight as Theramenes envisaged him. On the other hand is the poor farmer, living far from the city, coming only rarely to the assembly, bowed with toil, and respectful of his betters. This is the man whom the oligarchs were able to overawe in 411 (Th. 8. 66.). It was the second type of peasant that the conspirators needed in order to carry through their plans in 411 and again in 404. But it was the first who figured in their speeches and theoretical programmes.

Euripides tells us twice that the *autourgos* is the saviour of the State. He can mean that by taking up arms against the invader the *autourgos* literally preserves it, and he can also mean that by conducting the political life of the city in a more sober, dignified, and low-key manner he preserves it from the violent upheavals and see-saws, U-turns and frenetic activity, of the radical democracy.

The most coherent statement of this view is given by Aristotle:

Whenever the class of farmers and those of a moderate substance is sovereign in the State they govern according to traditional laws. For they have a livelihood if they work, and so cannot be at leisure. So they preserve the traditional laws and have meetings of the assembly only when necessary.

(*Pol.* 1292[b] 25)

Compare this with another passage: according to Aristotle there are four kinds of common people. Of these the rural type is best:

The rural *dēmos* is best . . . for, since they do not own much property, they have little time for leisure, and hence do not often meet in the assembly.

(*Pol.* 1318[b] 10)

Aristotle classes the farmer together with the man of moderate substance, which may or may not be land. The element of stability associated with infrequent meetings of the assembly is also what appealed to the authors of the oligarchic constitutions. Aristotle insists on the element of property-ownership: this is the key to stability in the State. Large divergences of fortune lead to social strains (*Pol.* 1295^b 30); the middle station is the best, and so Aristotle's solution for social harmony is to collect together all the revenues of the State and to distribute them in lump sums to those in need, to enable them either to buy a small property or, failing this, to set themselves up in business as tradesmen or husbandmen (*Pol.* 1320^a 37). Aristotle distinguishes here between a *gēdion* (smallholding), and a humbler *emporion* (trade or business) or *georgia* (husbandry). The *georgia* is something less than the smallholding, and may be the cultivation of rented land or perhaps a market garden.

In his description of the different kinds of democracy, Aristotle tells us that the worst sort is where there is a large element of artisans, market people, and wage-earners (*thetes*) loitering about the market-place, since these types of people find it easy to attend the assembly (*Pol.* 1319^a 24 ff.). These are the same as Plato's 'drones', and Aristotle's purpose in sharing out the city's revenues is to empty them out of the city into the country, and secure them to a piece of ground. Once there, preoccupied with making a living, they will have little time to think of politics. Thus Aristotle will have achieved his preferred kind of democracy, which meets seldom and governs according to traditional custom. Incidentally, it is truly extraordinary, at this late date, to find Aristotle recommending the sharing-out of the city's wealth among its citizens, an idea which we have traced back to the *Iliad*; it indicates, as I said earlier, how rudimentary was the idea of the State as we understand it, even at this time when the city-state was about to be swallowed up by Macedon for ever.

Aristotle recognizes that the possession of property has a calming and sobering effect, conducive to a state of *apragmosynē*, which in its turn brings a quieter, more stable society, and it is the small farmer who is the ideal citizen in this respect. There does not appear to be any historical evidence for extreme poverty among farmers in Attica in the Classical period. The upheavals

or wanton and random destructiveness which accompany it in
early nineteenth-century England are absent; neither is there
the cry for redivision of land such as there had been in the time
of Solon.[28] The two examples of the poor farmer, in
Aristophanes and Euripides, are introduced for dramatic
purposes. Poor farmers must have existed, but they were not
the majority and though the majority were poor enough, they
were not up against absolute poverty. The moderate, even
modest, farmer is noted for his *apragmosynē*, but the farmer
reduced to utter destitution and starvation is far from *apragmōn*.
He is a prime source of sedition, or social discontent, and
upheaval, which is precisely what we do not find in Classical
Attica. The upheavals of early nineteenth-century England were
the result of the expropriation of a once-proud yeoman class and
their reduction, largely, to the status of poor, landless, labourers.
Again, though there was a steady movement from the country
to the town in Attica, in the hundred years down to 330 BC, it
did not result, as in Italy, in the creation of large estates in the
hands of wealthy magnates.

The small proprietor is a constant phenomenon during the
Classical period, a majority of the citizen population owning their
own land.[29] The consequence is a way of life concentrated on
staying alive and producing a small profit, in which the farm
takes a central place. The farmer is a man who lives anything
up to a day's walk from Athens, and whose life is lived out in
his village. Here are enacted the various festivals and ceremonies
which make up the country calendar. Politically, it is the deme
and the phratry, rather than the assembly in Athens, which are
significant in this life. The city, in all its aspects, is something
to be escaped from at the earliest opportunity; the very variety
which Plato grudgingly admired (*Rep.* 557 B) and which was
analysed earlier into some of its components, from sycophants
to cheating fishmongers, from fluent lawyers to beardless youths,
all comes under the heading of *pragmata*—bother, business,

---

[28] Arist. *Ath. Pol.* 11. 2 and 12. 3.
[29] On the basic stability of rural life in the fifth and fourth centuries see V. N.
Andreev, 'Some Aspects of Agrarian Conditions in Attica in the Fifth to Third Centuries',
Eirene, 12, 22–3: 'Athens maintained a large middle group of land owners which preserved
stability in the upheavals of the fourth century'.

trouble, expense. All the same, the peasant is in business, cash business, if only to a limited extent, and is compelled to have some dealing with the city economy. He produces goods to sell, whether grapes, figs, olives, or other market produce.

Aristotle classes the farmer together with the *banausos*, and politically there is little difference. It is the possession of property which produces that calming, sobering, effect which the oligarchic theorists desired. The *banausos*, as Xenophon saw, has no time for the assembly, and the oligarchs, in constructing their theoretical constitutions, never confined the franchise to the peasant. But every one of them did have as its aim to exclude the poor without property, the 'drones' whom their authors had seen loitering in the market square of Athens.

It may be asked why the *autourgoi* have such a fascination for the oligarchic authors—for all the authors we have considered must be regarded as belonging in the oligarchic part of the political spectrum—when, from a political point of view, as Aristotle shows, they are analogous to the tradesmen and artisans. The reason must be mainly cultural; Xenophon despised the tradesman for being cramped indoors all day in front of a fire, crooked in mind and body. The peasant, by contrast, is out in the air. Then there is the element of tradition and continuity: the peasant is tilling the soil his father tilled before him. Culturally, change is slower in the countryside than in the town, which is exposed to new influences from abroad. In the Peiraeus they may worship Attis and Bendis, but at Brauron they keep the original wooden statue of Artemis.

Most importantly, the peasant respects his betters (and knows who they are), and is in favour of peace, for he is the one who suffers most from war. The city-dweller was safe behind the walls, but it was the peasant's vines and olive trees the Spartans destroyed. It is not coincidence that on the two occasions when there was an influx of peasants into the city (431–424 and 412–404 BC) foreign policy turned towards peace: in 429, in the aftermath of the plague, there was an embassy to Sparta, and in 411, with the navy in Samos, the oligarchs were able to overawe the predominantly country population again in Athens and to set up briefly an oligarchy dedicated to concluding a quick peace with Sparta.

Lastly, the oligarchic thinkers, the aristocrats or squires of

Attica, must have felt some sort of cultural affinity with the 'sons of the soil' who, having most to lose, would fight most tenaciously to keep it. They had certainly fought most tenaciously in the past; a favourite theme of Aristophanes' early *parabases* is that of the *Marathōnomachoi* — the men who fought at Marathon. At that most glorious moment, Athenians had stood shoulder to shoulder — as hoplites — rich and poor alike, to save Greece from the Persian. Then there had been no navy, no 'drones', no Empire, no sycophants, no lawcourts; then every man knew his place. Marathon, in a word, encompasses everything the oligarch longed for and sought to restore, and it was in the peasant that he saw his ally and support.

5

Rich Quietists

In the year 421 BC, peace was achieved between the Spartans and the Athenians, due, on the part of the Athenians, as Thucydides says, to Nicias son of Niceratus:

Nicias the son of Niceratus, who at the time was the most respected of all the generals, wished, while he was still well thought of and had suffered no ill luck, to preserve his good fortune and give both himself and his fellow-citizens a rest from their toils and to leave behind him the name of one who had never failed his city. He thought this could best be achieved by avoiding risks and trusting as little as possible to luck, and that only in peace could risks be avoided.

(5. 16. 1)

Six years later in 415, when Nicias attempted to prevent the Athenians sailing for Sicily, it was for reasons perhaps not unconnected with these. It seemed to Nicias that he was at the end of his career; he had come thus far without bad luck; his services to the State had been successful from start to finish; now was the time to stop, when things were going well. These factors must have influenced what Alcibiades calls his *apragmosynē*.

The difference in age between them is stressed by Thucydides: Nicias appeals to the older men in the audience not to allow themselves to be browbeaten (6. 13. 1); Alcibiades boasts of his youth. His fearlessness, his rashness, he claims, are in the tradition which made Athens great. But in recalling the words of Pericles, he distorts them. In 430, Pericles had said: 'If you bide your time, take care of the navy, do not try to add to the Empire during the war, and do not run the city into dangers, you cannot be beaten.' (2. 65. 7.) Now, in 415, Alcibiades turns this on its head: if the city remains at rest, he says, it will wear out (6. 18. 6). In 430, Pericles had said: 'Nor is it any longer possible for you to give up the Empire.' (2. 63. 1). Now Alcibiades says not merely that they cannot give up what they have got, but that they must continually seize more in order not

99

to lose what they have: 'We are now in a position where we must plan new conquests and yield to no one, for there is a danger that we ourselves shall fall under the rule of others if we do not rule over them.' (6. 18. 3.)[1]

Just as Pericles had attacked his enemies (or those who opposed his policies) as *apragmones*, so does Alcibiades, and this time we know at least one of his opponents — Nicias. Do not be put off by his arguments for sitting tight and doing nothing, says Alcibiades:

> The city, like anything else, will wear itself out if it is left in idleness, and its skill in everything will grow out of date; if it is in a state of conflict, on the other hand, it will forever be gaining fresh experience, learning how to defend itself not in words but in action. Generally speaking, my experience is that a city which is active by nature will soon come to ruin if it changes to a life of idleness.
>
> (6. 18. 6)[1]

Alcibiades' characterization of the Athenian people as essentially active, questing, innovative, is in accord with the description of them in Book 1. There Thucydides had set out an antithesis: Athenian/Spartan = active/idle (*hēsychos*). The same active/idle antithesis underlay Pericles' attacks on the *apragmones* and the justification of his own policy, and it is used yet again by Alcibiades in the justification of his policy. But this is on the surface: underneath, Alcibiades' policy represents the contradiction of Pericles'. Pericles had urged the Athenians to hold on to what they had, but not to attempt more, and for him the man who wanted to give up the empire was *apragmōn*; now Alcibiades is saying that the Athenians must be continually striving for more, and that the man who opposes them is *apragmōn*. Thucydides represents the dynamism and vitality of Athens, previously seen in an attractive light, as being now under the influence of insane folly (*atē*),[2] and the position of the *apragmōn* appears reversed under the impact of events. Pericles had represented his enemies as *apragmones*, but the *apragmosynē*

---

[1] J. de Romilly, *Thucydides and Imperial Athens*, 210 ff., discusses this speech in relation to Pericles' last speech, but without appreciating the shift of emphasis from a policy of, as it were, *sōphrosynē*, to one of *hybris*.

[2] See F. M. Cornford, *Thucydides Mythistoricus*, 188 ff.; ibid., 197, on Alcibiades deliberately misleading Athens; Th. 4. 65. 4 on Athenian hopes.

of Nicias and his friends now consists in maintaining Pericles' position.

It is only in Thucydides that the term *apragmosynē* is used of city-states. This is in accord with his view of states, that to a large extent (if not entirely) they constitute simply the aggregate of their citizens, and behave therefore like an individual citizen, and their actions can be described in moral and psychological terms. The essential difference is that whereas within states actions are regulated by laws, between states there is anarchy, tempered by occasional *ad hoc* agreements.[3] The extreme example, and Thucydides deliberately spells it out, is in the Melian dialogue. All the terms of judgement and reference are those used between individuals, but because the dispute is between states and not individuals, the Athenians can say almost at the beginning 'This is a dispute between the strong and the weak; leave all talk of justice aside'. (5. 89).

In a similar way *apragmosynē* can be applied, as a term, to the actions of states as well as to those of individuals. The stakes are higher because the individual has recourse to justice if he is wronged, the State none.

It is also only in these speeches that the term is used derisively. It has been claimed that *apragmōn* is always elsewhere a term of approval.[4] That is largely true, but the reality is rather complicated, and the attitude of juries was ambivalent when a plaintiff described himself as *apragmōn* (see below). More importantly, the speeches of both Pericles and Alcibiades, with their vigorous and robust tone, very much in the same key as the description of the Athenians in Thucydides' Book 1, suggest that they are carrying their audiences with them, and that their view of the *apragmones* is shared by their listeners, at least for the present.

Nicias appeals to the older men in the audience not to be browbeaten by the younger men around them in coming to a decision. This is a reflection of what appears to have been a 'youth culture' in Athens at the time. It is an interesting fact that although eligibility for the generalship was open only to the over-thirties and that generals could expect to exert a great deal

---

[3] So too de Romilly, op. cit., 210 n. 4.
[4] Ehrenberg, *JHS* 67 (1947), 46–76; Gomme, *HCT*, on 2. 63.

of authority in the assembly, young men were making their mark as speakers from the age of twenty onwards, and were, in some cases, a force to be feared. This seems to me to be in opposition to the general tendency in Greece, which was that age took precedence over youth: a point which Aristophanes brings out in the *Clouds* (993 ff.). It is interesting that after the Sicilian disaster, the Athenians reverted to the norm and appointed a council of elders of their own — the *probouloi* (minimum age forty).[5]

Nowhere is allowance made for Nicias on account of his age.[6] He had had a successful career and wanted to stop now while he was winning. But then why did he come forward and offer his advice on Sicily? Why did he allow himself to be elected general of the expedition? He was under no obligation to stand,[7] nor even to attend the meeting. Nicias was notorious for his retiring disposition, his timidity (Plut. *Nic.* 2), qualities which might have qualified him for *apragmosynē*, yet he possessed what Plutarch calls 'a certain vulgarity and ostentation aimed at increasing his prestige and satisfying his ambition' (*Nic.* 4). Nicias in fact embodies the qualities both of *philotimia* and *apragmosynē*. The *apragmōn* side of his character was perhaps the principal element which recommended him to public favour, which made his *philotimia* acceptable in the eyes of the *dēmos*. He had also been extremely shrewd in his military campaigns; it was this instinct which led him to avoid the Pylos campaign. Cleon never imagined Nicias would actually give up command of the expedition; he understood Nicias to be making a debating gesture. This is a measure of the instinct for *timē* among the Athenians. Nicias' genuine willingness to hand over command to Cleon is unique in the history of the assembly.

Nicias, then, represents an interesting paradox. His ambition is consonant with the prestige and importance of *timē* discussed in Chapter 1; at the same time, he is rather cautious by temperament. But it is this latter quality which makes him so popular. The more he tries to avoid the Sicilian command, the more it is pressed upon him. Nicias is both *philotimos* and

---

[5] The *Lysistrata* represents them as old dodderers.
[6] Compare too Ar. *Ach.* 1128 on Lamachus in a similar plight.
[7] Plato, *Rep.* 557 E.

apragmōn, and this contradiction in his character, it may be said, was responsible for his defeat and death.

Nicias is useful in this discussion in a more general way because he is an outstanding example of a very rich Athenian, and he exhibits the characteristics shared by 'rich quietists'.[8] The retiring quality which, in Nicias, was so popular with the assembly, is also found in, or assumed by, plaintiffs and defendants before the assembly in its other manifestation as lawcourt. There it has the same pleasing effect.[9]

The first characteristic is lavish spending on liturgies. Liturgies included, in peacetime, the funding of dramatic contests, choral recitals, religious ceremonies, processions, and sacred embassies, while in wartime there were also the trierarchies—the equipping of warships—the greatest expense of all.[10] While such services were obligatory, the wealthy took care to extract the maximum use-value from their contributions. In particular, if they were compelled to go to law, their liturgies served as character witnesses, and they made quite sure the jury was acquainted with their contributions. One defendant tells a jury of his liturgies, performed in the last years of the fifth century:

I reached the age of eighteen in the year Theopompus was archon, and being appointed to produce a tragic drama I spent 3,000 drachmas; two months later at the Thargelia I won a victory with a male chorus, when I spent 2,000 drachmas. In the following year I spent 800 drachmas on Pyrrhic dancers at the Great Panathenaea. At the Dionysia in the same year I had a victory with a male chorus, and spent 5,000 drachmas, including the dedication of the tripod. In the following year I spent 300 drachmas on a cyclic chorus at the little Panathenaea. In the meantime I was appointed trierarch for seven years and spent six talents [i.e. 36,000 drachmas].

(Lys. 21. 1)[11]

This does not exhaust the list of the speaker's services to the State. Minimum costs were laid down, but individuals strove

---

[8] The phrase is taken from S. C. Humphreys, 'Public and Private Interests in Classical Athens', *CJ* 73 (1977–8), 97–104.

[9] Cf. Isocr. *Antid* 15. 4.

[10] See article in *RE*. In 355 BC there were perhaps sixty or slightly more recurrent liturgies every year at Athens. See too J. K. Davies, 'Demosthenes on Liturgies: a Note', *JHS* 87 (1967), 33–40.

[11] The total expenditure in this case was over ten talents (60,000 drachmas).

to outdo them—or claimed they did: 'Of those sums I have enumerated, had I chosen to limit myself to the letter of the law, I should not have spent one quarter' (Lys. 21. 5). The reward of a big outlay was *timē*: 'Liturgies, though burdensome to those to whom they are assigned, do convey a certain distinction (*timē*).' (Isocr. 12. 145.)

There is no doubt that *timē* played an important part in motivating those appointed to perform liturgies. But it was not, it seems, the only factor which influenced the amounts laid out. Consider this extract:

> I have been trierarch five times, fought in four sea battles, contributed to many war levies and performed my other liturgies as amply as any other citizen. But my purpose in spending more than was enjoined upon me by the city was to raise myself the higher in your esteem, so that if any misfortune should befall me I might stand a better chance in court.

(Lys. 25. 12)

This is, so far as I know, the only occasion on which the speaker actually admits this defensive use of liturgies. But if the thought at least was common, and I think it must have been, it betrays a motive very far indeed from the lust for *timē*. It shows the rich citizen not as exulting in his wealth and prestige, but rather taking out an insurance policy against a possible appearance in court.[12] The implication is that the court will be essentially hostile to him. The rich man is on the defensive. The origin of liturgies lies in a pre-democratic past when such spending was the accompaniment of an appropriate public position.[13] But from the time of Ps.-Xenophon, at least, the emphasis is reversed. The rich are *required* to perform liturgies for the benefit of the poor, 'so that they [the poor] may have money, and the rich become poorer' (Ps.-X. *Ath. Pol.* 1. 13).

Nicias was famous for the sums he lavished on liturgies: 'on a scale more expensive and sumptuous than anything ever seen in Athens before' (Plut. *Nic.* 3). Plutarch details the gold-plated

---

[12] Cf. Davies, *APF* intro. xvii. On cost of being rich, compare X. *Oec.* 2. 5; and Theophrastus' Oligarchical Man who complains of being ruined by liturgies and trierarchies, reminiscent of Ps.-X. *Ath. Pol.*

[13] Aristotle dates liturgies to Hippias (*Econ.* 1547ª); Demosthenes to Solon (42. 1). Cimon, being extremely rich, performed sumptuous liturgies (Arist. *Ath. Pol.* 27).

statue of Athene on the acropolis; the dramatic choruses, so many and never beaten; the shrine in the precinct of Dionysus; above all, the elaborate ceremony at Delos when a special bridge of boats was constructed to allow the gorgeously apparelled procession to cross, dry-footed, from the neighbouring island at dawn.[14] The speaker of the passage last quoted seems to share Nicias' two-edged attitude to the *dēmos* — prestige and fame sit uneasily side by side with an *apragmōn* nervousness about public opinion, a need to conciliate the *dēmos* in advance of any possible trouble.

It was this uneasy relationship which enabled the sycophants to flourish.[15] After the exile of Themistocles in 472 'when the *dēmos* was becoming more insolent, there sprang up a mass of sycophants who brought suits against the men of power and influence, working on the envy of the people, who were exulted by their good luck and power.' (Plut. *Arist.* 26.)[16] This may not be too early, considering the prosecution of members of the Areopagus (Arist. *Ath. Pol.* 25; cf. Jacoby's comm. on 342F12). The earliest historical reference to sycophants is, I think, the Ps.-Xen. *Ath. Pol*, which describes how Athenians sailed out to lay charges against wealthy citizens among the allies (1. 14). The identical phenomenon occurs in the *Birds* of Aristophanes where, in a parade of democratic undesirables, we meet a sycophant-cum-summoner,[17] who has hit upon a cunning scheme to deliver summonses to citizens in the islands, fly back to Athens and gain a verdict before the unfortunate victim has had time to sail to Athens, and then fly back to the island to distrain upon his goods. The wealthy, whether they dwelt in Attica or elsewhere in the Empire, were the prey of sycophants.

Nicias was a famous victim of sycophants: 'He gave no less to those capable of doing him harm than to those by whom he benefited, and generally speaking his cowardice was as much a source of income to scoundrels as his generosity was to upright

---

[14] This was a liturgy. See Davies, 'Demosthenes on Liturgies: a Note' (above, n. 10), 38. Nicias was *architheōros*.

[15] Ps.-Xenophon, for one, believed the poor hated the rich (2. 19).

[16] Plutarch quotes Krateros of Macedonia, Jacoby, *FGH* 342F12.

[17] *Birds*,1422. Generally speaking, a plaintiff delivered his own summons, and called on a friend or bystander to act as witness.

men.' (Plut. *Nic.* 4.)[18] Plutarch quotes these lines from Telecleides on the sycophants and their power:

Charicles gave him a hundred drachmas to stop him telling how he was his mother's first child, born out of wedlock, but Nicias, Niceratus' son, gave him 400. I'm not telling why (though I know); the man's my friend, a careful, prudent chap.

(Plut. *Nic.* 4)

The threat of disenfranchisement, which is what Charicles has been threatened with here, is third only in significance to the death penalty and exile. There need have been no political grounds for the threat of such a prosecution, as the passage demonstrates, and it may be that in a majority of cases the sycophant preferred his victim to be a harmless *apragmōn* private citizen who would pay rather than be dragged into the harsh light of a lawcourt.[19]

It is, in fact, a common opening to a lawcourt speech for the speaker to say that he is unfamiliar with lawcourts. The inference is that those who were familiar there could expect to be unpopular.[20] The earliest such plea, and in fact the earliest example of a man claiming, or even boasting, of being *apragmōn*, occurs in one of the *Tetralogies* of Antiphon:

It is clear to me now that misfortune and necessity can compel a quiet and peace-loving man (*apragmōn*) to appear in court, and those who have never given offence to be bold and generally to speak and act in a manner contrary to their nature.

(2. 2. 1)

Whether these speeches are the work of Antiphon is not our concern here; what is important is to establish the date of their composition. On this subject, scholarly opinion is unanimous in placing them far back, perhaps in the 440s.[21] The language, with its balanced antitheses, recalls that of Gorgias, Corax, and

---

[18] Cf. Ar. *Birds*, 285 on Callias, and Theophrastus' Oligarchical Man.

[19] This point is made by S. C. Humphreys in 'Public and Private Interests in Classical Athens', *CJ* 73: 2 (1977–8), 103.

[20] Like Antiphon. Cf. Th. 8. 68. 1 and above, Chapter 3.

[21] e.g., Kleine Pauly; G. Zuntz, 'Earliest Attic Prose Style: on Antiphon's Second Tetralogy', *Class. et Med.* 2 (1939), 140 ff.; K. J. Maidment, intro. to Loeb edn of Antiphon, 46; K. J. Dover, *Lysias and the Corpus Lysiacum*, 189.

Teisias, while the subject of the *Second Tetralogy* here—the apportioning of guilt after a boy had been struck accidentally by a spear in a gymnasium—recalls the discussion which Pericles is said to have had with Protagoras, and, in general, the rethinking of Archaic views on pollution and guilt. The evidence of style is probably stronger than that of the issue of pollution, which was alive and well in the 420s and later.[22]

But if this speech is indeed of the 440s, it has important consequences for a study of *apragmosynē* and the lawcourts. The lawcourts, as they existed during the democracy, had taken their final shape soon after 462 when Pericles introduced pay for jury service.[23] It was this pay which ensured a democratic majority in the jury, and was responsible for the servile and humble manner adopted by litigants towards the jury. The early date which seems inevitable for this speech indicates that this relationship towards the jury existed almost from the start. This is important, because all the rest of the evidence from speeches comes from the fourth century, and it might otherwise possibly be concluded that the wealthy *apragmōn* was a post-war phenomenon. That he is, on the contrary, a democratic one and in existence, so far as we can see, almost from the date the democracy achieved its final form (that is, from the overthrow of the Areopagus) is the inevitable conclusion from this passage.

The power which juries exerted, the fear they induced in litigants, are well known from the 430s onwards: Pericles in tears at Aspasia's trial, Philocleon on piteous defendants in the *Wasps*, and so on. The motif of the wealthy gentleman dragged unwillingly into court continues through the fourth century in many examples. Consider the victim of an action in Lysias' *On the Olive Stump*:

Up till now, gentlemen, I had always thought it possible, for anyone who wished, to lead a quiet life and have nothing to do with the law and affairs. But now that I have so unexpectedly found myself the target of accusations by disreputable sycophants, I could almost believe that even those not yet born should be apprehensive about what may be

---

[22] Cf. Antiphon, *On the Choreutes*, 36, on pollution and its legal effects.
[23] So Hignett, *Hist. Ath. Const.*, 342.

in store for them. Thanks to these men, those who have led a blameless life are in as great danger as those who have committed every crime.

(7. 1)

The unfortunate gentleman who has fallen thus unexpectedly among *pragmata* is wealthy; later in the speech (30 ff.) he describes the zeal and munificence of his liturgies: his trierarchies, choruses, contributions to war taxes, and other duties enjoined upon the very rich. He had laid out more than he was officially required to, he says, possibly with an eye to just such an eventuality as this. He had fought many battles (7. 41) on behalf of his country, both by sea and land, and had shown himself an orderly citizen both under the democracy and the oligarchy.

The case against him was a very flimsy one: it concerned the stump of a sacred olive tree alleged to have been on his land. Even the stump of a sacred olive tree was protected by law and its removal was punishable by exile and the confiscation of property. However, there was no stump to be seen, and while the prosecution alleged that the defendant had dug it up, he for his part denied it had ever been there. The prosecution brought no witnesses; further he had chosen an accusation in which, if he failed to gain a fifth of the votes, he was not liable to any forfeit. Such an example of malicious prosecution is explained by the defendant's opening words: he was a man of wealth pursuing a quiet life while performing sumptuous liturgies to ensure himself a good name. The prosecutor clearly depended on the defendant's fear and dislike of lawsuits or any kind of public business; such a man would be prepared to pay a sycophant to desist. The fact that on this occasion the sycophant was mistaken in his victim does not alter what is, on the evidence of Lysias' speeches, a rule.[24]

Consider another example: the case of the speaker's father in Lysias' *On the Property of Aristophanes*. During the speech, the speaker contrasts the characters of his father and his brother-in-law, Aristophanes — the retiring private citizen against the public figure:

---

[24] And not only in Lysias. Cf. V. Albini, 'Antifonte Logografo', *Maia* 10 (1958), 45. He compares Ant. 1. i; Lys. 12. 3; Isaeus 1. i, 8. 5, 9. 35 and 10. 1; Isocrates, 15. 26; Dem. 27. 2, 29. 1, 41. 2, 55. 2; [Dem.] 48. 1.

There was not only a difference of age between them, but even more of character. For the one wished only to mind his own business, but the other, Aristophanes, wished to involve himself not only in private affairs, but in those of the State too. If he ever had any money, he spent it out of a desire for *timē*.

(19. 18)

'To mind one's own business' is clearly contrasted with the desire for *timē*. This is the same phrase we encountered in the discussion of Plato's *Charmides*, composed within a few years of this speech.[25] It is a definition of *apragmosynē*, and its meaning is clear from this context; it contrasts with the attitude of Aristophanes who was eager to serve the State and achieve honour. He had been on embassies, one to Syracuse, and had contributed freely to the cost of the trip. The *apragmōn* is prepared to contribute to the cost, without demanding any of the corresponding prestige. The amount of his contribution is detailed: he says he has spent twice as much on the State as on himself and his family (19. 9), and over a period of fifty years the sum had amounted to over nine talents (19. 59); this was in addition to providing dowries for the daughters of needy citizens, ransoming men home from the enemy, and paying for the funerals of others. It is, he says, the part of a good man to help his friends — a phrase familiar in definitions of justice, *aretē*, etc., in Plato's dialogues.[26] Near the end of the speech, the speaker turns for a moment to himself in order to show that he, like his father, has also led an orderly life, and has never once been seen in a lawcourt or council-chamber:

I am now thirty years old, yet I have never contradicted my father, nor have I ever been the subject of an accusation by a citizen. I live near the market square yet I had never once been seen in the lawcourt or the council chamber until this misfortune.

(19. 55)[27]

The rich man presents himself to a jury composed of men poorer than himself as one who has led a quiet, retiring life, one who minds his own business, endeavours not to give offence,

---

[25] The speech is dated 388/7; the *Charmides* to the 390s.

[26] e.g., *Rep.* 332 on justice; *Meno*, 71 E on *aretē*.

[27] And compare other speeches by Lysias: 3. 46; 4. 19; 5. 3; 12. 38; 16. 10; 26. 3.

or to thrust himself into the public limelight: this is the theme with which lawcourt speeches opened almost from the moment the democratic courts came into existence, and it continued throughout the fourth century. To say that it is a speech-writer's tool, a topos, is to miss the point. Why do speech-writers employ it? Presumably because it was effective, and if it was effective it must have some basis in fact. Juries were on their guard against speeches composed for litigants by professionals, and the profession of writing other people's speeches seems to have been regarded as degrading.[28] For this reason, whatever the degree of collaboration between the speech-writer and the man who had to stand up in court and deliver it, it was clearly in the client's interest for these kinds of details to be reasonably accurate. If the speaker said things either that the jury knew to be untrue, or which his opponent knew to be so, and could turn against him, he could do himself more harm than good. Script-writers, whatever tricks they possessed, had to be careful how they used them. For this reason I am inclined to question what Davies has called 'forensic inflation': the idea that figures for contributions to liturgies were falsely inflated to impress the jury.[29]

The property qualification for liturgies was three talents,[30] which was a great deal of money,[31] yet some of the figures already quoted show that there were men far richer than that. Further on in the speech last quoted (Lys. 19), the speaker discusses the fortunes of very rich men, and tries to convince the jury that they were not as rich as had been made out: thus Conon, who was thought to have been very rich, left no more than forty talents, while Callias' property at his death amounted to no more than fourteen talents. The writer here *is* trying to mislead the jury: if three talents made you a rich man, clearly both Conon and Callias died immensely rich, whatever the speaker is trying to imply to the contrary. For this, and the previous reason, I do not see why we need necessarily doubt the figures quoted.

---

[28] e.g., Antiphon. Cf. Dover, *Lysias and the Corpus Lysiacum*, 155.

[29] Intro. to Davies, *APF* intro. xxii. He admits that the scale of expenditure is probably not too misleadingly represented.

[30] Dem. *Against Aphobus*, 833.

[31] One talent = 6,000 days' wages for a skilled craftsman, approximately, according to the Erechtheum inscriptions. See Davies, *APF* intro. xxii n. 6.

I feel too that the claims to *apragmosynē* must have some basis in truth: those who funded the State festivities did not do so anonymously. The winner of a dramatic competition gained glory from it; it was effectively his victory, and the dedication afterwards was made in his name. In this context, there is an interesting variation on the same theme in Lysias' *On the Scrutiny of Evandrus*. The speaker, instead of making the usual claims on behalf of himself, anticipates that his opponent will make them:

He will tell you how much he and his family have spent on the city, and with what public zeal (*philotimia*) they have performed their liturgies, and how many splendid victories (in the dramatic or athletic contests) they have won under the democracy. And he will also tell you what an orderly life he leads and that he has never been seen in this place behaving in the brazen manner that others adopt, but has preferred to mind his own business.

(26. 3)

Here are the usual protestations about splendid victories, leading a quiet life, and behaving in an orderly fashion, yet the client is represented as possessed by *philotimia* as well as *apragmosynē*. If we claim that *philotimia* is the opposite to *apragmosynē*, then we must observe this caveat: the rich are compelled to perform liturgies, and however *apragmōn* they may be in their lives, they will make the maximum use of this duty to gain a good reputation.

Bearing this in mind, the impression is left that many rich men shied away from politics and the lawcourts, kept their heads down, and preferred to lead a quiet life: that they were, in fact, afraid of the people. If this is true, it is a remarkable aspect of the democracy, for throughout history, under all manner of constitutions and at all periods, the rich have been accustomed to power and influence out of all proportion to their numbers. Some rich men did exert power and influence in Athens, it is true, but this phenomenon of rich *apragmones* is not encountered in any other society. What evidence is there for them, outside lawcourt speeches? Are they actually anything more than a speech-writer's *topos*?

Consider the case of Crito, as described in Xenophon's *Memorabilia*. Crito complains to Socrates that it is no longer possible for a man to mind his own business, on account of sycophants:

I remember once Crito complaining to him how difficult life was in
Athens for anybody who wanted to mind his own business. There are
men, he said, who will take me to court, not because I've done them
any harm, but because they know I'd rather pay money than get mixed
up in legal business (*pragmata*).

(2. 9)

The solution which Socrates advises Crito to adopt is, so far as
I know, unique. He is to seek out one Archedemus, an excellent
speaker and man of affairs, but poor. He is an honest man, says
Socrates, not out to make money by underhand means.
Xenophon's opinion of Archedemus, if it be the same man, is
in such contrast to the character represented by the poet
Aristophanes, that it is difficult to decide whether Archedemus
has been maligned by Aristophanes, or whether Xenophon is
very naive, or whether Socrates is being very ironic. From what
other authors have told us, Archedemus was foremost in debate
in the closing years of the fifth century, both in the assembly
and the lawcourts.[32] Socrates may intend to set a sycophant to
catch a sycophant. Crito began very quietly sending Archedemus
presents of corn, oil, wine, wool, or other farm produce, and
invited him to sacrifices (i.e. feasts), so that, Xenophon says,
Archedemus came to regard Crito's home as a refuge, and
constantly paid his respects to him. He soon found out that
Crito's false accusers had much to answer for and many enemies.
He brought one of them to trial. The defendant, conscious that
he was guilty on many counts, did all he could to get rid of
Archedemus, but Archedemus refused to let him off until he
withdrew the action against Crito and compensated him.
Archedemus carried through several other enterprises of a similar
kind, and by this time many of Crito's friends were begging for
Archedemus' protection too.

---

[32] Aristophanes makes the standard sneer that he is not really of Athenian birth
(*Frogs*, 417). Lysias refers to him as a companion of the young Alcibiades, and as one
who had 'embezzled not a little of your [i.e. the *dēmos*'] property' (14. 25). Aeschines
says he corrupted the people by his largesse (*de F. Leg.* 76). Xenophon (*Hell.* 1. 7. 2)
represents him as 'watch-dog of the people' in 406, and the first to commence proceedings
against the generals after Arginousai. He brought an action against Erasinides, one of
the generals, for misappropriation of public funds and misconduct as a general.
Archedemus is seen here performing the central function of a 'watch-dog of the people'
in calling to account those in office, and specifically those who have charge of public
funds.

What had at first appeared to be a rather unusual relationship develops in the end into something more familiar—a network of friends (*philoi*) bound by ties of friendship, mutual aid, and dependence.

Consider also this passage from Aristophanes' *Knights*, in which the chorus address the Paphlagonian:

You squeeze the audit-passers, to see which are ripe,
Which are ripening, and which not ready to fall.
And if you find one who is *apragmōn* and gawping,
You summon him from the Chersonese, seize him,
Get a lock on him, twist his shoulder back and gulp him down.
And you look through the citizens for any who are
Lamb-like, wealthy, no villain, and fearful of *pragmata*.

(259–65)[33]

The gentleman described in the last two lines seems to be the very one I have been discussing above: he is rich, a 'gentleman', he is 'lamb-like' and he is 'fearful of *pragmata*'. An ancient commentator explains: 'Fearful of *pragmata*: to beware of getting involved in *pragmata*. Many men would rather pay than get involved in lawsuits, not through cowardice, but through their character and refined manners.' The scholiast is putting the best face on it, but all the same this idea of a certain cultural quality, an educated reserve, which inhibits a man from mixing in a common slanging match in a pulic debate was a quality of Hippolytus, and perhaps of many of Lysias' defendants too. The 'lamb-like' quality was what sycophants saw, or thought they saw, in the defendant in the case of the *Olive Stump*, and in Crito and Nicias too.

It is clear from this passage of Aristophanes that the rich quietist is a creation of the democracy, and not someone who only appeared in the fourth century. The two non-legal examples I have quoted show close affinities with Lysias' defendants, and make it clear that the protestations to the jury, though so oft-repeated and so similar in phrasing, were not merely a speech-writer's creation, but corresponded to reality.

---

[33] The last two lines seem to be in a rather unsatisfactory relationship to those preceding, and Brunck suggested putting them in after line 260. This would produce a double reference to *pragmata*, however, which is unattractive, and would further mean that it would be the citizen referred to in 264 who is to be summoned back from the Chersonese, which is not, I think, what Aristophanes intended.

The mention of the audit (*euthynai*) in the passage above brings us to a slightly different aspect of this subject. The *euthynai* were an audit undergone by all who had held public office at the completion of their year of service.[34] It might appear at first that those who held public office would not be eligible for inclusion in a discussion of *apragmosynē*, but I shall suggest (a) that in certain circumstances they are; and (b) that the rigours of the *euthynai* were such as to persuade otherwise public-spirited gentlemen from serving their country, and to encourage in them a tendency towards *apragmosynē*.

To take the latter point first. The *euthynai* were in two parts: a financial part, consisting of the scrutiny of the accounts if the magistrate in question had handled public money, and then a general review of his tenure of office in which anyone was free to bring an action for misbehaviour, especially if he were a general. In Chapter 2, I mentioned the prosecutions of generals during the 420s, some of which, like that of Paches, could have a spectacular ending. We also saw that a general might not return to Athens at once if his campaign had been a failure. He would have to face his *euthynai* in the end, but might consider it wise to wait until memories had faded a little.

In the passage quoted above from the *Knights*, it is not clear whether the man referred to in line 259 is a general or magistrate (or someone holding State money in some capacity, like a *tamias* — a steward). In the original Greek there is a pun on the word for 'fig' (which, in Greek, resembles the word sycophant) which suggests that Cleon, in feeling the fig to see if it is ripe enough to pluck, is weighing up the candidate to see if he should be prosecuted, or perhaps suggesting to the candidate that, for a bribe, he will go easy on him at his audit. Either way, Aristophanes sets out clearly the relationship of the sycophant to the man undergoing *euthynai*. The kind of man the sycophant is especially looking out for is the one who is *apragmōn* and 'gawping'. Here, then, is a man in office who is also *apragmōn*. What is he doing in the Chersonese? He may have been a general on duty in the region to collect tribute

---

[34] Cf. A. R. W. Harrison, *The Law of Athens*, 208; Hignett, *Hist. Ath. Const.* 203 ff.

or perform other duties in the area, or he may have been a magistrate holding office there.[35]

The Chersonese itself paid little tribute at this time; there had been Athenian settlers there since the time of the elder Miltiades around 520, and in 447, when Pericles planted a further thousand settlers, the tribute fell, presumably as the natives were displaced.[36] If he was a general, there are other indications in the *Knights* that Cleon would be hard on him in his audit: 'If you stand for general, I'll get you!' screams the Paphlagonian at the Sausage-seller (288).[37] Earlier, another character had outlined to the Sausage-seller the many advantages of being 'watch-dog of the people', one of which was the power to 'trim the generals' (166).[38]

Nevertheless, it seems more likely that the gentleman referred to was not a general. The ancient commentator enlarges on the subject a little:

The Thracian Chersonese was a tributary territory of the Athenians; it produced wheat in abundance and supplied Athens. The passage indicates that the inhabitants were private citizens, taken up with their own affairs, and hence it was easy to throw them into confusion, as Cleon is shown doing here, by violent abuse.

(schol. ad. loc.)

The clear implication is that the Paphlagonian's victim shares the general character of the inhabitants of the Chersonese: like the peasants of Attica, they are *apragmōn* private citizens, the easy prey of such as the Paphlagonian. The life of the settlers must have been even more *apragmōn* than that of the Attic

---

[35] The Chersonese was very rich. Blaydes, on this passage, quotes Xenophon (*Hell.* 3. 2. 10), and suggests it was just the sort of place Peisthetairos and Euelpides were in search of in the *Birds* — a nice quiet, peaceful place (*Birds*, 44). Neil, in a comment on this passage, thinks it may have referred to some actual case.

[36] In 447 BC the tribute from the Chersonese fell from fourteen talents to two talents. Cf. *CAH* v. 97 n. 1; Brunt, 'Athenian Settlements Abroad in the Fifth Century BC', 79.

[37] Cf. Nicias' speech in Th. 7. 48. The word used by Aristophanes here for attacking a political opponent is used by Thucydides of Cleon's conduct towards other generals: 4. 27. 4 and 5. 16. 1.

[38] Blaydes compares *Knights*, 358, and 355. There is a rich Attic vocabulary for the idea of vociferous abuse. Compare also *Knights*, 824 on the Paphlagonian and the *euthynai*, and 923, where he threatens to have the Sausage-seller assessed among the wealthiest for compulsory war contributions. See also *Wasps* 102, 571, on the rigours of the *euthynai*, also Ant. *On the Choreutes*, 43.

peasants, being proportionately further from the city. They were, none the less, not so far as to be beyond the reach of the sycophant as we see here, and above (Ps.-Xen. and Ar. *Birds*).

To come back to point (a): that under certain circumstances it might be possible to be a general *and apragmōn*; that not all generals used the office as a route to power and prestige. There seem to have been some at least who regarded regular soldiering as a profession, and were in other respects *apragmōn* citizens. One such was probably Lamachus. We know that he was poor, and that, in his *euthynai*, he had to account for expenditure on clothing and shoe leather (Plut. *Nic.* 15). The fact that this is mentioned points to its being a rare occurrence, and it is unique in surviving records. Moreover, because of his lack of means, Lamachus was obliged to give way to others less experienced than himself on questions of military strategy: 'Lamachus was a brave and experienced soldier, but he lacked weight and standing on account of his poverty'. (Plut. *Alc.* 21). Plutarch is probably following Thucydides here, for the latter makes the same point. Despite his greater experience, Lamachus was compelled to yield to Nicias and Alcibiades when drawing up a plan of operations for Sicily. Thucydides makes it clear that Lamachus had the best plan, yet he is forced to abandon it and support one of the other two (6. 49. 1).[39]

It seems that Lamachus was what we would call a regular soldier. He is first recorded as general for 436 BC (approximately),[40] and, if we may trust Aristophanes, had been serving regularly in the army in a paid capacity since the war began. Aristophanes regards it as a means of making a living at the expense of the *dēmos*, almost disreputable. Dikaiopolis taunts him: 'You only stand for general because of the money!' 'The people chose me!' blurts out Lamachus. 'Yes — three gowks!' retorts Dikaiopolis (Ar. *Ach.* 597 ff.). In this exchange Lamachus is a man of few words, and Dikaiopolis monopolizes the scene. Aristophanes is seeking to distinguish between those who serve their country out of duty, and those like Lamachus who, he implies, are in it only for the money. But was he general? In

---

[39] Cf. X. *Mem* 3. 4, where a seasoned officer is defeated in the election for generals by a man who has never done anything except make money.
[40] Plut. *Per.* 20. Cf. Fornara, *Athenian Board of Generals*, 50.

a later scene Dikaiopolis is about to set off to keep watch on some
snowy pass, on the orders of the generals (1071 ff.). The
implication would appear to be that in the spring of 425
Lamachus was not general but in some lesser elected post. In
fact the generalship for Tribe VI was held by Sophocles son of
Sostratides in that year.[41] Lamachus may have been taxiarch or
Aristophanes may have chosen him simply because he was a well-
known soldier, one who had been in service since at least 436.

Lamachus is a soldier of many years' experience who, because
of his lack of means, has no political weight, whose only defence
against Dikaiopolis' insinuations is 'The people chose me!', and
who is otherwise clearly lacking the impudence and self-
confidence that Aristophanes regularly attributes to the
demagogues. In fact, he cuts a rather pathetic figure. Such a
man might be described as an *apragmōn* general.

Another could be Laches. He stands somewhat higher on the
social ladder than Lamachus. He is represented as a colleague
of Nicias in the lists of generals for 427/6, 426/5, and 418/7,
when he was killed at the battle of Mantinea. Plato also associates
them in his dialogue the *Laches* which has a fictional date between
422 and 418. In this dialogue, Laches sets himself among those
who have to do with the affairs of the city (180 B), but the only
recorded reference to such activity is the proposal of peace with
Sparta in 423 BC (Th. 4. 118. 11). In proposing peace he joins
hands again with Nicias, who was to carry the same policy
through to fruition two years later with his support (Th. 5. 43. 2).
He would thus have been grouped together with Nicias by
Alcibiades as an *apragmōn* in foreign affairs. In his record of the
treaty, Thucydides emphasizes the contrast of youth and age,
which is brought out later in the debate over Sicily. It is Nicias
and Laches with whom the Spartans prefer to treat. They are
older men, and the Spartans look down on Alcibiades' youth
(though he was by now over thirty). Plato too in his dialogue
underlines the generation gap (178 A ff.).

Although Laches, like Nicias, takes an active part in politics,
it should be pointed out that there is no middle term between
polypragmosynē and *apragmosynē*. Whereas it is easy enough to
identify the two extremes, it is possible that Laches, like Nicias,

---

[41] Fornara, op. cit., 58.

occupied a kind of middle ground: born to a high place, and bred to take a leading role, yet not propelled by the intense lust for fame and glory that characterizes other public figures. The Athenians did look for something very like selfless devotion to duty in their public servants, and this is in fact how Aristophanes presents Laches in his parody court-scene in the *Wasps*. This is emphasized because he is contrasted with Cleon; Laches is presented in the guise of the dog Labes and Cleon as 'Kuon' (which means 'dog' with a play on Cleon as 'watch-dog of the people'). Laches has undergone his *euthynai* in the summer of 425 without, so far as we know, being impeached. The implication of this scene is that Cleon would have liked to impeach him for embezzlement of public money during his tour of duty round Sicily (cf. line 924). The dog Labes is charged with having eaten a Sicilian cheese, without giving Kuon a share. Bdelycleon presents the defence: 'He's a good dog, and drives away wolves.' 'He's a thief and a conspirator' says his father. 'He's the best dog you've got,' says Bdelycleon, 'and fit to guard any number of sheep [i.e. the Athenian people]. He fights your battles, guards your door; the best dog altogether. If he's a thief, yet oh forgive; he never learned the lyre.' Labes, the defence continues, is always on the go, lives on odds and ends, while the prosecutor (Kuon) sits at home and when anything is brought in, demands his share (949 ff.). In characteristic style, Aristophanes does not deny the charge (in which case he is abusing Laches almost as much as he is Cleon) but seeks to extenuate it. Again, this leads to further comic abuse of Laches; the reference to the lyre is an insinuation that Laches had never been educated.

Nevertheless, the message of the scene is that while Cleon sits at home and greedily demands a share of everything that is brought in, Laches is out sailing the seas, working away on behalf of the Athenian people and living on odds and ends. Philocleon's accusation of 'conspirator' may be no more than a reflex action at this time, directed at anyone the *dēmos* suspected. Elsewhere Aristophanes suggests that Cleon used the term as a means of attacking his enemies (*Knights*, 624 ff.). It would be fair to call Laches *apragmōn* on the evidence of this scene, because he is contrasted with Cleon, the very soul of *polypragmosynē*; it is stressed that he is away at sea serving the people, not sitting at home stirring up *pragmata*. The defence entered on his behalf by

Aristophanes is, in fact, not unlike that offered on behalf of wealthy citizens, which we have been considering: a zealous public servant, unambitious for himself.

So far in this chapter, I have discussed wealthy citizens' aversion to the lawcourts. I have also touched on the generation gap between the supporters of Nicias and Alcibiades. We have seen, too, how fear of the *euthynai* could be a powerful disincentive to public service among people traditionally accustomed to a leading role in the administration of the State. Finally, I have briefly discussed sycophants and suggested that they and the 'watch-dogs of the people' might in some cases be the same people, that in the role of watch-dog their over-zealous prosecution of public servants was what caused fear of the *euthynai*.

All these factors come together in the period of the Peloponnesian War in the figure of the young prosecutor, often known as *synēgoros*, and it will be useful to this discussion to examine the *synēgoros* and what made him so powerful.

Consider first this fragment from the *Banqueters* of Aristophanes:

Son: You're just coffin-fodder! Myrrh and headbands!
Father: There! 'Coffin-fodder' — you got that from Lysistratus.
Son: You'll soon be knocked out by Father Time, I bet.
Father: That 'knocked out' is from the public orators.
Son: Trust you to hoard up all these phrases.
Father: You got that 'hoard up' from Alcibiades.
Son: Why such condemnations? Why attack men who only seek to behave in a gentlemanly way?
Father: Oh heavens, Thrasymachus! Who of all the *synēgoroi* taught you to warble in that way?

(198 κ)

The father is teasing his son for using phrases he has picked up from public speakers and *synēgoroi*. The reference to myrrh and headbands is reminiscent of the sarcastic taunts with which the Wrong Argument ridicules the Right Argument in the *Clouds*, and later on Pheidippides attacks his father (*Clouds*, 984–5; 1353 ff.). The dispute conforms to a pattern familiar in Aristophanes: Youth versus Age.[42] It seems likely, however,

---

[42] e.g., Dikaiopolis' defence of the old Acharnians' (*Ach.* 599); the Knights versus Cleon; Philocleon versus Bdelycleon. After *Wasps* this antithesis does not appear again. The subject is discussed by W. G. Forrest, 'An Athenian Generation Gap', *YCS* 24 (1975).

that this is not merely a comic device of Aristophanes, but reflects a social reality: a generation gap, to which there are scattered references in the literature of this period. The young man is accused of copying his phrases from public speakers and *synēgoroi*; what were *synēgoroi*?

The term *synēgoros* has several meanings: basically it signifies one who pleads in court alongside someone else. That is to say, a plaintiff or defendant, though required to plead in person, was also permitted to bring others to plead on his behalf. He might therefore prevail upon someone who was experienced in such matters to compose and deliver a speech in his favour which would carry more weight with the jury than his own. Such a man would not be permitted to charge a fee but could be recompensed in other ways, as Crito recompensed Archedemus.

Beside this root meaning, *synēgoros* took on special meanings: (a) public advocate, chosen to defend laws against proposed changes before the *nomothetai* (e.g., Dem. 24. 36); (b) one who conducts a public prosecution (also, and more commonly, open to anyone who wished); (c) one of ten *synēgoroi* who were appointed annually, by lot in Aristotle's day, to represent the State at the *euthynai* of generals (*Ath. Pol.* 54. 2).

It is with these two last meanings that we are concerned. *Synēgoroi*, it appears, are a kind of public prosecutor. Although chosen by lot in Aristotle's day, it seems unlikely that this was so in the fifth century, unless it was from a limited list; their technique, their powers, their high-handed manner, all bespeak a privileged, educated background. Consider the following passage from the *Acharnians*, where the old Acharnians lament the fate of old men trapped into legal proceedings by younger men and hopelessly outmanœuvred with legal tricks:

Now we have the eager youngster, leading for the prosecution,
Quickly into action closes, striking us with pithy phrases,
Pulls us up with awkward questions, setting little verbal traps.
Poor old men like us are muddled, flurried, shook, and quite bamboozled.

(685–8)

The young man has eagerly sought the task of prosecuting, and Aristophanes implies there is something unseemly about his enthusiasm.[43] A few lines later, Aristophanes gives an instance of this young man at work. Old Thucydides, son of Melesias, is in the clutches of Cephisodemus — 'a Scythian wilderness' (suggesting that he was not a true Athenian) — and, more importantly, a *lalos synēgoros*. Another mentioned is Alcibiades, also *lalos*. *Lalos* is a term often associated with these young men: they are 'chatterers'. This 'chattering' is to be distinguished from public speaking as normally understood, as in the famous judgement on Phaiax: 'He can chatter very well, but he's no good as a speaker' (Eupolis, *Demes*, fr. 95). This chattering might be disliked by an older generation but it could be very effective in court. There is a passage in the *Knights* where we hear how Phaiax 'chattered' himself out of a capital charge:

Demos: Those striplings in the perfume-mart who sit
And prattle to each other stuff like this:
That Phaiax, clever fellow, did you see?
Acquitted, saved his life, and very neatly;
Polemic, logic, analytical,
Sophistic, casuistic, paradoxical —
Sausage-seller: You're most satirical about this twaddle.

(1375–81)

Aristophanes refers contemptuously to these youths: they are mere 'striplings' (*meirakia*).[44] The young man mentioned above in the fragment from *Banqueters* is no doubt to be found among them. They spend their days in that quarter of the market square occupied by the perfume-makers, chattering: 'Phaiax got off that capital charge very neatly — very clever (*dexios*)'.[45] Aristophanes must be talking of some actual event, though no record of it survives. The string of adjectives which follows illustrates, in the Greek, the fashion for abstract and philosophic formulations

---

[43] *Spoudazo* is the same as *speudo*; it implies an unseemly enthusiasm in seeking public posts: Ar. *Ach.* 595; X. *Smp.* 1. 4; Plat. *Theaet.* 173 D; Th. 6. 9. 3; Eur. *Ion.* 599.

[44] According to Hippocrates' division of a man's life into seven stages, *meirakion* comes third, and represents the ages fourteen to twenty-one (Pollux, 2. 4).

[45] *Dexios* is an interesting word. In its original meaning it is full of good omen: right-handed, boding well, hence neat, clever, witty, useful. Out of forty-one uses in Aristophanes, a majority have this favourable sense. But a second, minority, meaning, emerges during the 420s: cunning thought, skill in the lawcourts, hence moral disreputability. It is often linked with *kompsos*.

in '-*ikos*' which were coming in.[46] The Sausage-seller rounds off the list and points up its ludicrous side. Whereupon old Demos responds 'Now by God I'll make them all go hunting and put a stop to all this decree-making!' (1382–3.) Demos, in his reformed state, recommends hunting the hare as an admirable *apragmōn* pastime.

Consider too the passage in the *Clouds* where the Right Argument warns young Pheidippides to stay clear of the market square, where young men idle their time away, prattling of 'marvellous prickly disputes' (Rogers), and not to get dragged into court through some 'footling matter which is greedy, pettifogging, barefaced and knavish' (1003–4). This idea of being caught in disputes, tricked, and outwitted, is what the *apragmōn* most feared in legal *pragmata*.

The Right Argument, only a few lines later, turns to the peaceful and contented existence at the Academy which he proposes as an alternative; a life well appreciated by the Hippolytuses of the period, characterized by *apragmosynē*.

There is also a passage in the *Wasps* where the poor jurymen are given their orders by an arrogant and effeminate young man, who later reappears to collect his fee as *synēgoros* (687 ff.); and Cleon, in the *Knights*, vows he will put a stop to all the effeminate young men, whereupon the Sausage-seller asks him if he does that, where are they going to get any public speakers? (*Knights*, 877 ff.). The idea that these young men were homosexual runs through many of the references to them in Aristophanes, and fits in with the picture of *palaestra* life which Plato showed in the *Charmides*.[47]

It will be as well to pause here and sum up the evidence Aristophanes has provided on the subject of lawcourts and *synēgoroi*. There is in existence by 428 BC a race of clever young

---

[46] Cf. C. W. Peppler, 'The Termination -*ikos* as Used by Aristophanes for Comic Effect', *AJP* 31 (1910), 428–44.

[47] It is possible that for Plato and Aristophanes, homosexuality has a nostalgic, reactionary, quality. This is the view of O. Murray (*Early Greece*, 207), who identifies it as an aristocratic activity. Dover (*Greek Popular Morality*, 213–16; *Greek Homosexuality*, 140 ff.), thinks homosexuality was normal. His main point is that a man would be ridiculed not for homosexuality as such, but for submitting to being the passive partner; to be buggered, in short, and this is the abusive element in many words which can be translated as 'capacious-arsed'. The abusive element comes from playing a woman's part. Effeminacy in men is generally ridiculed by Aristophanes

orators who particularly pride themselves on the use of new words, or words used in new ways. Their skill with words and logic, their ability to confuse and bamboozle an older and simpler opponent, has made them feared by ordinary citizens. Their skill with words is expressed in the verb *lalein*.[48] The line from Eupolis' *Demes* quoted earlier refers not to the difference between conversation in private and oratory in public, but between older and newer kinds of oratory. We saw above what it was to be *lalos*: it was to be *dexios*, clever, nimble-witted, skilled in newly coined phrases. These young men constitute an intellectual élite in the market-place; they despise traditional pastimes, and open-air sports in particular. They seem to come from educated upper-class backgrounds, and to be homosexual in some cases. Their youth is stressed, and they are frequently referred to as 'striplings', and 'youths'. They speak as orators in the assembly, but the evidence above applies particularly to the lawcourts; they are very ambitious to be chosen as public prosecutors either in magistrates' audits, or in public prosecutions (often the outcome of an audit). The evidence suggests, though not conclusively, that at this period the *synēgoroi* were chosen by some kind of election rather than by lot, as was later the case. The force with which they attack their opponents has been stressed in the evidence of Aristophanes, and gives a vivid impression of what a would-be magistrate or litigant might have to face.

Thucydides also mentions these young men. In Cleon's speech on the fate of Mytilene, before coming to the main topic, he makes some general remarks about the Athenian assembly, and in particular attacks a certain kind of speaker who is clever but undisciplined, intelligent but anxious to appear cleverer than the established laws, and in reality more of a liability than an asset:

Untutored common sense is more profitable to a city than unbridled cleverness, and on the whole cities are better run by the man in the street than by intellectuals. For these always want to appear cleverer than the established laws, and want to come out on top in every public

---

[48] Aristophanes also accuses Euripides of teaching the young to *lalein* (*Frogs*, 89). These young men may be the 'shivers and fevers' afflicting old folks in their *apragmōn* beds (*Wasps*, 1037).

debate, since there is no greater occasion to show how clever they are, and it is these men who very often bring ruin on their cities.

(3. 37. 3)

But, adds Cleon, the fault lies with the people themselves for 'stupidly instituting these competitive displays. You have become regular speech-goers . . .'. I suggest that Cleon is talking about the young men we have been discussing. The speech quoted here was written very close in time to the plays from which I quoted earlier. Although Cleon makes no mention of the age of these speakers, there is another discussion which does refer to young men in a hurry, in a situation reminiscent of that in Athens. During a debate in Syracuse on the eve of the Athenian expedition to Sicily, a speech is made by Athenagoras, who, according to Thucydides, occupies a position similar to that of Cleon. There is a sizeable and prominent oligarchic element in Syracuse, he says, which is forever aiming at power over the people and causing party strife. The oligarchic element consists largely of young men; in accusing them of aiming at unconstitutional power, Athenagoras is reminiscent of Cleon with his cry of 'conspirators':

An oligarchy is quite happy to share the dangers with the people, but when it comes to the good things it not merely wants the largest share, but seizes the whole lot. And this is what the powerful men and the young men among you are after, but they'll have no luck in a great city.

(6. 39)[49]

Thucydides must have been aware of the parallels between Syracuse and Athens in this respect, and of the parallel roles played by Athenagoras and Cleon. Athenagoras is the 'watch-dog of the people' just as Cleon was.[50] And, just as in Athens, there are young men, accused of oligarchic leanings, and claiming a monopoly of intelligence (ibid.). In Athens, Alcibiades was only the most famous of the young rhetors to be suspected of conspiracy against the democracy in 415. Lysistratus was another.

One must be careful: both Athenagoras and Cleon make these accusations partly as a tactic—to keep the opposition on the

---

[49] This speech is discussed by W. G. Forrest. See note 42.   [50]Th. 6. 35. 2.

defensive. Plato gives a clue here when he observes that the rich are driven into conspiracy because of the vehemence of the attacks by popular leaders (*Rep.* 565 B). The situation is not easily analysed along class lines, however. If Plato asserts that it is the 'drones' and their leaders who attack the rich in lawcourt and assembly, the evidence we have seen suggests that those who came forward to make a name for themselves as politicians and lawyers, who in reality constituted a threat to the 'rich quietists', and who used the legal machinery of writs and summonses as a ladder to their own political advancement, were in fact themselves from the same cultural and financial background as those they were attacking.

Before concluding this chapter there are two other aspects that should be touched on. One is the famous misanthropist of Athens, Timon. He was certainly a 'rich quietist' of a sort, though not representative. He was the son of Echekratides, of the deme Collytos, in the city. He was a citizen, lived around the time of Pericles, and was sufficiently well known for stories to gather about him. Plutarch mentions an incident concerning the young Alcibiades: passing him in the street, Timon went up and spoke to him, a thing most unusual for him: 'You are doing well, my boy; carry on like this and you will ruin the lot of them' (Plut. *Alc.* 16). He cursed his fellow-citizens and retired outside the walls to his 'solitariness', which is presumably the tower described by Pausanias as being near the Academy. Pausanias comments: 'He was the only human being who could find no happiness except in flight from the rest of humanity.' (1. 30. 4.)[51]

But if he was a legend in Pausanias' time, he was becoming one in 411: 'There was a man called Timon . . .' sing the chorus of the *Lysistrata* (807), citing an extreme example of misanthropy. Plutarch records a possibly apocryphal story of how Timon fell and broke his hip, and died because he would allow no doctor near him. He was buried at Halimous, by the sea (Plut. *Ant.* 69–70).

So Timon was famous in his own time and for centuries after.

---

[51] *RE* puts the tower in Kollytos deme, but Traill's map puts Kollytos deme inside the city walls ('Political Organisation in Attica', *Hesperia*, suppl. 14). Pausanias says the tower is near the Academy, on the road to modern Dafni, a little way outside the walls to the west of the city (trans. Levi, Penguin edn., p. 83 n. 172).

It was his uniqueness that made him so. Pausanias said he was the only man who had ever retired from the company of men; the chorus of the *Lysistrata* single him out as a special case. He is, therefore, an eccentric individual rather than representative of any group or class of citizens.[52]

I should also like briefly to discuss the metics. The metic was someone who had given up the full rights of citizenship in his own country and accepted a reduced status in Athens in exchange for the various advantages Athens could offer, principally the opportunity to make money. The difference between a citizen and a metic is stated by Aristotle: 'A citizen, above all, is one who has a share in the honours of the state; as Homer puts it: "Like an alien without honour—"'. That is, one who has no share of public honours is like an alien resident in the land [i.e., a metic].' (*Pol.* 1278ᵃ 37.) The essence of citizenship is to partake of *timē*, and of being a metic, the inability to do so. This brings the discussion back to the theme of the first chapter, where it was maintained that honour was the highest prize a citizen could look for. Nowhere is the central function of honour, its defining character, stated quite as baldly as here. The metic is excluded from that which defines citizenship, even though he is indispensable to the city (*Pol.* 1326ᵃ 18).

There is an interesting psychological expansion of the above passage in the *Eudemian Ethics*: 'No one would say a metic is *mikropsychos* (small of soul) because he does not consider himself fit to hold office but rather to be subject to those in office, though they would in the case of a well-born citizen who regarded high office as something valuable.' (*EE* 1233ᵃ 28.)[53] In the *Nichomachean Ethics, mikropsychia* is the opposite, not of *megalopsychia* (greatness of soul) which Aristotle regards as the mean, and hence as the normal and proper state, but of *chaunotēs*, (vanity) (1107ᵇ 21). It is as normal for a citizen to take a proper pride in the dignity of citizenship, with its rights and duties, as it is for a metic to take a modest and humble, and otherwise un-Athenian, attitude. The modesty and humility which the citizen looked for in the metic are well set forth by Euripides in

---

[52] Dienelt maintained that Timon was the type for the *apragmones* attacked by Pericles (*Wiener Studien*, 1953).

[53] The connection between these two passages is made by D. Whitehead in *The Ideology of the Athenian Metic*, 59.

his *Suppliant Women*. In talking of the seven champions sent by Argos, Adrastus comes to Parthenopaeus:

> The child next of huntress Atalanta,
> Parthenopaeus, a youth unmatched for beauty;
> Arcadian born, but, coming to the banks
> Of Inachos, was brought up there in Argos.
> So, educated there, he bore himself
> Amongst us as a stranger [metic] should, he gave
> No trouble, no resentment nursed against
> The city, was not quarrelsome, which is
> Offensive both in citizens and foreigners.
> Defending our land, like an Argive, in
> The ranks he took his place, and when the city
> Prospered he rejoiced, lamenting if its fortunes fell.
> He is careful to commit no crime, and he
> Has many friends, as many among women
> As men.
>
> (888–900)

This description is 'a blue-print for the ideal metic, permanently installed and permanently on his best behaviour'.[54]

Parthenopaeus was not troublesome, nor arousing jealousy, nor engaging in contentious argument. He was prepared to go out and fight for Argos, though possessing no tangible stake in it; he rejoiced with the city in its prosperity, and lamented its misfortunes. He had many friends and took care not to give offence.

The question may be asked—was the metic *apragmōn*? In the civic sense, in which *pragmata* are the city's affairs and the business of the citizen he had no choice (other than to go home and participate in the affairs of his own city—which I feel must have lain behind the attitude of the Athenians towards the metics). If by *apragmōn*, however, we mean not one who is prohibited but one who *abstains*, then the metic cannot be included. As far as citizens are concerned, all *apragmones* abstain; there may be difficulties in their way, but, theoretically at least, they are free to play a citizen's part.

In the legal sense of *pragmata*, the fact is that metics could go to law, could initiate actions, and could in turn be prosecuted.

<hr>

[54] Ibid., 37.

The difference was that whereas it was harder for the metic to bring a legal action, since he had to operate via his patron (*prostatēs*), and Athenian law regarded him as less than a citizen,[55] the rich metic, at least, made a correspondingly more inviting target for sycophants. The man who was in Athens on suffrance, on his best behaviour, was more likely to pay than to fight. The most striking example of the vulnerability of the metic was in 404 BC when the Thirty, in order to get money, resolved that each of them should seize one of the metics, put him to death, and take his property (X. *Hell.* 2. 3. 21). There would therefore be a strong case for the metic to play the *apragmōn*; if it was wise for the wealthy citizen to make the kind of plea in a lawcourt which I discussed earlier, it would be even more so for the metic.[56]

This tells us something very significant, however, about the *apragmōn* citizen. To go back to Aristotle's judgement on metics, that is *mikropsychos* not to aspire to office and honour, the average citizen must have regarded the *apragmōn* in a somewhat similar light. The opening phrases of those speeches of Lysias, then, on being a modest, retiring citizen and so forth, are not really a boast, but more an act of supplication and conciliation. They are not the act of a *megalopsychos*. It is perhaps misleading, therefore to say that *apragmōn* is normally a favourable term; the jury is flattered to be addressed in this way by the *apragmōn* citizen, but it will hardly respect him for it.

Conclusion

This chapter has been in two parts: in the first part I dealt with the *apragmosynē* of wealthy citizens, their claims to mind their own business, while in the second I looked at what it

---

[55] The murderer of a metic was brought before the court of the Palladion, which also tried the unpremeditated murder of citizens, and which had the power of banishment only. Cf. Whitehead, op. cit., 93.

[56] Aristotle talks of metic sycophants (*Ath. Pol.* 43). This is a puzzling passage; it could, however, be supported by the passage in Ar. *Wasps*, 1037–42, in which the *apragmōn* citizen, afflicted by 'fevers and shivers', jumps out of bed and runs to the polemarch. The 'fevers and shivers' are legal figures of some sort, since they resort to 'counter-oaths, summonses and witnesses', and could possibly be called sycophants (see note 51, above). But are they metics? Macdowell, in a note on this passage, thinks so. Alternatively, it is possible the polemarch had some power to deal with sycophants in 422 which he no longer had in Aristotle's time.

was that could deter them from a public role, or litigation. First I considered the case of Nicias, and with him, to some extent, Laches. Nicias had been called *apragmōn* because he did not want the State to embark on fresh military ventures, because he wanted it to maintain a moderate and peaceful attitude to foreign states and especially to Sparta. *Apragmosynē* here represents not so much a state of being as an attitude: Nicias would have Athens adopt an *apragmōn* attitude toward Sparta. The rich quietists, on the other hand, were in an *apragmōn* state, of non-participation, so far as was possible in the public life of Athens. The evidence of fourth-century speech-writers shows that it had become a common opening to a speech to claim to be, on the one hand, a generous benefactor to the *dēmos* in fulfilmr. . of statutory obligations, and on the other, a tame and harmless citizen. To what extent this plea corresponded to reality must, of course, have varied from client to client. The speech-writer, however, and his client, must have believed that it would create a pleasing effect with the jury. And if we accept that Antiphon's *Second Tetralogy* dates from the 440s, it means that, almost from the moment when the democracy achieved its final form, from the moment when jurymen first began to receive pay, and hence juries took on a genuinely popular character, the rich went on to the defensive; they began to supplicate and conciliate the jury. The *apragmones* were not only Athenian citizens but from the Empire, too, though whether as clerouchs or as allies is not clear. In either case they were subject to the courts and could be summoned back by sycophants. Sycophants preyed especially, perhaps exclusively, on the rich; it was the first intention of the Thirty, so they claimed, to eliminate them.

Apart from the rich citizen who was prepared to pay to be left alone, another important victim of sycophants was the general or other official of State undergoing his audit. In these cases the prosecutor though often called a sycophant, especially by a comic poet, may be what was known as a 'watch-dog of the people', or else a politician aspiring to that role, by calling to account those who have charge of public money. Generals and State treasurers often represent the most ambitious of politicians, so that these prosecutions are part of the political fight for pre-eminence. Nevertheless it is possible that some generals were just soldiers and no more, not interested in using their position for political advancement; that there existed a tradition of public service and that they were in other respects *apragmōn* private citizens.

The wealthy citizen, either in a private capacity or as general or treasurer, had not merely sycophants to deal with. The sycophant could not have existed except in a climate of public opinion which was basically hostile, suspicious, and critical of its elected servants, which could be capricious and cruel.

A further aspect of the scene in the 420s and 410s was the emergence of a kind of young politician, ambitious, and using the public audits as a ladder to prominence. Aristophanes calls him a 'stripling'. Greek society as a whole paid respect to age; care of their parents was the first duty of offspring; a defendant boasted that he never contradicted his father. Age carried authority; the Areopagus had been stripped of its powers less than twenty years before Aristophanes was born. The emergence of youth, its assumption of powers, its ambition, its intolerance and arrogant questioning of traditional values, above all its aggressive attitude in the lawcourts and assembly, must have been a shock to the older generation. It brought to public life a whole battery of new attitudes, concepts and techniques for debate. Opponents were demolished in completely new ways. Behind these young men was not simply a school of rhetoric but an entirely new kind of philosophical outlook, often the property of visiting teachers. They are not the subject of this essay, but as their pupils made their attacks, as they climbed into political prominence, they were frightening away others who in an earlier age might have been in political life. Political existence became more dangerous and inevitably many citizens preferred to stay away.

6

The Contemplative Life:
The Presocratics

The *Bios Theōrētikos* (Contemplative Life) was a fourth-century
rationalization—an interpretation in philosophic terms—of the
political and social phenomenon of *apragmosynē*. In Chapter 1
it was seen that the urge to honour and glory—the competitive
spirit—remained the single most characteristic quality of the
Greeks down to and throughout the fourth century. Plato, in
his triple division of society, places this quality of ambition
alongside that of money-making, and then introduces the
philosophic life as distinct from these two. The philosopher is
he who refrains from, or even despises, the activities of seeking
after honour and making money. Most of this book, in its analysis
of *apragmosynē*, has been devoted to exposing the political and
social factors which Plato transformed in formulating his concept
of the *Bios Theōrētikos*. Before coming on to examine the genesis
of that concept in detail in the next chapter, however, it will be
useful to look at the Contemplative Life as it was practised, or
not practised, by some of the Presocratic philosophers. It will
be seen that between the time of these men and Plato the term
underwent a change of meaning, although Plato would have us
believe that what he understood by the *Bios Theōrētikos* was not
simply a creation of his own, but had a respectable pedigree,
and had been practised by many of the wise men of old.

Thus, Plato tells us that the majority of those who, in olden
times, had a reputation for wisdom, refrained from political
activity, amongst whom he names Pittacus, Bias, Thales, and
Anaxagoras. He also recounts the famous anecdote about Thales,
so engrossed in contemplating the heavens that he does not see
what lies before him, and falls down a well.[1]

Yet it is not difficult to show that, of these, Pittacus, Bias,

---

[1] Plat. *Hipp. Maj.* 281c; *Theaet.* 174.

and Thales at least were all political men, and may not have
been above making money either (indeed they would not have
recognized Plato's distinction between the two activities). The
evidence, significantly, is earlier than the fourth century. Pittacus
was tyrant of Mytilene, which automatically disqualifies him from
being *apragmōn*. Bias is encountered twice in Herodotus: first,
he gives shrewd advice to Croesus, dissuading him from attacking
the islands of Ionia. Then again, after the subjugation of Ionia,
at the Panionium, he makes what Herodotus regards as an
admirable suggestion, namely that the Ionians should unite and
sail to Sardinia to found a new community. These stories may,
or may not, be historical, but they show the kind of action Bias
was credited with in the fifth century.[2] There follows a similar
story of how Thales advised the Ionians to set up a common
centre of Government on Teos; the other cities should continue
as before, only subject to the central Government, rather on the
Attic model. Herodotus also recounts, though he says he himself
doesn't believe it, the common account of how Thales transferred
the army of Croesus across the river Halys, by digging a trench
and causing the river to divide and run in two channels, so
making each half fordable. Again, even if this story is not
historical, it shows what the fifth century looked for in a sage.[3]

The simple distinction between those anecdotes of the fifth
century and earlier which make out the Seven Wise Men to be
law-givers and men of practical affairs, and those of the fourth
century which present them as contemplative philosophers
withdrawn from the world, has already been made elsewhere;
in particular, Werner Jaeger has pointed it out.[4] He suggests
that the stories of the unworldly philosopher neglecting his
material concerns — stories applied indiscriminately to Thales,
Democritus, and Anaxagoras — [5]were either the product of the
Platonic and Peripatetic schools or at least came under their
influence.[6] This approach, which will be particularly important

---

[2] So How and Wells on Hdt. 1. 27. 2; they also mention Bias arbitrating between
Priene and Samos.

[3] So H. Fraenkel, *Dichtung und Philosophie des frühen Griechentums*, 275.

[4] Werner Jaeger, *Über Ursprung und Kreislauf des philosophischen Lebensideal*. Also in an
English translation as an appendix in his *Aristotle* (London, 1948).

[5] For Thales, see note 2 above; for Democritus see *DK* 68A15; for Anaxagoras, see
below.

[6] Jaeger, op. cit., 5, and 5 n. 4.

in the discussion of Pythagoras below, only seems to run into trouble with those stories which seem, as far as one can judge, to be genuine folk-tales, such as the story of Thales and the well. They would appear to reflect a popular attitude towards those who turn their attention towards *theōria*, and by implication away from worldly concerns. Aristophanes represents such men as imposters (see below on Socrates).

Pythagoras

The evidence on Thales is polarized between fifth-century and earlier sources, and those of the fourth century; the weight of probability is with the earlier evidence. This polarization is also evident in the case of Pythagoras, if anything more so: on the one hand those stories that show him as leading the Contemplative Life; on the other those that show him as statesman, governor, tyrant. Jaeger's chief point in his essay was to trace these two traditions back to the successors of Plato and Aristotle: the unworldly philosopher to Heraclides of Pontus, the practical politician to Dikaiarchus and Aristoxenus.

Evidence for Pythagoras as contemplative philosopher comes, for example, in the story of his visit to Leon, tyrant of Phlius, according to which Leon asked him in what art he placed most trust.[7] Pythagoras replied that he knew no art, but was a philosopher. He explained that life was like a fair or market: some came to buy and sell, and make money; others came to show off their strength and gain fame; and there was a third class of those who were in quest of neither fame nor wealth, but came as spectators, to admire the holy places and works of art, and characteristic displays of prowess in word and deed. In the same way, in life some men strive after wealth and luxury, whilst others seek political power and position. But the most uncorrupted are those who are contented with the contemplation of that which is most beautiful. This is the contemplation of the universe, and how the stars that move in it are ordered: this is participation in the 'First Principle' (or 'Cause') (*to prōton*), and

---

[7] Iamblichus, *VP* 58-9; Cic. *Tusc. Disp.* 5. 3. 8-9. Joly, 'La thème philosophique des genres de vie', 21 ff., makes a careful comparison of these two versions, printing them side by side. While the two versions are very similar, only Iamblichus contains the paragraph which develops the idea of contemplation into a metaphysical system of 'First Cause' etc.

the 'Intelligible' (*to noēton*). The 'First Principle' is the 'Nature of Number and Reason', which is dispersed everywhere, and according to which everything is ordained with the greatest care. Wisdom is true knowledge, and concerns itself with the Beautiful, the Holy, the Pure, and the Unchanging. By participation in these things, one may be able to speak of the Beautiful, and philosophy is the seeking after this contemplation (*theōria*).

Should this anecdote be accepted as true, or is it a backward projection of Platonic ideas onto Pythagoras? Some scholars, in particular Burnet, accept it.[8] The problem is that all our information comes via Plato's pupils and there is no independent account of Pythagoras' philosophy.[9] We can accept that observation of the stars (*theōria*) and an interest in numbers were among the interests of Pythagoras, but in this anecdote they are merely the platform for a complex metaphysical statement abounding in abstract terms and concepts. *Theōria* is equated with *philosophia*; observation of the ordering of the stars along with a participation in the 'First Cause' and the 'Intelligible'. This 'First Cause' is the 'Nature of Number and Reason' by which the whole of the universe is ordered.

This transcendental element is particularly Platonic, and, I think, can be shown not to go back to Pythagoras: it is the idea of the Forms, the idea that there is, immanent in physical reality, an ideal reality, to which the physical reality but imperfectly corresponds.[10] The philosopher, by training himself, can pass from the contemplation of the real physical order to the ideal order. This is the theory put forward in the *Republic*, in the name of Socrates.[11] The triple division of occupations — money-making, politics, philosophy — to which Pythagoras referred in the anecdote, must also, I think, be the work of Plato; in the *Republic* it forms the foundation of his whole analysis of contemporary society.[12] There is a passage in Plato where he seems to be referring to Pythagoras: 'Some ingenious person,

---

[8] Burnet, *EGP*, 4th edn., 1930.
[9] Cf. W. Burkert, *Lore and Science in Ancient Pythagoreanism*, 93.
[10] According to Aristotle (*Metaph.* 987ᵃ 19), the Pythagoreans held that 'number is the essence of all things'. Again (987ᵇ 1 ff.) Plato seems to have been following Socrates in his search for definitions when he devised the 'Forms' or 'Ideas'. Cf. Burkert, op. cit., 73.
[11] Plato, *Rep.* 532 A.
[12] *Rep.* 580 D; *Phaedo*, 68 B-C.

probably Sicilian or Italian' (*Gorg.* 493), but here he attributes
to him a doctrine of the soul by which it contains an appetitive
part, and could therefore be said to contain two parts—the
'Appetites' and the rest—but by no means three parts. Since
his own theories, set out in the *Republic* and the *Phaedo*, specify
a threefold division in the soul—corresponding to the threefold
division of society—it seems clear that while Plato was familiar
with Pythagorean ideas, his own differed from them.[13]

The use of *theōria* to mean the study of the heavens, what we
would understand as scientific study, is known in connection
with Anaxagoras, but its development to mean the contemplation
of the invisible order, something more real than reality, is the
work of Plato. There is an anecdote about Pythagoras which runs:
Pythagoras was once asked what was the point of life, and he
replied, 'The contemplation of the heavens'. He was himself,
he said, an observer of nature, and it was for this that he lived
(Arist. *Protrept.* fr. 11). However the identical story is also told
of Anaxagoras (Arist. *EE.* 1216ᵃ 11). This similarity must make
any student of the Presocratics extremely wary; but whether it
was Pythagoras to whom the story originally referred, or as I
think more likely, Anaxagoras (or someone else), the important
thing is that there is no metaphysical dimension. Furthermore,
Aristotle knew of the Forms as Plato's exclusive property and
did not accept them himself.[14]

Again, Burkert maintains that the word *philosophos* is used
anachronistically in the anecdote about Leon and Pythagoras.
According to him, it is Heraclides who maintains that Pythagoras
was a *philosophos*, yet there is no earlier evidence to show
that *philosophos* was a Pythagorean expression, and in fact,
from Homer down to Plato, this prefix *philos-* could not
mean a 'seeking after'.[15] Plato had learnt it from Socrates
and his *aporia*. Even if Burkert can be shown to be wrong
when he says that the prefix *philos-* never meant a 'seeking
after' before Plato, the concept of philosophy as a search, which

---

[13] Dodds on this passage: 'No tripartition of the soul is intended here.' Cf. also R.
Mondolfo, *L'origine del ideale filosofico della vita*, 124.

[14] *Eth. Nic.* 1096ᵃ 11 ff. If they were Pythagorean he could have said so. He mentions
the Pythagoreans a few lines later, 1096ᵇ 5.

[15] W. Burkert, 'Platon oder Pythagoras?', *Hermes*, 88 (1960), 169.

he thinks Plato derived from Socrates, seems convincing.[16]

If this anecdote seems almost certainly the work of the fourth century, what of the other tradition, of Dikaiarchus and Aristoxenus, presenting Pythagoras as a practical politician? According to them, Pythagoras comes to Croton where, by his sage counsels, he establishes a powerful reputation; by his legislation he wins renown for himself and his pupils; they administer the city so well that it becomes virtually an aristocracy. Despite Cylon's attacks, their prestige is undimmed and the cities continue in their desire to be governed by the Pythagoreans. Later, when there is a threat of war with Sybaris, Pythagoras is capable of turning the judgement of the whole assembly. Yet, when their house is burnt down, the Pythagoreans get no support; the citizens show contempt for them.[17]

Burkert said that there is not a single detail in the life of Pythagoras which stands uncontradicted, and the task therefore is to attempt to pick out from the jumble of ancient testimony some few strands that seem more reliable than the rest.[18] The society of Pythagoras' followers constituted a powerful political force in the city. They had no official standing, since there was a council of a thousand members of the aristocracy when Pythagoras arrived, but it seems Pythagoras drew his followers from the ruling families, and, constituted by him into a society, bound to one another by customs and observances, they came to exert a powerful influence in the Government and virtually to dominate life in the city. Their attachment to one another and contempt for everyone else is remarked in the sources (e.g. Iamblichus *de Vita Pythagorica* 254).[19] The tradition that their Government was accepted by all is understandable, coming from members of the Pythagorean sect. The tradition that there were one or more risings against them is also understandable, given their position in the city.

The devotion of the Pythagoreans to their master is well known. In fact, the greatest problem lies in trying to decipher

---

[16] The word *philotimia* must mean a 'seeking after *timē*' as early as Pindar (fr. 209) and Aeschylus (*Suppl.* 658).

[17] A detailed study of Pythagoras' political career is to be found A. Delatte, *Essai sur la politique Pythagoricienne*, (Liege and Paris, 1922).

[18] Burkert, *Lore and Science*, 109.

[19] Ibid.; Grote, IV. 87.

what he himself said, since his disciples and followers habitually attributed their own ideas to him and a mass of various ideas grew up around his name, obscuring whatever may have been his original conceptions. But if Pythagoras dominated the life of the society, what was his relation to the city? He was an alien in Croton, yet the sources speak of his tremendous moral influence; did he also control the political influence of his followers, or was that another, separate, aspect of their corporate existence? It has been asserted that Pythagoras himself was only interested in his private sect, devoted to moral, religious and scientific instruction and study, his pupils linked together by a common mode of life.[20] But there is another tradition, in which Pythagoras is presented, not as a wise and benevolent governor, but as a tyrant. A fourth-century historian, Theopompus, talking of the tyrant Athenion of Athens, compares him to Pythagoras; Athenion had been a member of the Peripatetic school he says, but at the first opportunity he had cast aside the mask of philosophy and become a tyrant, thus illustrating the philosophic system which the 'noble Pythagoras' had introduced.[21] There is also a reference by Diogenes Laertius to a 'Pythagoras the Crotoniate, a tyrant', said to be a contemporary of the philosopher, a 'desperate attempt to get rid of the tradition of Pythagoras as a tyrant'.[22]

If the tradition of the central political role played by the Pythagoreans in Croton is well attested, it would be difficult to keep Pythagoras himself out of it, and the weight of probability must lie with the view that Pythagoras was involved in the political life of the city. At the same time he was also occupied with scientific and speculative thought and observation, and, in Plato's time, long after the original sect had been dispersed from Croton, there were to be seen, wandering through Greek cities, the *Pythagoristai*, who claimed to adhere to the master's teaching: a species of unwashed mendicants and ascetics, the butt of comedians.

---

[20] Cf. Plato, *Rep.* 600 в. Delatte believes that Pythagoras held aloof from the political activities of his pupils.

[21] Theopompus quoted in Jacoby, *FGH* 115F73; cf. Burkert, *Lore and Science*, 118.

[22] Burkert, op. cit. It was Pythagoras too who was supposed to have said that it would be better to be a bull for a day, than a cow for a lifetime. Cf. Jacoby, loc. cit.

Heraclitus

With Heraclitus we get possibly the first mention of someone who grew dissatisfied with public affairs. The evidence, however, often appears fanciful, and must be treated with caution.

He was of a noble family with hereditary rights,[23] but these rights he renounced in favour of his brother. He traced his family back to Androclus, son of Codrus, founder of Ephesus, and 'the family are still called kings and have certain rights, a front seat at the games, a red badge of the royal house, a staff in place of the royal sceptre, and the priesthood of Eleusinian Demeter'. These honours he resigned to his brother out of a 'loftiness of spirit' (*megalophrosynē*).[24] To go with these details, which are probably true (at any rate one cannot see why they should have been invented)[25] there are anecdotes to show his aloofness and arrogance:[26] asked to frame laws for the citizens, he haughtily refused on the grounds that the city had already been ruined by a worthless constitution. Again, he went to play knucklebones with the boys in the temple of Artemis. The Ephesians came to wonder, whereupon he rebuked them: 'What are you staring at? Don't you think I'm better employed here than governing the city with you?'

These qualities come out too in the fragments: fragment 1, on the incapacity of men to understand his *logos*; or fragment 29, where the best people seek after one thing, eternal fame, while the masses chew the cud like cattle; or fragment 104: 'What mind or understanding have they? They believe what the bards tell them, and the crowd is their teacher. They do not realize that "the many are base, the few noble." '[27]

At last, out of his hatred for mankind, he withdraws to the mountains to feed on grasses and plants, and from here on the story degenerates into fiction, based on well-known sayings of his: his vegetarianism from a mention of blood pollution (fr. 5);

[23] DK 22A1 (DL 9. 6); DK 22A2 (Antisthenes, Strabo, 14. 633).

[24] The root of *megalophrosynē* is self-confidence, as in Plat. *Smp.* 194B; cf. Hdt. 7. 24 and Hdt. 7. 136: we can choose between 'courage', 'magnanimity', 'ostentation', and even 'arrogance'.

[25] Cf. Kirk and Raven, *The Presocratic Philosophers*, 184.

[26] DK 22A1.

[27] And see frs. 69ᵃ, 97, 121; cf. DK 22A1 (DL 9. 1).

the fatal dropsy from his assertion that 'it is death for a soul to become water' (fr. 36).[28]

It is likely that these utterances were made at different stages of his career: that fr. 29, in which the best people (*aristoi*) seek after eternal fame, might belong to the period when he still counted himself one of them. It is the utterance of the aristocrat which Heraclitus was. At what stage of Ephesus' history his family had been kings we do not know, but the hereditary priesthood places him in the highest circles. The actual position of Heraclitus in Ephesus around 500 BC is not known. Before the conquest of Croesus the city had been governed by tyrants; then, after the Persian conquest in 546, tyrants were installed in all the cities of the coast sympathetic to themselves. When the Persians had regained control after the Ionian revolt in 492, the cities set up democracies,[29] and we can assume that from this time until 478, the cities were at least internally self-governing. This is the context in which the meagre facts known about Heraclitus' life must be fitted. The family continued to enjoy its privileges under both tyrants and democracy.[30] It is possible that when the democracy was established in 492, the people turned to him to participate in the Government, or assist in framing a constitution. What the 'worthless constitution' was that he referred to cannot be known — perhaps he had the tyranny in mind. Nevertheless, the stories of Heraclitus refusing to participate in the Government or help in framing a constitution must belong to the period of the democracy and go with the details of his resignation of his hereditary priesthood to his brother. This is the single most important piece of evidence we have on Heraclitus: given the status indisputably associated with the function, its public character, together with the other honours, the red badge, the staff — to resign all these trappings of aristocratic, quasi-kinglike status and retire into private life, would appear to an Athenian of the late fifth century the act of an *apragmōn*. At the same time, there is no suggestion of contemplation, nor of transcendentalism. Heraclitus does not represent or belong to any social group; he is not an example

---

[28] So Kirk and Raven, op. cit., 183.
[29] Hdt. 6. 43; 4. 137.
[30] The family still enjoyed its privileges in Strabo's time (DK 22A2).

of any social movement. As far as we can tell, as a scientist or philosopher he stands in a tradition of speculation and research, but as a social phenomenon he stands on his own.

Parmenides and Ameinias

Among the few details of Parmenides' life, it is recorded, in what has been accepted as a reliable tradition,[31] that he was a legislator for his native city of Elea, but that, although of a wealthy and distinguished family himself, he preferred to associate with the Pythagorean Ameinias, a man poor but of noble character, and was converted by him to a quiet life (*hēsychia*).

As a legislator, Parmenides stands with other wise men of the sixth and fifth centuries—Solon, Thales, Pythagoras, Zeno, Heraclitus. The character of Ameinias is a mystery, though it is likely he is genuine, since he was substituted in one source for the well-known Xenophanes, and is himself otherwise unknown.[32] The problem lies in the phrasing: the idea that a man might be 'poor but noble' does not occur, to my knowledge, before Euripides' *Electra*, and is otherwise post-Socrates and popular with oligarchic theorists. Again, the term used here for noble (*kalokagathos*) is used in the late fifth century for the oligarchic nobility. Socrates uses it as a term of moral approval in the *Apology* (21 D) for, I think, the first time. Secondly, the phrase 'converted to a quiet life' is meant to imply that he was converted to a *philosophic* life, Ameinias being a Pythagorean. This is another example of transporting fourth-century ideas back into the fifth century. There is no fifth-century evidence for poor philosophers other than Socrates in the *Clouds* (if he is meant to be poor), least of all in the Old Comedy, where we should most expect to find it.

If we accept the existence of Ameinias, and of some relationship with Parmenides and possibly the introduction of the latter into the Pythagorean circle, it is doubtful if we can go much further.

---

[31] DK 28A1.

[32] According to Aristotle, Parmenides was a pupil of Xenophanes (DK 28A6). Diogenes must have had some good reason to substitute the little-known Ameinias for the better-known Xenophanes. See Kirk and Raven, op. cit., 265.

Democritus

In his pursuit of *genres de vie*, Joly quotes several fragments of Democritus' *Ethics* to suggest that the philosopher was interested in, or recommending a life of, *theōria*, or that, at least, there was more to life than wealth, power, and reputation.[33] He quotes, for example, from fr. 194: 'The greatest pleasure comes from the contemplation of noble actions.'

This fragment cannot, however, be made to mean that Democritus was recommending a life of contemplation, as opposed to activity, any more than when Pericles in the Funeral Speech exhorted the Athenians to fix their eyes every day on the greatness of Athens and to fall in love with her, he meant it as anything other than a spur to action — to contemplate the beautiful, not as an end in itself, but in order to emulate it oneself.[34] Other fragments recommend intelligence and prudence in the management of one's affairs but in no sense the abandonment or withdrawal from an active life.[35]

Anaxagoras

More important that all the philosophers we have considered so far as possible models for *apragmōn* behaviour, or forerunners of the *Bios Theōrētikos*, must be Anaxagoras.[36] The first important point about Anaxagoras in Athens is that he was there as an alien. Unlike the sophists, however he did not set himself up as a teacher of *aretē* (prowess, specifically in the political sphere).[37] To what extent he was a teacher at all is unclear. He had *mathētai* (pupils): Pericles was one, Archelaus another, and

[33] Ibid., 57.

[34] Th. 2. 43.

[35] Democritus, frs. 40, 77, 157, 282.

[36] The dates of Anaxagoras' sojourn in Athens are disputed. The main discussions are in A. E. Taylor, 'On the Date of the Trial of Anaxagoras', *CQ* 11 (1917), 81–7, who argues that Anaxagoras arrived in 480 and was banished in 450; J. S. Morrison, argues that he arrived in 456 and was banished just before the Peloponnesian War broke out ('The Place of Protagoras in Athenian Public Life', *CQ* 35 (1941), 1–16, esp. 5 n. 2). J. A. Davison suggests that there were two trials, first in 456, then in the late 430s ('Protagoras, Democritus, and Anaxagoras', *CQ* NS 3, 1953, 33–45). Most recently, J. Mansfield argues for Anaxagoras' arrival in 456, and trial in 437 ('The Chronology of Anaxagoras' Athenian Period and the Date of his Trial', *Mnemosyne*, 4: 32 (1979), 39–69; ibid., 4: 33 (1980), 17–95).

[37] In his own time the word 'sophist' was used indiscriminately of wise men in general: cf. Hdt. 1. 29 (Solon) and 4. 95 (Pythagoras); Isoc. 15. 235 (Anaxagoras).

Euripides a third, and he published a book, although the remains of his writings do not include anything on ethics. He was the guest and intimate friend of Pericles; it was he, according to Plutarch, who coached Pericles in oratory and was responsible for the 'majestic bearing, more potent than any demagogue's appeal'. Pericles, in his association with Anaxagoras, steeped himself in natural speculation (*meteōrologia*) and grasped the 'true nature of mind and folly'. Again, to Pericles, Anaxagoras was a 'trusted counsellor in matters of government'.[38]

Then there is the famous anecdote of the time when Pericles, busy with affairs, neglected to send the philosopher his allowance, and Anaxagoras, by now an old man, and too proud to remind him of it, wrapped himself in his cloak, took to his bed, and prepared to starve to death. Fortunately, Pericles remembered in time, and hastened round to save his friend. Anaxagoras told him 'If you want to keep a lamp going, you must fill it with oil.' (Plut. *Per.* 16.)

Anaxagoras, then, was a source of inspiration to Pericles, possibly even a political adviser, but was not growing rich from the fees of *mathētai*, like his contemporaries the sophists.

Indeed, Anaxagoras announced his rejection of money early in his career. He came of a good family — that is, one with wealth and a pedigree — but gave away his wealth to his relatives out of *enthousiasmos* and *megalophrosynē* — just like Heraclitus.[39] (For the meaning of *megalophrosynē* compare note 24; *enthousiasmos* is a wild passion, almost possession.) When his relatives remonstrated with him for neglecting his property, he retorted 'Very well, take care of it yourselves'. Finally, he withdrew to devote himself to the contemplation (*theōria*) of nature, and took no interest in politics.[40] When someone asked him why he did not concern himself with his country he replied that he did so very much, and pointed to the heavens.[41] He left Ionia at the age of twenty to settle in Athens to practise philosophy.[42] Someone asked what was the point of life; he replied, to study the heavens.[43]

38 Plut. *Per.* 4–5; Plat. *Phaedrus*, 269 E with Lanza's note; Plut. *Per.* 16.
39 Plut. *Per.* 16; Plat. *Hipp. Maj.* 283 A. On *enthousiasmos*, cf. Plat. *Tim.* 71 E.
40 DK 59A1 (DL 2. 7); cf. Plat. *Hipp. Maj.* 281 C.
41 DK 59A1 (DL 2. 7).
42 Ibid.
43 DK 59A29–30

Such an attitude naturally struck people as odd, and there are anecdotes relating the attitude of the man in the street towards Anaxagoras: Anaxagoras, Thales, and others like them may have been wise (*sophos*) but they were not sensible (*phronimos*) since they neglected their own advantage; their knowledge was exceptional, marvellous, wonderful, clever, supernatural (perhaps referring to Anaxagoras' supposed prediction of the meteorite at Aegospotami) but useless for all that because they were not seeking ordinary human 'goods' (*anthrōpina agatha*). Anaxagoras was also said to have been left a great fortune but to have neglected and lost it; in fact he might have been a philosopher, but he was also a fool. Anaxagoras is said to have recognized this himself when he remarked that he did not hold wealth or power to be happiness, and he wouldn't be surprised if people thought him a simpleton.[44]

Although he professed to take no part in politics, and had deliberately chosen to live in Athens where, in any case, he was debarred from participating in public life, he did nevertheless make an impact on the Athenians by reason of his scientific speculations. The Athenians were puzzled by his rejection of all that they considered valuable in life, yet he was able to disturb them sufficiently by his questioning of what they held to be the unquestionable facts of the universe, as to lead eventually to condemnation and exile. The prosecution may have been brought against him as a way of striking against Pericles, but the jury were more likely voting against Anaxagoras himself. His assertion that the sun was a mass of red-hot metal was perhaps the best-known thing about him, sufficient for Socrates to remark on it nearly thirty years after Anaxagoras' death.[45] Plutarch is thinking of Anaxagoras, among others, when he writes 'Men could not tolerate those who investigated natural phenomena or who held forth about the heavens, since they reduced to power of the gods to irrational cause, blind forces, and the action of necessity.' (*Nic.* 23.)[46] This passage occurs in a description of Nicias' notorious superstition, but it illustrates how a man who was ostensibly withdrawn from public life in the sense in which

---

[44] Arist. *Eth. Nic.* 1141[b] 3; Plat. *Hipp. Maj.* 283 A; Arist. *Eth. Nic.* 1179[a]13.
[45] DL 2. 12; Plat. *Apol.* 26 D; DK 59A2.
[46] 'On 'Necessity', see below, and Ar. *Clouds*, 369–407.

it was normally understood found himself interfering in the lives of the citizens at a more profound level, and at some danger to himself. Diopeithes was sometimes asserted to be mad[47] but his motion to outlaw those who did not honour religious observances, and taught about the heavens, was passed by the assembly (Plut. *Per*. 32).

By rejecting their values and institutions, Anaxagoras is rejecting the Athenians themselves, and if at first they regard him with amusement and contempt, their feelings turn at last to hatred and fear. This hatred is something against which an alien has always to be on his guard. Anaxagoras had renounced his own city: why should he be loyal to Athens? Someone once asked him whether he wouldn't prefer to be buried in his own land when he died. 'The road to Hades is the same everywhere' he replied.[48] Perhaps he loved to shock; perhaps it was part of his *megalophrosyne*.[49] It could also reflect the growth of a cosmopolitan attitude among intellectuals, of which there are other traces at the time.[50] Hippias of Elis, for example, on a visit to Athens, addressed a meeting of friends and pupils as 'kinsmen, fellow citizens, by nature, not by custom', a view echoed by Antiphon the sophist.[51] According to one version of his trial, Anaxagoras was accused not only of impiety, but of 'Medism' for good measure.[52]

The evidence from the anecdotes, then, is that he (*a*) renounced his own worldy affairs; (*b*) renounced politics; (*c*) renounced his own country; (*d*) devoted himself to *theoria*.

How reliable are these anecdotes? Werner Jaeger, in the article referred to above, suggests they were either the product of the Platonic and Peripatetic schools, or had at least been shaped by them. He points out that the motif of the absent-minded professor neglecting his fields is applied indiscriminately to other old *sophoi*,

---

[47] Ar. *Knights*; 1085; *Wasps*, 380 with Macdowell's note.

[48] DK 59A1 (DL 2. 11).

[49] Other anecdotes suggest he had little time for public opinion: DL 2. 10; and cf. DK 59A33.

[50] Cf. Nestle, 'Apragmosyne', *Philologus*, 81 (1926), 133.

[51] DK 87B44. B1. Compare Euripides, fr. 1047, and fr. 1113N: 'Our [human] nature is our [true] fatherland'.

[52] DK 59A1 (DL 2. 12). Wade-Gery believes such a charge would have been obsolete in 433. Hence, either the trial took place in the 450s, or else Thucydides was getting out of touch (W-G's view — 'Thucydides Son of Melesias', *JHS* 52 (1932), 220).

Democritus and Thales. He admits, on the evidence of the *Antiope* (see below) that there was some sort of philosophical/practical debate in progress before Plato began writing, but insists that it was Plato who first introduced the contemplative philosopher as an 'ethical problem' in philosophy. It was seen above how many of the old philosophers contrived to be socially useful; it might also be argued that as a friend and counsellor of Pericles, Anaxagoras was close to the centre of political life. Nevertheless, Jaeger is on much firmer ground with the earlier figures than with Anaxagoras.

First, Anaxagoras had left his native Clazomenae, and was therefore, as an alien, debarred from political life. Then he is said to have renounced his personal wealth. This is a difficult point; Anaxagoras' decision is recorded in terms almost identical to those of his fellow Ionian Heraclitus, and the unworldly philosopher is a figure so especially beloved of the fourth century, that we must be on our guard. All that can be said is that the stories are unanimous, and that although they are sometimes told of other wise men, it is about Anaxagoras that they chiefly cluster.

Finally, he is said to have devoted himself to *theōria*. There is nothing implausible about this: he stood in a tradition of Ionian speculation, which continued after him. *Theōria* meant for him, of course, observation, and with it speculation about natural phenomena. It was the beginning of science, and was based on what we would understand as a scientific attitude: that statements about the natural world should be based upon observation (not received belief or superstition). Understanding *theōria* in this sense, then, it would be fair to say that Anaxagoras lived a life of contemplation, a *Bios Theōrētikos*, though this is not what Plato and the fourth-century thinkers meant by the term.[53]

As a stranger living in Athens, Anaxagoras represented a threat to the Athenians on two counts: his presence in Athens was a negation of conventional patriotism (he appears to have been the first to have recognized this) and in this respect he stands at the head of the cosmopolitan tradition of later centuries. His rejection of political life was also a threat. But also, and most

---

[53] Cf. Nestle, op. cit., 132; di Benedetto, *Euripide: Teatro e società* 308; Ehrenberg, 'Polypragmosyne', *JHS* 68 (1948), 54.

importantly, his apparently disinterested pursuit of scientific truth
was a threat because it undermined the commonly accepted and
unquestioned basis of most people's lives. For many years such
a man may be tolerated, laughed at perhaps, or despised, even
admired by a few, but at some critical moment, often unforeseen,
the people turn on him with a ferocity which seems out of all
proportion to the man and his work. Such was the fate of
Anaxagoras.

Among so much evidence from the fourth century, we are
fortunate to have one testimony which dates from within a year
of Anaxagoras' trial, and which seems to glance obliquely at the
man. This is a speech in Euripides' *Medea*:

> No man of sense should bring up his children
> To be cleverer than their fellows. For apart
> From a reputation for uselessness, they will
> Incur the hostility of their fellow-citizens.
> If you offer new ideas to fools, you will seem
> Useless and foolish. If you are thought to know
> More than those considered to be intelligent you
> Will only give offence. I have experienced it myself:
> I am wise, and while to some I am an object of
> Envy (to some I am leading a quiet life, to others
> The opposite) to others I am an enemy.

(294 ff.)[54]

Medea's complaint touches on what we have been discussing at
several points: she, like Anaxagoras, is an alien; she is reputed to be
clever—Anaxagoras was called 'Intelligence Personified' (*Nous*);
Medea is adept at *pharmaka* (magic potions)—Anaxagoras, like
Hippocrates, seems to have been dabbling in what it would have
been safer to leave alone;[55] Medea arouses in the citizens a
mixture of fear and envy—so did Anaxagoras.

What is especially interesting is the view the citizens have of
Medea: apart from being skilled (*sophē*) she is considered
unproductive (*argos*) and useless (*achreios*). Later she forestalls
criticism of being idle (*hēsychaia*) and lazy (*phaulē*): if this is what
the citizens think of her, she says, that she is nothing but an

---

[54] Cf. Festugière, *Contemplation et vie contemplative selon Platon*, 38; Joly, op. cit., 54;
line 304 (in brackets) is repeated at 808, and is therefore deleted by some editors.
[55] Cf. Verrall's note on *argia* and *pharmakia*.

intellectual layabout, she most strongly rejects the charge; let no one say she is not capable of being a bane to her foes and a boon to her friends.[56] These are the terms in which an Athenian was accustomed to define what he considered the intrinsic worth of a man, and they are a measure of the seriousness of the charges levelled against Medea and Anaxagoras.

It is important that this contradiction — the wise man who is useless — had been consciously formulated in 431, even more so, in fact, than any parallels between Medea and Anaxagoras, which should not be pushed too hard. After all, as an Ionian he was hardly a foreigner, simply debarred from political status; she was a beautiful young woman, he an old man. At the same time, much of what she has to say in this speech does not really apply to her dramatic situation. Even if we drop the connection with Anaxagoras we are left with the picture of an *apragmōn* intellectual drawn in 431, possibly soon after the trial of Anaxagoras.[57] Medea was accused of being idle and useless: such were the public criticisms of Anaxagoras; that he was a combination of wisdom and foolishness (an apparent contradiction), people could not understand that a man should be clever, have ability, and yet not put it to practical, useful ends.

Finally, let us attempt to estimate what influence, if any, as models of *apragmosynē*, the men we have considered in this chapter may have exerted in the last third of the fifth century. I have already observed that writers in the fourth century were eager to find forerunners of the *Bios Theōrētikos* among philosophers in the previous two centuries. Plato had even tried to enrol such eminently practical men of the world as the Seven Wise Men under the banner of the Contemplative Life, without much success; there was too much evidence to the contrary from the sixth and fifth centuries.

Heraclitus and possibly Parmenides seem to have taken some such step as the renunciation of worldly ambition and chosen a life devoted to speculation and thought. Both, however, remain

---

[56] *Med.* 807–9.
[57] Within a very few years, if we accept Plutarch and Sotion's view that the trial took place shortly before the Peloponnesian War broke out.

individual cases which do not appear to have produced any effect on those around them, or on those who came immediately after them. Pythagoras and Anaxagoras are different, and there is some evidence of their influence in the period under review. To take Anaxagoras first: it was said that Euripides had been a pupil of Anaxagoras.[58] Let us therefore consider reflections of Anaxagoras' cosmological teaching in Euripides' plays, and then go on to ask whether Euripides also adopted an *apragmōn* role in Athenian public life.

There are a number of instances in his plays where Euripides has been thought to express Anaxagorean ideas about the universe. The most obvious are those in the *Orestes* where the sun is called a 'rock slung on swinging golden chains midway between sky and earth' (982) and in the *Phaethon* where the sun is called a 'golden lump' (fr. 783) and a 'hot flame' rising above the earth (fr. 782). These clearly refer back to Anaxagoras' famous statement that the sun was a mass of red-hot metal.[59] Another is the fragment of the *Melanippe* (fr. 484) according to which earth and heaven were all one, and only after they had divided were all the things—trees, birds, animals—which are nourished by the sea, produced, together with the race of men. Diodorus, quoting this fragment, says Euripides was the pupil of Anaxagoras and so implies that he is reproducing Anaxagoras' ideas.[60] Undoubtedly the most famous fragment in this context is fragment 910 from the *Antiope*:

> Blessed is the man who gives his
> Attention to researches, not aiming
> At the misery of citizens, nor to
> Commit crimes, but contemplating the
> Ageless order of immortal nature,
> Its manner, origin and purpose.
> Concern for shameful deeds never
> Sits near such things.

---

[58] DL 2. 45 (Lanza, a 4 a); D. H. *Rhet. Art.* 1. 10 (Lanza, a 7); Schol. Pind. *Ol.* 1. 91 (Lanza, a 20 a); *Theol. Arithm.* 6. 18 de Falco (Lanza a 20 b); Aul. Gell. 15. 20 (Lanza, a 21); DL 2. 10 (Lanza, a 1).

[59] Fr. 944 is more doubtfully ascribed to Anaxagoras' influence; so too fr. 964 and *Alcestis*, 903.

[60] Diodorus, 1. 7. 7 (Lanza, a 62).

It may be objected that this fragment could apply to any other cosmologist,[61] but then Euripides was not the pupil of any other cosmologist, and even if later writers had only deduced from his writing that Euripides had been Anaxagoras' pupil, it makes no difference: the influence is there.

If Euripides took an interest in *physikē*—the study of nature— did he also adopt an attitude of *apragmosynē* in the city? Many scholars hold the opinion, derived from his plays, that he did. Thus Nestle: 'Die *Apragmosyne*, der von Sokrates geübte und empfohlene *theoretikos bios*, ist sein Ideal . . .', and 'mit sichtlicher Freude malt er im Ion das zurückgezogene Leben des jungen Mannes.'[62] Or Martinazzoli: 'Poichè era in fondo il suo carattere raccolto e la sua *apragmosyne* ad alimentare la sua grandezza d'animo, la sua audacia spirituale . . .'[63] Or Festugière on Hippolytus and Ion: 'Si l'on veut connaître l'âme religieuse d'Euripide, c'est ici, et dans l'Ion qu'il faut chercher . . . le sage du Théétète est le frère d'Ion et d'Hippolyte.'[64] Goossens thinks Euripides is *apragmōn* 'par sentiment de son impuissance devant les intrigues et l'incompréhension de la masse par crainte de ridicule'.[65] He develops a theory that artists and intellectuals through the ages have, for these reasons, preferred a life of speculation and contemplation. Critics have detected too in the fragment of the *Erechtheus*: 'let my spear lie there, gathering cobwebs . . . while I sit here, unfolding the voice of the tablets, in which wise men are made famous' (fr. 369), a longing for peace and retirement from affairs in a man now over sixty.[66] The *Antiope* (discussed in detail below) undoubtedly provides the strongest evidence for *apragmosynē* on Euripides' part. Critics have often assumed that Euripides is taking Amphion's part—the poet and student of nature against the practical man of affairs: 'Amphion ist sein Gegenbild' (Pohlenz);[67] 'Euripide a voulu donner à Amphion la meilleure parte' (Goossens).[68] Since Euripides did actually go off to Macedonia when he was

[61] Burnet, *EGP*, 4th edn., 255.
[62] *Euripides der Dichter der Aufklärung*, 23.
[63] *Euripide*, 422.
[64] *Contemplation et vie contemplative selon Platon*, 465–6.
[65] *Euripides et Athènes*, 496.
[66] di Benedetto, op. cit., 149.
[67] *Die Griechische Tragödie*, 411.
[68] Ibid., 651.

nearly eighty, we can agree that in a manner of speaking he did eventually retire into *apragmosynē*. At such an age, however, his decision can be accounted for on other, more straightforward, grounds. At the age of eighty, one can be forgiven for wishing to retire, and we cannot construe any other plausible motive. His retirement to Macedonia may reflect on the Athenian democracy, or it may not. Socrates, who received a similar invitation, characteristically chose to stay.

But if we consider his career as a playwright, about fifty years long, can it be called an *apragmōn* existence? That would be to mis-understand the function of playwrights in Athens. Euripides came of a noble family: he was 'cup-bearer' for the dancers in honour of Apollo, who were themselves young men of good family. It was a hereditary function. His mother was also of very high birth. As a young man, Euripides was victorious in the games, and there is an anecdote that he practised very hard at boxing and the pankration because his father had received an oracle that his son would win the garland in the contests, not realizing that Apollo was referring to the *dramatic* contests. There was in fact nothing *apragmōn* about being a playwright; the dramatic festivals were as hotly contested as the games or any other Greek contest. To enter a competition and to endeavour to win was the Greek norm of behaviour, and in his fifty years of entering the dramatic competitions, Euripides conforms to the usual practice. In fact he goes further, because throughout his career he took it upon himself in his plays to comment upon current affairs. It was an oblique comment, dressed in mythological guise, but it may be because his audience was present at a religious festival that he enjoyed a freedom almost unknown to public speakers. Neither was he timid or retiring, as Goossens thinks; throughout his career he never ceased to shock his audience — one need only think of the procession of beggars through his plays to which Aristophanes took such exception.[69] In Aristophanes' own *Frogs* he actually makes Euripides say that a poet's function is to make better citizens, and considering the attacks which he makes on Euripides in this and other plays (which betray the care with which Aristophanes had studied his works) this statement has some foundation.

[69] e.g., *Acharnians*, 418 ff.: Oineus, Phoenix, Philoctetes, Bellerophon, Telephus, Thyestes, Ino.

Euripides never occupied, so far as is known, any public position, and contrasts with Sophocles, whose plays are on the whole free of topical references, but who performed public duties on several occasions as general, as *proboulos*, and in religious capacities. Given the freedom which Euripides exercised in his plays, however, perhaps he felt no need to.

On the whole, then, I feel it would not be right to call Euripides an *apragmōn*. He was aware of the phenomenon, as is apparent from his plays, but his own role must be regarded as a public one. Anaxagoras may have stimulated in him an interest in *physikē* but he did not convert him to the Contemplative Life.

Another important witness to the influence of the philosophers is Aristophanes' *Clouds* (423 BC). Here we may detect the influence of both *physikē* and possibly of the Pythagoreans. As to *physikē* the 'Thinkery' abounds in examples: in Strepsiades' guided tour of the establishment, Aristophanes takes the opportunity to satirize various kinds of scientific experiments (to find out how far a flea jumps, for example), as well as research into natural phenomena—astronomy, geography, and so on. Socrates himself is discovered suspended above the ground in order to study the sun more closely. In their conversation, Socrates explains that thunder is caused by the clashing together of clouds through necessity (*anankē*). While Aristophanes is indulging in a general satire of scientific research and speculation, and presupposes on the audience's part some vague knowledge of these activities, he is also alluding specifically to Anaxagoras, and Democritus after him. The 'celestial whirl' (*dinos*) was originally Anaxagoras' idea, though Democritus may have coined the term. Anaxagoras was also responsible for the theory that thunder was caused by the clashing of clouds, and the concept of necessity was prominent in fifth-century cosmology.[70]

It must be said, however, that although this picture fits well with what is known of the Ionian scientific tradition, there is never any kind of metaphysical element or any transcendental 'wisdom', and although these activities are presented by Aristophanes as being manifestly useless (the attitude of which Medea complained), the denizens of the 'Thinkery' are shown as cunning charlatans rather than harmless *apragmōn* eccentrics.

---

[70] Cf. Dover on *Clouds*, 376, 380.

Later in the play, Socrates is happy to cast his researches aside and to teach the young man the notorious sophistic technique of 'making the worse cause appear the better', a recipe for worldly success.

It was mentioned earlier that Socrates had been the pupil of Archelaus, who was in turn said to have been the successor of Anaxagoras.[71] It has been suggested that Socrates was himself the successor to Archelaus, and in the years before 423 was in some way or other the centre of a group of pupils.[72] There is no evidence to support this idea, other than the *Clouds* itself and those dialogues like the *Phaedo* which portray him surrounded by a group of like-minded friends. According to the *Phaedo* (95 E) Socrates had studied *physikē* and Anaxagoras' concept of mind (*nous*) before rejecting them as insufficient, for the reason that Anaxagoras could offer no 'Final Cause' for natural phenomena. It is through hints like this that we can see Plato making his way towards a supernatural, or transcendental, account of reality.

Socrates also suggests that the typical picture we have of him, arguing in the market-place or the public gymnasiums, only dates from the time when Chaerephon came back from Delphi with the oracle proclaiming him the 'wisest of men' (though we do not know when that was). 'I set myself, with considerable reluctance, to test the truth of it', he says (*Apol.* 21 B).

The question of how much money Socrates had, and whether, even though he did not actually receive fees from his friends, he might have received quite a lot in the way of presents and hospitality, is a difficult one. There is one reference to a sum of money he is supposed to have lent out to Nicias at interest. The testimony of Old Comedy, however, is unanimous on this point. Socrates is a 'bare-foot babbler', or 'idle beggar'; his bare feet and his apparent idleness were alike notorious in Athens.[73]

This raises the related question of Pythagorean influence. The *Pythagoristai* were well known in the fourth century and after: they are bare-foot, pale-skinned charlatans, according to the comedians. The pale skin refers to the philosophers spending their time indoors, instead of out in the fresh air like any normal man. It is axiomatic that what they engaged in is a lot of worthless

---

[71] Lanza, a 7.   [72] Woods, *Class Ideology and Ancient Political Theory*, 85.
[73] Ameipsias, *Gobbler-up*, fr. 9; Eupolis, frs. 352, 353 K.

rubbish, and there is a strong presumption that they have other more sinister ends in view.[74]

As a matter of fact, these three qualities are precisely those which characterize the students of the 'Thinkery' (*Clouds*, 102–3), and the comic stereotype thus established enjoyed a remarkably long life, flourishing over several centuries. But if the students of the 'Thinkery' shared this stereotype with the *Pythagoristai*, are there any other references in the *Clouds* to Pythagorean influence? As a matter of fact, there are two possible such references. When Strepsiades is first brought into the presence of Socrates, the student refers to Socrates as 'Himself' (218–19). Now although in Greek homes the servants might refer to the master as 'Himself' (e.g. Men. *Sam.* 41) the disciples of Pythagoras were known always to refer to their master as 'Himself', and this could be an echo of it. Again, later in the play, Socrates rushes out of the 'Thinkery' in desperation, exclaiming 'Oh breath! Oh Chaos! Oh Air!' (627). A work beginning with these words was attributed to Pythagoras, though it is not known whether it was circulating in Athens in Aristophanes' time. In fact this is the central problem: the Pythagoreans were dispersed around 450, but we have no independent means of knowing whether they had reached Athens by 423. What should be our most certain evidence, the Old Comedy, makes no mention of them (by name) and it is difficult to believe Aristophanes would allude to them without mentioning their name. On the other hand, certain characteristics have defined themselves: the students of the 'Thinkery' are pale-skinned and bare-foot. At the same time, they are not philosophers in the sense of later centuries: their concern is with natural phenomena—the study of the heavens, map-making and so on. The contrast between the inherently superior philosophic way of life and the ordinary life is not made consciously. In fact, so little is Aristophanes aware of such a contrast that any unworldliness implied earlier in the 'Thinkery' is soon brushed aside by a thoroughly cosmopolitan, sophistic element, determined on worldly, financial, and political success.

[74] Cf. Cratinus, fr. 5; Euboulus, fr. 36; Antiphanes, frs. 135, 160, 227; Mnesimachus, fr. 1; Alexis, frs. 196, 220, 221; Aristophon, frs. 9–13 on the vegetarianism of the Pythagoreans. For later writers, cf. Alciphron, 3. 14 and 1. 3; Theocritus, 14. 5; Lucian, *Iupp. Trag.* 1.

While, therefore, we can certainly detect the existence of *physikē*, of men whom we would call scientists, speculating on natural phenomena, sometimes unworldly and neglecting their own concerns in their enthusiasm for their research, what we do not see is the conscious presentation of a philosophic life as against a worldly one, a life which rejects worldly values and which is concerned with a supernatural reality as Plato evolved it. And although Plato often attributes a *Bios Theōrētikos* to earlier generations of wise men, the sense of that phrase for them was the contemplation of the natural order, what we would call scientific investigation. For Plato, on the other hand, it involves the contemplation of an invisible, higher order of reality, and is therefore a kind of inner contemplation, which turns away from the real, natural order to an inner, superior reality.

7

The Contemplative Life: To Plato

The study of the Presocratics is a frustrating business, the evidence having been refracted through so many ideological prisms before reaching us. This is one reason why it is better to try to seek another approach to Plato's view of the Contemplative Life. In any case, it is my belief that Plato did not arrive at his philosophic position through the inspiration of previous philosophers (Socrates aside), but rather derived it out of the social and political circumstances of his own time; in other words, that his version of the Contemplative Life—the *Bios Theōrētikos*—was a philosophic rationalization of the social and political phenomenon of *apragmosynē*, though his own particular cast of mind, his psychological make-up, in short his genius, is also a significant factor. In deriving Plato's Contemplative Life it will be safer too, I feel, to confine myself to contemporary evidence, and, by way of an opening, to go back to the year 413 BC, when Plato would have been fifteen.

Euripides' Ion

Around the year 413, Euripides produced his play *Ion*.[1] Together with the *Iphigeneia in Tauris* and *Helen*, both of them produced about this time, it has a certain 'Never Never Land' quality, which is evoked at the beginning. After the prologue,

---

[1] At one time the play was dated earlier, around 419: Murray, Delebesque, Dindorf, Hermann, Wilamowitz. Latest opinion, however, sets it around 413. In particular, the play has important similarities to the *Iphigeneia in Tauris*, and *Helen*, and a parody of *Ion* has been detected in the *Lysistrata* (909–13). The most conclusive evidence comes from an analysis of resolved feet. E. B. Ceadel places the *Ion* between the *IT* and *Helen* (414–412 BC) ('Resolved Feet in the Trimeters of Euripides and the Chronology of the Plays', *CQ* 35 (1941), 68 ff., esp. 78). It should be observed that this method is not entirely consistent; nevertheless, it seems the strongest evidence for the comparative dating of the plays.

Ion comes out of the great temple on a bright morning and in a long monody (100 lines) creates a vision of an enchanted world of calm and tranquillity, of a life which goes contentedly and without fret, undisturbed from day to day. There may even be a touch of humour in his stage business with the bow and arrow to scare off the birds. Ion is a young man, probably in his late teens;[2] he has been brought up in the temple by a priestess and has never known any other life. He is proud of the responsibility which has been entrusted to him — for he is the temple steward, and has charge of Apollo's gold.[3] In a sense, unofficially, his life has been consecrated to the god. In this he resembles Hippolytus, who also felt himself devoted to a divinity. Ion's life is very different from Hippolytus', however: whereas Hippolytus is away in the fields and woods with his friends, far from cities and men, Ion's life, though protected and tranquil, is full of variety and incident. He may not live in the world of business affairs, of cities and governments, but he hears about it from a stream of visitors, and he is constantly encountering the human problems of those who have come to seek guidance from the oracle.[4]

However, Ion is remarkable not merely for his devotion to Apollo, but for the humility, the positive self-abasement, with which he throws himself into the humble tasks he performs. His monody in this first scene is a panegyric of his lowly life in the service of Apollo. Ion serves, he labours, he sweeps, he is a humble servant of the god, he takes delight in his labour: it is noble, famous, he never tires, and so on. For his devotion to a god we may compare Hippolytus, but for this exultation in menial tasks there is no precedent. Certainly this must be the first and last time in the history of drama that the protagonist apostrophizes his broom.[5]

If we look for a precedent, it must be to the same author's *Electra*, in which Orestes discerns the innate worth of the simple

---

[2] Line 53: he has taken on man's shape; he is guardian of the gold, and faithful steward of the temple. Again, line 316: 'Did you come here as a boy, or as a young man (*neanias*)?' Owen in his edition of the play, refers to him as a 'boy' and 'this older boy, in his teens' (intro. xxvi).

[3] *Ion*, 54.

[4] *Ion*, 301 ff.; 640 ff.

[5] *Ion*, 112. Some have detected here a touch of comedy. Cf. H. Rohdich, 'ruhrenden Farce', referring to the bow and arrows (*Die Euripideische Tragödie*, 111).

peasant. Nevertheless, Orestes' point is that true nobility resides within, despite an unprepossessing exterior; even in a life of toil, a man can be noble. The life of toil in the *Electra* is painted in very unglamorous colours, and if a man can rise to nobility, it is despite his labours. Ion's life, by contrast, is exalted because of its toil. Ion is not a hermit; he is well aware of the world, its affairs and its problems, and he is content with his lot. This combination of a consciously sheltered life, together with a steady round of toil, could be called *apragmosynē*,[6] but, in the terms of this study, it is the *apragmosynē* not of Hippolytus, but of the peasant farmer. It is an *apragmosynē* associated too with tradition and continuity, represented by the institution of the oracle. This quality lends it much of its charm. It was tradition and continuity in the peasant's life that made it attractive in the eyes of a cosmopolitan intellectual.

This speech provides the background for Ion's scene with his newly discovered father, Xouthos, and explains his initial rejection of the King's offer to take him back to Athens as his son and heir — to transform his position from the bottom to the top of the social ladder. Ion's speech in reply to Xouthos' offer is, like other key speeches in Euripides, somewhat ambiguous. Ion is Xouthos' son, and according to the legend, goes back with him to Athens, amongst other things to found the Ionian people. This is a given referent in the story which Euripides cannot change. At the same time, given the character of the play's opening, Ion is bound to make some initial remonstrance before he accepts Xouthos' offer. Whatever his intentions in framing the play in this way, Euripides has set the scene for one of those speeches which occupy an ambiguous place in many of his plays: it contains a critique of contemporary Athenian politics, and cannot be justified in terms of the needs of the play. It has been most convincingly accounted for as a kind of parallel to Aristophanes' parabases.[7]

The speech is in three parts. The central part refers to reactions within the family and does not affect this discussion. The first part is a denunciation of the excesses of democratic Athens, while

---

[6] So C. Wolff, 'Design and Myth in Euripides' *Ion*, *HSCP* 69 (1965), 172

[7] Cf. M. Imhof, *Euripides Ion: Eine literarische Studie*, 74 n. 2. See too F. Solmsen, 'Euripides *Ion* im Vergleich mit anderen Tragödien', *Hermes* 69 (1934), 409.

the third part is an account of his personal reservations about life in a mythical kingdom as a tyrant. Euripides does not, therefore, have any concern for consistency at this point. The speech opens: 'Things look differently to one standing further away, than to one closer up.' This could be the voice of the poet standing apart from the press of political life so as to gain a clearer view. A few lines later he begins a perceptive analysis of political life in the Athenian democracy:

If someone seeks high office in the State he is hated by those having no power. Success is always unpopular. The more useful, capable sort are wisely silent, and do not seek to meddle in affairs.[8] I shall be laughed at by them if I do not keep quiet in a city full of fear.[9] If I try to rise in the city I shall be warded off by the votes of those clever men who run the city.[10] This is what it is like, father; those who have rank in the city are most hostile to their rivals.

(595–606)

This is a good example of the freedom which Euripides exercised in writing his plays. The speech is strictly gratuitous to the story; instead, the author has taken this opportunity to unburden himself of some opinions of the contemporary political scene, the opinions of a member of a certain section of the upper class. They are the justification, or part of the justification, for a member of that upper class abstaining from political life in 413.

The speech reveals three kinds of men in the city: (*a*) those who are powerless in political matters; (*b*) those who have ability, and who under normal conditions, as it were, would take a controlling place in the State, but now consider it wisest to refrain from politics: the *apragmones*; (*c*) those who hold power and are jealous of those who seek to wrest it from them. Ion's, and Euripides', sympathies are with group (*b*). These people have all the right epithets: they are useful (*chrēstoi*) and capable (*dynamenoi*) — terms which carried political significance at the time, as we have already seen. They are people who are not only

---

[8] I follow Verrall (ed. *Ion*, Cambridge, 1890) in putting a comma after *einai* instead of after *sophoi* (Murray). Murray's punctuation makes the *chrēstoi* capable of being *sophoi*. In so doing, he ignores the political weight of the term *dynamenoi*. These terms are political catchwords, and indicate men of power and influence. But at this moment they show their political acumen by keeping silent. Owen thinks this 'too ingenious'.

[9] Fear: *phobos*. Some read *psogos* — envy.

[10] Or 'those who can use arguments'.

rich, but educated; they are the natural Government of the city. Ps.-Xenophon had referred to them as those obliged by their position to perform numerous and varied duties for the city while remaining at the beck and call of the *dēmos*. But whereas a generation or so earlier these men were in political circulation, by now they have 'grown wiser', and they seem to regard anyone who does try his luck in public life as a fool. There is a kind of tension in the condition of a man referred to as 'capable' but yet reduced to a nullity. Such a condition is especially significant in the year 413.

Xouthos had offered to restore Ion to his rightful place as his son and heir at Athens: a golden sceptre, wealth, power and position would all be his.[11] In the third part of his speech, Ion sets forth his objections to this — the tyrant's — life:

> You praise a tyrant's life to me in vain; the outside is fair enough, but misery lurks at home. How can a man be happy and prosperous who lives in fear, dragging out his life, eternally on the watch for an assassin?[12] Rather than a tyrant, I would be a prosperous commoner;[13] a tyrant is surrounded by criminals, but he hates honest men for fear of death.[14] You say gold outweighs this, and love of wealth? I would not like to have to guard my wealth with my hands, listening for suspicious noises, beset with worry.[15] Let me have a moderate portion, so it bring no grief. Let me tell you the great advantage of my life, father; I have leisure, man's greatest boon. The people behave with respect to me and do not elbow me aside in the street; if there is one thing I cannot tolerate it is to have to give way in the street to the low rabble.[16]

(621 ff.)

In a state which had not witnessed a tyrant for a hundred years, the arguments for and against tyranny were well rehearsed, and nowhere more so than on the tragic stage. Hippolytus had

---

[11] *Ion*, 578.

[12] Cf. Creon in *Oedipus Tyrannus*, 583 ff; X. *Hieron*, 2. 6 ff.; the tyrant in Plato's imperfect State, *Rep.* 567.

[13] Cf. Eur. *Hipp.* 1017.

[14] *Esthlos* more likely means 'noble' here. It is not good or honest men the tyrant fears, but the disgruntled aristocracy. The tyrant had come to power as the champion of the common people. Cf. Hdt. 3. 80 and Arist. *Pol.* 1314[b] 14.

[15] *psophous* is the MS reading: 'noise without sense'. Paley reads *psogous* — 'blame, envy' which makes more immediate sense.

[16] This jostling is described by Ps.-Xenophon (*Ath. Pol.* 1. 10) and Plato (*Rep.* 563 c).

previously rejected the position in terms very similar to those used by Ion. Ion, for all his humble station at Delphi, clearly sees himself moving in respectable circles at Athens: he does not want to be a tyrant, but associates himself with prosperous citizens and the *esthloi*—the upper class who have been superseded by the tyrant. Euripides here understands tyrants as they were commonly understood by political theorists, that is as commoners who have seized power in the name of the people. Ion's sympathies are with the better sort of people and against the rabble of whom the tyrant is only a special case.

His objection to wealth is on account of the worry it would bring: a lowlier station, a moderate estate, attract less envy. His objections to tyranny are very similar to those which he levels against democracy. In both cases it is prominence above the throng which brings trouble—envy, treachery, worry. Perhaps Ion regards those who control the democratic city as tyrants of a kind—the idea which Plato develops in the *Republic* (*Rep.* 565). His attachment to the better sort is especially strongly brought out towards the end of this passage: to be elbowed aside in the street is especially degrading. This aspect of democratic Athens had been remarked on by other writers of an oligarchic, or pro-Spartan, turn of mind.

Yet what is it that Ion chooses as the single most important aspect of his life at Delphi? What is the thing he is most loath to give up? He tells us that the one thing political power cannot give him is leisure (*scholē*). This is, so far as I know, the first time anyone has ever claimed it as a good. Now, leisure is a first requirement of the *Bios Theōrētikos*—the Contemplative Life—but it is not yet that life itself. This is important, because some writers have detected a parallel between Ion and Socrates.[17] I discuss Socrates in more detail below. Here it may be pointed out that Ion is not recommending a Contemplative Life; indeed he gives us no clue as to what use he might put his leisure. Nevertheless, the appearance of leisure here is important because it provides a significant link in the chain that connects *apragmosynē* with the *Bios Theōrētikos*.

Conflating these two passages, we find Ion associating with the

---

[17] Rohdich, 'Die Socratische Idee: Das Tempelidyll' in *Euripideische Tragödie*, 111. Snell (*Scenes from Greek Drama*, 82) takes the opposite view.

better sort, those who are wisely silent, those who mock anyone who attempts a public career. At the same time, he refuses a tyrant's throne in favour of a moderate station in society (though not a low one). In fact, he despises the poor, and would hold aloof from them. The most precious aspect of his present life is leisure.

The condition of these people of a 'better sort' seems to have deteriorated even since the time of Hippolytus or Ps.-Xenophon. Here, in the *Ion*, as in the *Orestes*, they are simply silent.[18] They have retired into *apragmosynē*, but not out of choice, nor do they have any ideological reason for doing so. They have simply been forced out of public life. The reasons are practical: the hatred of the masses, and the dominance of those sort of demagogues described in the *Orestes*—the men with the 'unstoppable mouths', the men who would keep Ion out of office if ever he tried to gain it. Although Euripides distinguishes between the 'better sort' and the demagogues, the political vocabulary of the period no longer distinguishes an aristocracy as such—that is, government by those who, in addition to personal wealth, are distinguished by high birth. Euripides makes this distinction, then, on the more tenuous grounds of culture and style of life.[19] This would explain why Nicias was *persona grata* to the upper class, while Cleon was not, when they both came from similar backgrounds. It is possible that this culture, whatever it was, was linked with the leisure which Ion prizes.

Ion concludes his long speech with these words:

Duty (*nomos*) and nature (*physis*) alike have made me fit for Apollo's service. Weighing these things together I find life here better than what you offer me, father. Let me live on here! The reward is equal, whether enjoying greatness, or being happy with little.

(643 ff.)

The harnessing together of *nomos* and *physis* lends an intellectual and contemporary note to Ion's argument. In Chapter 2 it was seen that *physis*—human nature—which was juxtaposed to *nomos* (traditional law) in contemporary arguments, was advanced as a justification for ignoring the traditional demands of patriotism.

---

[18] Eur. *Or.* 930.
[19] Euripides uses *eugenēs* of *Ion* but it may be consciously archaic.

According to a fragment of Euripides, 'our [human] nature is our [true] fatherland',[20] and Hippias the sophist addressed his friends as 'fellow-citizens by nature, not custom'. Ion is giving his argument maximum effect, therefore, by harnessing the terms together. The final sentence is also full of philosophic import, though it looks forward to philosophers of later ages, to whom the idea of being happy with little was especially congenial. Plato's philosopher in the *Theaetetus* would have been especially sympathetic (see below).

Euripides, in choosing the Ion story, was constrained by the myth. Ion must go to Athens. The Ionian people must be fathered. It is particularly interesting, therefore, that he has chosen to introduce these political issues into his play, when they are, strictly speaking, gratuitous. At the same time, the fact that Ion must go to Athens may indicate that for Euripides the state of *apragmosynē* was not an ideal one, and that the political field remained the legitimate place for those suitably adapted to it, while he registered the difficulties placed in their way in contemporary society.

It has been suggested that Ion's life at Delphi is one of hedonism, and that the idleness of the 'wisely silent' is also hedonism: a deliberate giving up of political duty in favour of an easy life.[21] Ion's arguments, first in his opening monody, and then in his speech to Xouthos, are not entirely consistent; at first, his life at Delphi is described as one of untiring labour. Later, to Xouthos, he says it is leisure he enjoys most. Ion's labour cannot, except by a most perverse logic, be called hedonism, though he enjoys working for Apollo, and in the analysis of contemporary Athens, as we saw, the *chrēstoi* with whom Ion sympathizes are enjoying an *enforced* leisure. To substantiate such an argument, one would have to demonstrate that there was some *positive* pleasure or advantage to be got from *apragmosynē*, and although Ion has hinted at it in the term *scholē*, we have not yet arrived at a worked-out alternative to political activity: we have not yet arrived at the *Bios Theōrētikos*.

[20] Eur. fr. 1113N.
[21] di Benedetto, *Euripide: Teatro e società*, 284. Cf. C. Wolff, op. cit., 175, and Paley on line 646.

Euripides' Antiope

The *Antiope* was acted within a year of 409.[22] Like the *Ion*, it is an aetiological play, and has a happy ending. I shall deal principally with the famous debate between the two brothers Zethos and Amphion, who, though sons of Zeus by a mortal woman, have been brought up by a humble shepherd in ignorance of their origin. None of this affects the debate, which, like that in the *Ion*, is concerned with contemporary political and social issues, far removed from Mount Cithaeron and mythological times. The play survives only in fragments, and in the following paragraphs I shall present my own reconstruction of the debate between the two brothers.

After some kind of prologue, and probably the entrance of the chorus, Amphion comes on and sings a cosmogonic hymn, of which fragment 1023 is probably part: 'Air and Earth I sing, the mother of all'.[23] The fragment 910, which is thought to belong to this play, may belong to a chorus commenting on Amphion:

> Blessed is the man who gives his
> Attention to researches, not aiming
> At the misery of citizens, nor to
> Commit crimes, but contemplating the
> Ageless order of immortal nature,
> Its manner, origin and purpose.
> Concern for shameful deeds never
> Sits near such things.[24]

What Amphion is chanting is here called *historia* — 'researches' — which we called '*theōria*' — contemplation — in the previous chapter.[25] It is the investigation of the heavens and the cause of things, as understood by Anaxagoras and the Ionian 'researchers'. According to Euripides here, it is specifically directed away from the 'misery of citizens': it is an *apragmōn* activity. Anaxagoras, in his sojourn in Athens had been, whether he liked it or not, *apragmōn*, as an alien. This fragment recalls

---

[22] Schol. *Frogs*, 53. Cf. Goossens, *Euripide et Athènes*, 628 n. 62; Webster, *The Tragedies of Euripides*, 163; Kambitsis, ed. *Antiope*, intro. xxxiv.

[23] This fragment was first shown to belong to this play by Wilamowitz.

[24] Cf. Kambitsis for a full review of discussions of this fragment.

[25] Cf. Snell, op. cit., 94; di Benedetto, op. cit. 307.

the anecdote about Anaxagoras, that when asked what was the point of existence, he replied: 'The study of the heavens and the order of the entire universe', and the influence of Anaxagoras seems certain here. Alternatively, the phrase 'Blessed is he . . .' may recall Pythagoras.[26] What must be of great significance in this discussion, however, is that *theōria* is contrasted with a political career, and that the political career is expressed in pejorative terms — aiming at the misery of citizens and to commit crimes.

At the end of this hymn Amphion's brother Zethos enters, on his way to go hunting.[27] The contrast between them is one that we have encountered before.[28] Most reconstructions of this scene give the first speech to Zethos, and this seems right.[29] The debate starts over *mousikē* — either music specifically, or more likely, education in general, before moving on to a general discussion of wisdom and *aretē*.[30] Zethos accuses his brother of cultivating a muse that is idle, fond of wine, and no good in practical matters (frs. 395 and 184). His prejudice against Amphion's muse is an old and tough one: he is neglecting his own concerns; the criticism that was made of Anaxagoras, that he was neglecting 'human goods' (*anthrōpina agatha*).

Euripides establishes at the outset that the debate has got nothing to do with shepherding or Mount Cithaeron, but is set in contemporary Athens amongst the sort of characters who might have been found in the gymnasia or the market-place. Amphion is one of the 'beardless youths' criticized by old Demos in the *Knights* (1382 ff.).

Zethos enlarges his argument:

> Any man of substance and property
> Who neglects the affairs of his house,
> Running after the pleasures of music and dance,
> Will be useless both to his house and the city,
> And no good to his friends. It ruins his
> nature (*physis*) when he gives way to pleasure.

(Fr. 187)

---

[26] Kambitsis, op. cit., devotes a long discussion to antecedents of this phrase.

[27] Horace, *Epistles*, 1. 18, 39–40.

[28] In Chapter 5. Cf. Ar. *Knights*, 1382.

[29] Kambitsis, xxiii; Snell, 82; Goossens, 649. Kambitsis in his reconstruction of this debate, which I do not follow, gives a full review of previous opinions.

[30] Anon. *Rhet. ad Her.* 2. 27. 43.

Zethos is addressing his argument to Amphion, and it is he who is the 'man of substance'. Amphion and his brother are, for the purpose of the debate, young men about Athens. Zethos specifies three ways such a man must prove his worth, his *aretē*: to his house, his city, his friends. This is the traditional definition of *aretē* as it is encountered in the Socratic dialogues; it is a social quality. That quality is also associated with *physis* in this fragment. *Physis* has aristocratic overtones: it was regarded as something that a gentleman's son just grew up to; it 'rubbed off' on him from his elders.[31] This *physis*, and the whole aristocratic life associated with it, is undermined by running after pleasure, and yielding to the desires of the body.[32]

Again, Zethos becomes more specific in another fragment:

You are neglecting what you should not;
The gods bestowed on you a noble nature (*physis*),
Yet you make yourself conspicuous in a womanish shape.
. . . You could not take your place in battle with the hollow shield,
Nor offer vigorous counsels on behalf of others.

(Fr. 185)[33]

Amphion has been born with an aristocratic nature (which is the force of *physis* both here and in the previous fragment, but it has here been strengthened by the unequivocal *gennaian* — noble), but such a nature is being spoiled by taking on an effeminate form — either physically through the lack of hard exercise associated with Zethos and the hunt, or through the wearing of effeminate clothing (such as Aristophanes pictured in the *Thesmophoriazousai*, in the character of Agathon), or both.[34] The consequence will be that he will be unable to perform the part expected of a member of the upper class in time of war, nor will he be in a condition to offer vigorous counsels on behalf of his friends in the assembly and lawcourts. The term translated by 'vigorous' here — *neanikos* — is particularly interesting since it has a slightly ambiguous quality, denoting on the one hand youthful high spirits and vigour, the qualities which Zethos thinks Amphion lacks, and on the other a note

---

[31] *Physis* has aristocratic overtones; Snell, op. cit., 84; Plato, *Meno*, 92 E.
[32] See Xenophon, *Mem.* 4. 5. 11.
[33] This is a reconstruction from the quotation in Plato, *Gorgias*, 485 E.
[34] Ar. *Thesm.* 136.

of insolence, vehemence, and forcefulness, a quality not necessarily in accord with aristocratic *sōphrosynē*, but necessary to survival in democratic debate. Zethos is criticizing his brother for not equipping himself as a member of his class needs to in order to survive in democratic Athens.

The destruction of Amphion's character is also touched on in another fragment: 'How can this be wise, to take a man well endowed by nature (*euphyēs*), and make him worse?' (Fr. 186.) The aristocratic note is struck yet again in *euphyēs*. In another fragment, which might come at the end of the speech, Zethos advises his brother to sing of useful things—ploughing, the care of flocks, and to leave these useless subtleties, which can ruin a man:

> Believe me. Cease these pointless activities,
> And cultivate instead the healthy muse of labour.
> You will seem sensible, if you sing of digging,
> Ploughing the land, and the tending of herds.
> Leave over-ingenious subtleties to others, for they
> Will bring nothing but ruin on your house.
>
> (Fr. 188)[35]

The care of one's estate, one's property—this has been the dominant theme of these fragments: taking care of 'human goods'. This is the base from which a man can operate; once this is in good shape he is in a position to help his friends and serve the city.

The 'human goods' are contrasted with 'over-ingenious subtleties' (which may also carry a note of moral ambiguity) which are not useful in these three vital respects: house, friends, city. It is specifically in contrast to these subtleties that Zethos urges a conservative reticence:

> A decent reticence shows well in a man of worth.
> This idle prattling is all pleasure;
> It is a bad companion, and the city is weakened by it.
>
> (Fr. 219)

---

[35] There is rather similar fragment from Aristophanes' *Banqueters*: 'You waste your time with pipes and lyres, and then tell *me* to go out and dig the fields?' The fragment of the *Antiope*, fr. 188, is another reconstruction from the *Gorgias*.

The 'decent reticence' (*kosmos sigēs*) is 'almost proverbial'.[36] It seems to refer not simply to silence, but rather to silence at the right time, just as *lalein* is not simply chattering, but doing so inopportunely.

It was the custom in this kind of 'contest of speeches' (*agōn logōn*) for the reply to take up points raised in the previous speech. From the condition of the fragments it is not possible to do this with exactness. Nevertheless, some points of consonance do emerge.

Amphion seems at first to reject his brother's charges. He takes a loftier, more philosophic view, by comparison with which his brother seems a trifle naive; his is a rather pessimistic view of life, which paradoxically gives rise to a hedonistic attitude:

> Such is the life of wretched, struggling mortals:
> Not always fortunate, neither unfortunate;
> Sometimes prosperous, then again out of luck.
> When life is so full of uncertainties,
> Why should we not get as much enjoyment as
> We can, and avoid misery?

> (Fr. 196)[37]

This theme of 'that wretched creature, man' is a venerable one in Greek literature, and the consequent search for an untroubled life (*hēsychia*) familiar, especially in the sixth and early fifth centuries.[38] It brings into a discussion that is centred on a specific political and social climate a theme that is older and wider. *Apragmosynē* is a specifically Athenian idea, an expression of conditions in the late fifth century and after. *Hēsychia*, although in this period it may stand as a synonym for *apragmosynē*, has an older and wider history. It is found in the songs of Pindar, for example; here it introduces an atmosphere of archaic gloom into a specifically Athenian and democratic context. The hedonistic outlook is repeated in fr. 193:

> He who meddles in many things which don't concern him
> Is a fool, when he might lead a life *apragmōn*
> And free of care.

---

[36] Pearson ad Soph. fr. 64. 4.   [37] Cf. di Benedetto, op. cit., 304.
[38] Cf. Kambitsis on this fragment.

Why get involved in all sorts of public affairs which do not concern you, he is saying, when you can be leading a pleasant life at home? There is an antithesis here between a public career and a private life, which is in contrast to Zethos' position. For him, public and private life were inextricably entwined, and a safe private life depended on a vigorous public one. He had condemned Amphion as exposing himself to dangers by neglecting this public side of life.

If Amphion has any purpose in his *apragmosynē* (he has not yet mentioned his 'researches'), it may be detected in another fragment:

> If a man is prosperous, and enjoying a good life,
> And does not cultivate things of beauty (*kala*)
> At home, I would not call him fortunate,
> Just the guardian of his wealth.

(Fr. 198)

Amphion is responding to a persistent point of Zethos': you talk of riches, wealth, security, but all this is no use in itself; it must be the means to some end, and that must be *kala*—beautiful and noble things. Perhaps he means the leisure to pursue his 'researches'.[39]

Amphion takes up another of Zethos' accusations: that, in his way of life, he is letting his body get out of condition.[40] Physical prowess is not everything, he says:

> You reproach me for weakness and an
> Effeminate appearance. There is nothing unsound
> About this, however; it is better than
> Overdeveloped physical prowess.

(Fr. 199)

The 'soundness' (*eu phronein*) of which Amphion speaks has nothing intellectual about it. It is the 'wise counsels' that are useful to a city: never mind my weak body, effeminacy even; if I am of quick mind, and a useful counsellor, that is of more moment than a strong arm. In thus setting his brain power

---

[39] Kambitsis on this fragment: 'de s'adonner aux activitées intellectuelles'; cf. Arist. *Pol.* 1333ᵃ 33.

[40] Just the accusation of the unreconstructed Pheidippides against the inhabitants of the 'Thinkery' in the *Clouds*.

against his brother's emphasis on physical fitness, Amphion has made an important progression in his debating position. He is no longer arguing from a point of view of pure *apragmosynē*, of political passivity, but maintaining that he can, in certain circumstances, be more useful to the city than his brother. The remaining fragments of his speech all now argue this new position — that the *apragmōn* actually makes a better citizen than he who meddles too rashly or zealously in public affairs. But first, in another fragment, he again attacks those who overindulge in physical fitness — the 'professional athletes':

> Those who concentrate on developing their bodies
> To a high state of health, if they lack money,
> They make bad citizens. If a man becomes accustomed
> To the unbridled nature of his belly, how can he
> Break free of it?

> (Fr. 201)

It seems likely that Euripides had some personal grudge against such men.[41] In a perhaps slightly more humorous vein, Amphion takes the charge of ruining oneself by the wine-loving muse, of which Zethos had spoken earlier, and underlying which was the concept of upsetting some ideal balance represented by the aristocratic notion of *physis*, and turns it back on his brother: it is the athletes who are upsetting the balance — their addiction to exercise and eating shows their unbridled natures (*akolaston ethos*). He pursues this notion of balance, that the *apragmōn* makes the better citizen because he is less rash, and offers moderate and wise (and not *neanika*) counsels to the city. Consider fragment 194:

> The moderate man (*hēsychos*) is a staunch friend, and
> Serves the city best. He does not lead the people
> Into rash enterprises. Beware the ship's captain who
> Dares too far, and the people's leader too.

Amphion here answers the specific charge Zethos had made repeatedly against him — that of neglecting his affairs, and in consequence his friends and the city too. On the contrary, the *hēsychos*, says Amphion, serves his friends and city better than

---

[41] Cf. Chapter 1.

Zethos. For, by taking a moderate line, he avoids dangers, whereas the rash and headstrong Zethos (he implies), the one who dares too far, leads her into dangerous waters. The term for the leader of the city, here called the *prostatēs tou chthonos*, recalls the term commonly used for a popular leader, *prostatēs tou dēmou*. We are back in the territory of the debate in the *Ion* and the references in the *Orestes*. The 'man with the unstoppable mouth' is the leader who dares too far, whereas the better sort could, or would if they got the chance, offer sager counsels. There is clearly a complex relationship between the *apragmōn* and the city. He is not merely turning his back on it. He is a man naturally accustomed to govern, bred to it. The political climate is such, however, that he is unable to perform this role. He is forced into unwilling inactivity. Consider another fragment:

> With sound advice a city thrives,
> And so too a man's house, and it lends
> Strength in time of war.
> Wise counsel will always overcome the strength of many arms.
> Ignorance is the greatest evil with the mob.

> (Fr. 200)

Here is the sentiment of fragment 199 reiterated: the mind clever in counsel and stratagem will always overcome the arm relying merely on its strength.[42] Amphion is defending the faculty of thought not as something in its own right, or as a means to abstract speculation, but as the instrument for action, just indeed as it is regarded in Homer, in what might therefore be taken as a traditional attitude.[43] He is attacking his brother, then, entirely on his own ground—of advantage to house and city. His speech perhaps concluded:

> I hope I shall always have a sense of proportion (*aidōs*)
> And offer prudent advice, and so make no
> Disturbance which might harm the city.

> (Fr. 202)

Amphion's *aidōs* — a fitting respect for that which properly commands it — is to be seen in opposition to the 'daring too far'

---

[42] Cf. P. Huert, *Le Vocabulaire de l'analyse psychologique dans l'œuvre de Thucydide*, 309, on *gnomē* as thought directed to practical ends.
[43] Cf. Snell, op. cit., 89; di Benedetto, op. cit., 304.

which he attributes to a hypothetical opponent (not necessarily his brother); Zethos had posited a certain antithesis: the active man, looking after his house, the supporter of friends and city (Xenophon, as it were) versus a 'softy' or aesthete, given to pleasure, music, and abstract and useless speculation. To this Amphion poses a new antithesis: the moderate, thoughtful man, cautious but a true friend to the city and his friends, offering his mature judgement in place of the overheated ranting of the popular leader at the mercy of the ignorant rabble: the *chrēstos* as depicted in the *Ion* and the *Orestes*. Amphion in his reply says nothing about his cosmogonic or other researches. He adapts his arguments to those of his brother, though since his brother spoke first, he is bound by the rules of the contest of speeches (*agōn logōn*) to reply in his brother's terms.

Euripides is not composing a philosophic study, and we should not look for consistency when it may not be there. There is no reason to imagine that the Greeks in 409 BC used the term *apragmosynē* with scientific precision any more than we use catchwords nowadays. It is more likely that words slipped about, adopting different shades of meaning at different times and under different circumstances. Thus it is possible that *apragmosynē* as a term of disparagement can be used of a man who shirks his democratic responsibilities, acquiring a more severe tone in the case of a man who, by *physis*, is fitted for public life. On the other hand, and as a term of approval, it signifies the man, like the *autourgos* in the *Electra* who, though seldom in town, and shunning the market square (a blanket term for everything that is worst in democratic politics) is nevertheless the backbone of the nation. The term *apragmōn* does not signify shunning politics here, but keeping politics in a low key, coming only seldom to town, and to the assembly. This ambiguity has already been noted elsewhere in this study.

The character of Zethos has a strong aristocratic colouring. Having, in the discussion of the *Ion*, remarked that terms for the aristocracy had gone out of use, we find them here as key terms in Zethos' accusations. Amphion has by birth, he says, a noble nature, which he is ruining by an addiction to wine, pleasure, and song. The aristocratic character is drawn in terms of outdoor activities, of the hunt, and athletics; in terms of sound estate-management, to create solid prosperity, and in a three-way nexus of house, friends, and city. The solid basis of prosperity, grounded in an estate, is essential not merely to support one's friends and the city when necessary, but also to be able to defend oneself against enemies. It is essential, therefore, to be able to speak in public, either before the lawcourts, or in the assembly. Zethos' accusations against Amphion are in terms of this life: they represent the harsh, Periclean, view of *apragmosynē*. Amphion's addiction to wine, music, and pleasure, is not only ruining him physically, it is also weakening him drastically in areas where he dare not weaken: in his capacity to defend himself at law, and in the assembly, and above all, in his neglect of his worldly prosperity, the basis of everything. It may be characteristic of an aristocratic outlook (though it may also be dictated by the needs of the drama) that the sources of big wealth in the late fifth century — shipping, mining, etc. — are not mentioned. Worldly wealth is understood in terms of the landed estate.

The first part of Amphion's reply attempts a philosophical approach, a loftier, wider, view. It sees the fortunes and misfortunes of men, and takes a pessimistic view. Man is born to suffer, fortunes rise and fall, you might as well enjoy yourself while you can. What is the use of piling up wealth unless it is put to some use? That use is the enjoyment of *kala*, among which he may include leisure and study. He then turns to attack Zethos' emphasis on physical fitness, and with it he redefines the concept of balance which underlies Zethos' position. The athlete, he argues, is himself unbalanced since he overindulges in physical exercise and the appetite that goes with it. Proper balance, by contrast, is to be found in the moderate, restrained, citizen; the man who avoids dangers for the city, the man who stands in contrast to the rash and headstrong popular leader.

The argument which Euripides puts into the mouth of Amphion stands in a tradition — moderate democratic, or moderate oligarchic, according to point of view — which had been expressed by Nicias, and was to be summed up by Aristotle in his preferred constitution (see above, Chapter 4). It was an attitude which persisted therefore, as an upper-class, minority, opinion, for a hundred years.

It is important to note that in both the *Ion* and the *Antiope*, Euripides can see no future for complete *apragmosynē*. Ion goes to Athens to fulfil his destiny: to take up the sceptre and father a new people. Amphion is called on, at the end of the *Antiope*, to construct the walls of Thebes with the aid of his music.[44] Ultimately, there is no life outside the city; even fourth-century theorists, while setting the Contemplative Life above all others, still conceived it as something taking place within the context of city life. It is still a social existence. This lends weight to the view of *apragmosynē* outlined above, as a kind of moderate democracy; something conceived of by those who regarded the democracy as overheated and diseased.

Plato's Gorgias

It is likely that the debate in the *Antiope* reflected a debate going on in Athens at the time, and it is worth while going on to look at parts of Plato's *Gorgias* which quote from the *Antiope* and therefore reflect the same debate.[45] The dramatic date of the *Gorgias* varies from the early 420s down to 405, but in any case the date of composition must have been only a few years later, in the 390s.[46] The discussion in the *Gorgias* between Callicles and Socrates has important similarities to that in the *Antiope*; Callicles likens himself to Zethos, and like him speaks first. His basic point is that the study of philosophy is becoming at a certain age, but if pursued beyond that age it becomes contemptible. Concentrating on philosophy, a man finds himself ill-adapted to the world, and in some danger from enemies:

> If you are of good birth (*euphyēs*) and continue with philosophic studies beyond the proper age, you are bound to be ignorant of things of which you should have experience if you are to be a gentleman and of good reputation. You will know nothing of the traditional laws of the city, or of the habits of thought necessary for dealing with men both in public and private. You will be ignorant of the pleasures and desires of men, and altogether you will know nothing of human nature.
>
> (*Gorg.* 484 C)

This is the language of Zethos and probably of Pericles also. The first and obvious difference from the debate in the *Antiope* is that Socrates is blamed not for contemplation or researches, but for

---

[44] Pap. Inv. 485, Kambitsis fr. 48 D.   [45] So Dodds on *Gorgias*, 485 E 3.
[46] Dodd's introduction to his edition of the *Gorgias*, 17.

philosophizing. Socrates, as Plato reports elsewhere, had found the Ionian researches of Anaxagoras insufficient, and had turned his attention to ethical concerns; he had enquired into the nature of such terms as *sōphrosynē* (prudence, moderation) and *dikaiosynē* (justice). This enquiry may have been not only ethical, but also philological; at this period, when abstract formulations were coming more and more into use, there may have been confusion as to what exactly an abstract noun *was*. It may even be that abstract nouns such as these led Plato to develop the idea of the Forms.

As far as Callicles is concerned, however, these abstract speculations are pursued at the cost of much more important matters:

> Such a man, even if well born, is not a real man if he shuns the heart of the city and the market square, where, as the poet says, 'men win renown', wasting the rest of his life whispering in a corner with three or four young men, and never uttering anything big, bold, or effective.
>
> (Ibid. 485 D)

The logic of Callicles is straightforward: good birth is the foundation, and knowledge of the city's laws and of business, public and private, the thronging intercourse of the city, is the training to enable a gentleman (*kalokagathos*) to take his proper place in the life of the city. This is a view which never changed, and is an important reminder, if any were needed, of how far Plato stood outside the mainstream of Greek life. A tincture of philosophy—of abstract discussion—adds charm to one's conversation, but that is as far as it should go. That Socrates should continue to hold these discussions into middle age deserves a whipping. Callicles' indignation has a strong foundation: the man who is not conversant with the city's ways, who is not trained to speak in public, is in no slight danger from those who may wish to harm him. Dragged into court, he would gape and be helpless (Ibid., 486 B). Callicles finishes his argument with a plea to Socrates to give up his profitless existence and adapt himself to that which brings real profit: 'Stop cross-questioning people on these trifling matters, and concentrate on the things which bring life, good reputation, and all other goods' (Ibid., 486 C).

The whole speech is interesting in several respects: Plato knew

Euripides' play, and borrowed from it to make up Callicles' argument. Now, although Socrates was a well-known figure in Athens when Euripides wrote his play, it is not the figure of Socrates which is juxtaposed to Zethos, but one apparently closer to the Anaxagorean researchers. Socrates' attitude is very different from that of Amphion. His concern is ethical. His first, revolutionary, statement is that defence and retaliation against one's enemies are less important than a correct and innocent mode of life. To adopt such a mode of life, characterized by *sōphrosynē* and justice, is the overriding imperative, and to be abused, or even put to death, counts for less than failing to achieve such a life. He calls the pursuit of this existence the philosophic life, and he contrasts it with the political life:

> What kind of life should one lead; either the one you recommend to me, the life of a man who can address the assembly and has practised the speech-maker's art, and leads a political life the way you do, or, on the other hand, this philosophic life . . .
>
> (Ibid., 500 c)

Socrates does not define, in this dialogue, what he means by his two key terms *sōphrosynē* and *dikaiosynē*, and doubtless Plato himself was still struggling to evolve his philosophic system, and the idea of the 'good' which should stand in contradistinction to 'human goods', as commonly understood. Its character, however, must be in some way defined in opposition to the corrupt democracy which he mentions several times and censures in the most severe terms. Talking of the achievements of Themistocles, Pericles, and the earlier statesmen, he says:

> It is said they made the city great, but no one realizes that, thanks to them, the city is swollen, and underneath all is corrupt. The city has become stuffed with harbours, dockyards, walls, tribute, and all such rubbish. Prudence and justice are ignored.
>
> (Ibid., 518 E)

The entire achievement of Athens since the Persian invasion is dismissed as 'rubbish' and set in conscious opposition to *sōphrosynē* and *dikaiosynē*. This helps to throw a little light on the sort of context in which Socrates is struggling to define these words. That context is nostalgic, reactionary: Athens has been corrupted; *ergo*, she was once in a state of grace, perhaps possessed of justice and prudence. Also Athens has become more democratic; *ergo*, that state of grace was a less democratic one. The virtues which Socrates prizes are not democratic ones. Socrates can, and in other dialogues does, look abroad to other city-states, such as Sparta, where such virtues are apparently still held in respect.

Plato juxtaposes to the excesses of the democracy a life which he styles 'philosophic', but which is none other than the life of those 'wisely silent' in the face of public hostility, though bedecked with speculative trimmings. Speculation in the *Gorgias* is at a fairly primitive level compared with Plato's later work; nevertheless, in this book he begins the process whereby he introduces a transcendental system which will justify the *apragmosynē* of the philosopher. Towards the end of the book, he recounts the myth of the Last Judgement. This, like others of Plato's myths, is of such artistic vividness, that one is almost tempted to ask whether Plato himself believed it, or whether he was carried away by his own artistic powers. For the sake of this discussion, however, we shall have to assume that he accepted it. According to Socrates, this life is a preparation for that day of judgement when we shall stand naked before our judges in the underworld:

I shall leave on one side, therefore, the honours which men hold dear, and shall try to live according to the truth as it really is, to live as best I can, and when I come to die, to die as best as I can.

(Ibid., 526 D)

Everything which Callicles values is summed up in those 'honours', which Socrates rejects in the face of the 'greater assize'. It is before this Last Judgement that the philosopher will receive his just deserts; talking of the souls that come before the judges, Socrates says: 'Sometimes they see approach them, in reverence and truth, the soul of a private man, perhaps of a philosopher, who has minded his own business and not meddled in the affairs of others during his lifetime . . .' (Ibid., 526 C). Why is it that when this philosopher is brought naked before his judges, it is his *apragmosynē* which is stressed? Throughout the dialogue, the philosophic life is contrasted with the political one, and therefore the *unpolitical*, or *apragmōn* aspect of his life must have been uppermost in Plato's mind. The supernatural judgement serves an important role in the argument. Socrates, in urging a course of behaviour so extraordinary as not to seek to defend oneself in the Athenian democracy, must needs propose a reason sufficiently striking to convince his hearers. The supernatural judgement serves that purpose. In putting it forward he has lifted the whole debate about *apragmosynē* on to an entirely new plane.[47]

The mode of living proposed by Socrates in the *Gorgias* does not constitute contemplation, however. This final stage in the journey does not appear until the *Republic* and the concept of the Forms. Once Plato had evolved the idea of a supernatural reality, both invisible and superior to common reality, the task of his philosopher is revealed: it is to train himself to the contemplation of these Forms, and ultimately the contemplation of the Form of goodness itself. This is described in the celebrated parable of the cave in Book 7. The situation in the cave is described in the same kind of language as the democracy in the *Gorgias*. The condition of the prisoners, that is to say, and the constant parade of shadows which they are compelled to watch, are a metaphor for the political life under the Athenian democracy. There are honours to be won among the prisoners: 'There were honours, glory, and prizes for those among them who could most clearly perceive events going on around them, and could remember what had gone before, and what was most likely to happen . . .' (*Rep.* 516 c).

These honours, as we saw in Chapter 1, are at the heart of the democracy, of Greek life itself, and the man who rejects them is rejecting the most significant mark of a man's worth that the Greeks knew how to bestow. But it is these prizes that the prisoner who has escaped from the cave — i.e. the philosopher — no longer values once he has learnt to gaze on the sun itself, which is the metaphor for the contemplation of the Form of the Good — *hē tou agathou idea* (517 B). Plato admits that once his philosopher has become accustomed to absolute justice he will have a rough time of it under ordinary justice; to continue the metaphor, once the philosopher has learnt to gaze on the sun itself, if he should then return to the cave he will be as bewildered and disorientated as when he first emerged from it. As Callicles had said in the

---

[47] The notion of a supernatural judgement was in existence before Plato. Cf. Aesch. *Eum.* 269 ff.; Pindar *Ol.* 2. 57.

Gorgias, such a man, dragged into court, would 'gape and be helpless'.

Elsewhere, in another celebrated metaphor, the philosopher in the democracy is likened to a man standing under a wall during a driving storm of dust and hail (*Rep.* 496 D).[48] The *Bios Theōrētikos* which Plato elaborates in the *Republic* differs in a fundamental way from that of the Ionian researchers. For them it had meant observation of the real world, scientific study as we would understand the term. But for Plato it has nothing to do with the world. His philosopher withdraws his gaze from outward things and concentrates his mind inwardly, contemplating abstract ideas. In the world, men are constrained to achieve justice in whatever rough and ready manner they can, as occasion requires. The philosopher, on the other hand, withdrawn from the commerce of men, fixes his mind on the abstract concept of justice in the absolute. Whether Plato himself had any idea of what this concept was like, or what it consisted of, we do not know.

Plato's *Bios Theōrētikos* requires leisure, and the terms in which Plato values leisure are reminiscent of Ion: 'The free man always has time at his disposal to converse in peace at his leisure . . . the orator is always talking against time, hurried on by the clock . . . he is a slave disputing about a fellow slave . . .' (*Theaet* 172 D).[49] The 'free man' is, of course, the philosopher, as becomes clear in the description of the philosophic life which follows: the philosopher does not know his way to the market-place or the lawcourt, or council-chamber; he takes no interest in the rivalries of political cliques, meetings, dinners; it is only his body which sojourns in the city while his thought takes wing . . . he looks a fool if he has to appear in court, but he in turn laughs at things most people respect (*Theaet.* 173 D ff.). Surely this philosopher would have concurred with Ion when he told his father: 'The reward is equal, whether enjoying greatness, or being content with little' (*Ion*, 646–7).

The most revolutionary aspect of Plato's philosopher, however, the most paradoxical thing about him, is that, though incapable

---

[48] Cf. Dodds, 'Euripides the Irrationalist', *CR* 43 (1929), 201: 'The contemplative life . . . is a sheltered and beautiful one, but for all that, it is the refuge of despair . . .'

[49] Cf. Antisthenes, the friend of Socrates and one of the first 'bare-foot layabouts' positively attested, on *scholē* in X. *Mem.* 4. 44.

amid the reality of the democratic city, the laughing-stock of ordinary citizens, and preferring a life apart, the philosopher is nevertheless, precisely because he does not value worldy honours, the only man truly fit to govern. He must therefore be compelled to do so. This point is emphasized in the *Republic* and Plato returns to it several times: 'Good men will not consent to govern for cash or honour . . . they will not work for honour, they are not ambitious. We must therefore compel them . . .' (*Rep.* 347 B).

Again, the philosopher, after many years of arduous study and training, and not before the age of fifty, will have to take his turn at 'the weary business of politics' and do his duty as ruler, not for the honour of it, but out of necessity (*Rep.* 540 B). 'Our job as law-givers', says Socrates, 'will be to compel the best minds to attain what we have called the highest form of knowledge . . . but then to prevent them remaining in the upper world . . . and to compel them to return again into the cave, and share the labours (*ponoi*) and rewards (*timai*) of the prisoners.' (*Rep.* 519 C.)

To emphasize that his philosophic life is somehow more real than real life, Plato likens it to a waking state, while the masses are asleep, and only dream of life: 'The city for us will be wide awake, not, as now, in a dream: the masses squabbling for power amongst themselves in a sort of shadow-contest' (*Rep.* 520 C). It is the essence of Plato's philosophic life that it consists in the rejection of worldly honours; we have seen how, time after time, he returns to the struggles for power in the democracy, and the glory associated with it. Plato is proposing a transformation of the State from its most fundamental foundations upwards.

Plato's Political Career

Plato provides a comprehensive and coherent description of the philosopher and the *Bios Theōrētikos;* given the magnitude of the changes proposed, it would not be surprising to find that his own life corresponded but imperfectly to it. At the beginning of the *Seventh Letter*, he tells how, as a youth, he intended, like many others, to enter public life, 'as soon as he was master of himself', in other words, as soon as he was twenty.[50] In the revolution

---

[50] The authenticity of the *Seventh Letter* has been much disputed. 'Most scholars accept it as genuine' (Hamilton, intro. to Penguin translation, 1973). Finlay (*Aspects of Antiquity*, 80) does not accept it, nor does Edelstein (*Plato's Seventh Letter*, intro. 4).

of 404 the Thirty were installed, and he was invited to join them. Plato is vague about his relations with the Thirty, though he is writing fifty years after the event. 'I thought they would lead the city from her evil ways into justice; I watched them eagerly to see what they would do' (324 D). As he watched their abuses, he withdrew in disgust at these evils (325 A). He had been the friend and relation of several of them: Critias was one of the Thirty, Charmides among the Ten set over the Piraeus, but Plato was certainly not one of the fifty-one oligarchs. Neither, so far as we know, did they attempt to incriminate him as they did Socrates. If Plato was directly associated with the oligarch we know of no way in which he was implicated in their crimes, and he was never, so far as we know, attacked afterwards on that account (as were, for example, some of Lysias' clients). Nor was he compelled to lie low in the aftermath of 404; he goes on in the *Letter* to say that 'once again a desire to enter politics took hold of me' (325 A), and this was before 399. The Thirty had been a shock to Plato; his high expectations contrasted painfully with the reality. But then the restored democracy put Socrates to death, and this was a second severe shock. Plato still had, or thought he had, designs on a political career, but the more he looked, and the more he understood, the less confidence he had of being able to do anything:

Nothing could be done without friends and companions, and such men were not easy to find, since our city was no longer administered according to the standards and practices of our fathers . . . Further, the written law and the customs were being corrupted at an astounding rate.

(325 D)

As he gazed upon the 'whirlpool' of political life, he felt 'dizzy', and he kept waiting 'for favourable moments, and finally saw clearly in regard to all states now existing that without exception their system of government is bad' (326 A).

Plato was destined to a public career by his family, his education; his forebears, his uncles, cousins, his brother, all had held, or were holding, or about to hold, prominent positions in the State. It was assumed by all that Plato would do so too. The experiences discussed above, however, show Plato undergoing that process of self-discovery by which his mentor had set such store. Plato was painfully coming to know himself; to know that the real world, the imperfect world, was not for him.[51] His first contacts with politics at the time of the Thirty and their activities are instinctively judged against an ideal standard; at each turn the real political world is judged and found wanting. Plato naturally inhabited a world of ideal states, and was not prepared to compromise himself by contact with real ones. Plato's withholding from a political career was principally a consequence of his temperament, which was scholarly, objective, shy of involvement. Yet this truth about his own nature was not one which he was able, for a long time, to accept. He continually promised himself that eventually he would become involved. The real politician, statesman, reformer, especially if he enjoys Plato's advantages, does not wait to be invited to participate. Yet Plato was over sixty when he received Dionysius' invitation to go to Syracuse. The overwhelming motive that compelled him to go was his own self-respect: he was afraid lest he should seem afraid to put his ideas into practice; that he should prefer to construct ideal states on paper, and yet shun the opportunity to construct them in reality. In addition, Plato had received the invitation at the urging of his close friend Dion. Not to go would have laid him open to the charge of deserting his friend. He would, he says, have incurred the most odious shame, which must at all costs be avoided. Plato, unlike his imaginary philosopher, is caught in an all too Greek dilemma: to desert or not to desert his friend.

How did Plato behave when he actually had the opportunity to put his theories into practice? Admittedly, Dionysius was not the most promising material out of which to construct the philosopher-king. Nevertheless, a man of Plato's intellect, if he had genuinely sought to improve conditions in Syracuse, and if he enjoyed the respect that Plato appeared to do for the first few months of his sojourn there, might have achieved something, however limited. He might have recommended some limited political reforms, as a start towards converting absolute tyranny into enlightened kingship.

Plato, however, thought more of his own pedagogic principles

---

[51] Edelstein draws attention to Arist. *Metaph.* 1. 6 which, in describing Plato's early years, makes no mention of any political career.

and moral standards than the welfare of the Syracusans. He persisted in viewing the situation as Plato- rather than Syracuse-centred. In defending the part he played in Syracuse (330 D–331 D) Plato characterizes himself as the doctor *vis-à-vis* the patient. But his attitude towards Dionysius was rather that of the confessor towards the penitent.[52] Before any practical reforms might be attempted, Dionysius would be required to undertake a long and arduous course of self-regeneration under Plato's tutorship. The ineptness of this approach is underlined by Dionysius' own complaint afterwards that he had been willing to undertake various limited reforms in his rule, but that Plato first required him to reform himself in accordance with Plato's principles.[53] The result was total failure for Plato, and worse for Dion.

Plato was over sixty; he had presided over his school in the Academy for twenty years. We must allow for a certain inflexibility; nevertheless it must be admitted that in Syracuse his political judgement was hopeless. In no sense can it be said that Plato's own political and philosophical studies had prepared him for real-life politics. On the contrary. His practical experiences contrast dismally with his theoretical programme in the *Republic*, where only after a lifetime of study and contemplation was the philosopher fitted to take on the wearisome business of government. Such a lifetime of study and contemplation had only turned Plato into, dare we say it, a stiff-necked pedant, plainly out of his depth in the real world.

We should dismiss, therefore, the popular notion that Plato was really dying to reform the world, but that unfortunately the world was not ready for him. His mind was of an imaginative and speculative turn; he saw the wider issues too clearly, and, by nature prone to think in terms of ideals, he was ill suited to take part in real politics. Yet, though he had no taste for it, he believed he ought to make the attempt, and he went to Sicily out of a sense of duty, and out of a fear of what others might think of a man who, while constructing ideal societies on paper, was afraid of the chance to put them into practice. This fear for his reputation bears witness to the extent to which Plato still felt bound by normal standards of behaviour.

---

[52] Grote, IX. 71.   [53] *Letter Three*, 315 D, 319 B; *Letter Seven*, 331 D.

Socrates

Before closing this chapter, it would be useful to enquire whether Socrates, the real Socrates in so far as we can identify him, was regarded in his lifetime as *apragmōn*. In previous discussions of *apragmosynē*, the name of Socrates has been invoked as an important, if not *the* important, figure in this context. Thus in the first article to bear the name *Apragmosyne*, Nestle concluded that 'es ist wirklich nicht einzusehen, warum es ausgeschlossen sein sollte, bei den *Apragmones* des Thukydideischen Perikles, auch an Sokrates und seinen Kreis zu denken.' (139.)[54] Wade-Gery, in a reply to this article, concluded: 'I cannot believe Socrates was a figure of any consequence in 430.'[55] The question was reopened in 1953 by Karl Dienelt who also denied Nestle's view, and claimed that Socrates had always been involved in the life of the city.[56]

Ehrenberg, in 1947, agreed with Nestle: 'With men like Anaxagoras and Socrates a new ideal of life came into being, which would appear as pure laziness to most people.'[57]

It is likely that Nestle comes nearest to the truth when he refers to Socrates' 'circle' as the *apragmones* to whom Pericles referred. As we saw in an earlier chapter, the kind of young men with whom Socrates consorted in, say, the *Charmides*, were very likely *apragmones*. What of Socrates himself?

In Plato's *Apology*, which must to a large degree represent Socrates' own views, Socrates tells the jury how he was prevented from entering public life by the admonition of his inner voice, since in politics an honest man would not last long (32 A). Again, after he has been condemned, he explains to the jury how he never cared for the things most men cared for — money, his household, the generalship, popular leadership, other magistracies and secret clubs, party organizations — thinking he was too strict in his principles to survive long in that sort of thing (36 B). Elsewhere Socrates is associated by Aristophanes with an 'idle existence' (*Frogs*, 1498), and such men as he are called 'idle fellows' and 'good-for-nothings' (*Clouds*, 316, 334). In the *Gorgias*

[54] Nestle, 'Apragmosyne', *Philologus*, 81 (1926).
[55] Wade-Gery, 'Thucydides Son of Melesias', *JHS* 52 (1932).
[56] Dienelt, 'Ápragmosyne', *Wiener Studien*, 66 (1953), 94–104.
[57] Ehrenberg, 'Polypragmosyne: A Study in Greek Politics', *JHS* 67 (1947), 46–67.

he describes how, being chosen by lot as *prytanis* and *epistatēs* (president of the assembly for the day), he caused a laugh when he found himself ignorant of the proper procedure for putting a motion to the vote (473 E).[58]

The evidence in Xenophon's writing is confused, and parts of what appear to be Socrates' own ideas are muddled up with the author's own preoccupations. In one anecdote, for example, Antiphon asks Socrates how he supposes he can make others into politicians when he abstains from politics himself. Socrates replies: 'How should I play a more important role in politics than by turning out as many competent politicians as possible?' (*Mem.* 1. 6. 15.) Even in Plato's *Gorgias*, Socrates had not been opposed to others at least performing a political role; his point was that they were not fit to do so until they had undergone 'philosophy's purification'. Xenophon elsewhere, however, states a contrary position: the true friends of Socrates, Crito and others, associate with him not that they might shine in the assembly or the courts, but that they might become proper gentlemen (*kalokagathoi*), and do their duty by their households, their friends, and the city (*Mem.* 1. 2. 48). Again, there is the anecdote about Charmides, in which Socrates tries to persuade him to take his rightful place in public life. He explains how the assembly is full of dunces and weaklings, and Charmides, who is on terms of intimacy with the first men in the State, should have no trouble addressing them.

My dear man, don't be ignorant of yourself, and don't make the mistake so many make; most people are so busy prying into other people's business that they never turn aside to examine themselves. Don't neglect this; strive to know yourself, and don't neglect the city's affairs . . .

(*Mem.* 3. 7. 9)

The emphasis on self-knowledge is clearly authentic — it is a theme in the *Apology* too. Xenophon has, however, unconsciously linked it to his own train of thought, with which it is really in conflict. This comes out clearly in a passage in which the virtue

---

[58] Dodds (ad loc.) believes Socrates is referring here to the trial of the generals after Arginousai. Xenophon says, however, that on that occasion he was opposing an unconstitutional motion (*Hell.* 1. 7. 15; cf. Plato, *Apol.* 32 B). It is inconceivable that the two could have been muddled up.

of self-control, the virtue by which the Platonic Socrates sets the greatest store, is made out to consist of all those qualities prized by Zethos in the *Antiope*: proper regulation of the body, household management, and to be useful to one's friends and the city (*Mem.* 4. 5. 10). This is Xenophon speaking. How could Socrates have gained notoriety peddling such banalities as these?

In the *Crito*, Socrates devotes a long speech to a defence of the city's laws, and the absolute necessity of obedience even at the cost of one's life. Again, he was the friend and confidant of many in the first rank of public life. Xenophon goes to some lengths to exculpate him from the crimes and excesses of Critias and Alcibiades. Like Euripides and others, he was invited to Macedonia around 408 by King Archelaos. He preferred to stay in Athens.[59]

Socrates explains in the *Apology* that, although debarred by his divine sign from actual participation in politics (other than as the lot decreed), he never ceased to go among the citizens and talk to them, asking them about goodness and other such things, examining himself and exhorting them to examine themselves: 'I go about privately discussing these things, a bit of a busybody, and making a nuisance of myself, but I would never dare to get up in the assembly to offer the meeting my opinion' (*Apol.* 31 C). The antithesis set out by Socrates is by no means a simple one, as shown by his vocabulary: he is a 'busybody' (*polypragmōn*) — in private.

Socrates, it seems is an *apragmōn*, but a very special case. He is debarred from political involvement, from addressing the assembly, by his divine sign. Yet he feels impelled to go about the city constantly accosting the citizens, questioning their accepted notions of commonly held ethical qualities — courage, and so on — but above all, wisdom and justice. He himself does not regard this as an *apragmōn* existence. Socrates is in fact both *apragmōn* and not. He is a case on his own.[60]

In closing, it will be useful to make one or two comments on the foregoing.

First, Plato's philosopher, as we meet him in the *Republic* and

---

[59] Arist. *Rhet.* 1398ᵃ 24.

[60] Cf. X. *Mem.* 3. 11. 16 where Socrates himself is aware of his unique status. See J. W. Roberts, *The City of Socrates*, 232–49, for a recent assessment of Socrates' general significance.

the *Theaetetus*, is not a portrait of Socrates. Although both Plato's and Xenophon's portraits of Socrates are, as it were, 'contaminated', an outline can be discerned of what seems to be the authentic man, and he, very much unlike Plato's philosopher, is an inhabitant of the democracy: his probing and questioning, his going about among the 'fullers and cobblers', even his confusion as *epistatēs*, everything that we know about him, could only exist in the democracy. His restless intelligence is itself characteristic of the democracy.

Second, to go back to Plato, it is clear that he derived his portrait of the philosopher as a reaction to what he regarded as the 'excesses' of the democracy. In almost every description of the philosopher, his mode of life is contrasted explicitly with the vigorous, competitive, vulgar but energetic, democracy, and his most characteristic quality lies in his rejection of the honours and prizes which the democracy bestows on its leading men. In fact, Plato constructed his philosopher precisely as a reaction to the democracy, as a new kind of man, who should be, first of all, superior to the attractions of those prizes and honours. In so doing, Plato was making one of the greatest revolutions in Greek thought. In our brief examination of his own career we saw how imperfectly he was able to match his own actions to his theoretical model, and how strong were the social pressures on even a man of his intellectual stature.

Third, and most important, it was seen that Plato derived his concept of the Contemplative Life, not from any previous thinker, nor from the *Bios Theōrētikos* of the Ionian 'researchers', but as a consequence of his own political experiences and in the climate of thought at the end of the fifth century. It was seen how the concept of *apragmosynē* had been articulated by Euripides, and how Plato, through the figure of Socrates, dignified the *apragmōn* existence by constructing a philosophic framework on it, and in particular how he validated it by the concept of a transcendental reality more real than vulgar reality.

Finally, it reminds us, if such a reminder is necessary, that Plato, in his way of life and thought, was absolutely untypical of Greek life, that his ideas were in contradiction to normal Athenian beliefs and thought, and that he would have been regarded by the man in the street, in so far as he regarded him at all, as a 'layabout', and a 'crank'.

8

Conclusion

Apragmosynē grew out of the Athenian democracy — as a product of it and as a reaction against it. Peasant farmers may have been quietly working their farms for generations before Ephialtes and scarcely given a thought to Athens. But once the radical democracy took its final shape the character of their lives changed — in so far as they did not respond to the new regime they had become *apragmones*. *Apragmosynē* as a contrary tendency within the democracy seems to have persisted until the eclipse of Athens by Macedon.

Apragmosynē was a contradiction of what was most characteristic in the democracy. The qualities in the democracy which most excited the animosity of its enemies — its energy, variety, innovation, ambition — qualities despised and repudiated by Critias and Plato and those who regarded themselves as conservatives and traditionalists; these qualities were in fact only the reinterpretation of a tradition which went back to Homer. To strive for fame and honour had been the preoccupation of the heroes, and though other Greek states might regard the Athenians as aggressive, competitive, greedy, even tyrannical, they had a perfectly legitimate precedent, which they did not hesitate to invoke.

The *apragmōn* is first attested in 431 BC, in circumstances not easy to clarify. Euripides' Odysseus seemed to be growing weary of the life of a *chrēstos*: the career of a leader of men, a general perhaps, seemed to offer no rewards other than fame and honour (which, in the speech, are in fact sufficient). Yet if Odysseus reaps no material reward in the execution of his duty, others, generals perhaps among them, were certainly prospering from the Empire at this time. The problem is plagued by lack of evidence, but the explanation may lie in a culture gap — Thucydides tells how after Pericles died a different breed of politician arose, of lesser stature, pandering to the crowd. None of these, so far as we know, drew their wealth from land, but from various kinds of quasi-industrial enterprises. It seems possible that at this moment, 431, there was taking place a transition — a new generation was arising, and that at the outbreak of the war attitudes had polarized. A new kind of rich man emerged who, not feeling constrained by traditional loyalties and values, could see more clearly the immense possibilities the Empire afforded. Investment overseas by Athenians must have been of a speculative nature, subject to the fortunes of war. In the event, the Athenians lost all of it. It is a question of mentality, of ideology — some men will hazard their money in risk investments; others will keep it safe in land, especially if it has been inherited.

So, if some men plunged into the Empire, others reacted differently. The 'internationalists' — aristocratic, reserved men out of tune with the imperial spirit, whose ideological sympathies lay with Sparta — these were the men who constituted the reaction against democracy. When we encounter them in the 420s they are indeed *apragmones*; the democracy offers them no channel for advancement. They feel displaced, since, ideologically, they are on the wrong side. In 428, Critias had no inclination for politics; Antiphon too chose not to become directly involved. According to Thucydides, men of education and refinement were liable to attack by a more populist kind of leader, a 'watch-dog of the people'. Antiphon and Critias are the two most interesting kinds of these *apragmones* in the early years of the war, when the war-fever was at its height.

There is a tension in the condition of these men who, bred to a leading place, are yet frittering away their lives in obscurity. This tension emerges occasionally, in Aristophanes for example, when Bdelycleon, he who loves to dress in an unpatriotic, Spartan, style, is accused in the street of aiming at the tyranny; or in Euripides in the period immediately after the Sicilian fiasco, when the playwright, describing a meeting of the Athenian assembly, and those such as the simple countryman or the loud-mouthed demagogue who address it, also notices the better sort, the *chrēstoi*, who are 'wisely silent'. In these years between the collapse of the Sicilian expedition and the oligarchic coup, they seem incapable of taking action within the machinery of the democracy.

In that same scene, Euripides points out that, though the

chrēstoi remain silent, they approve what the simple peasant has
to say, and it seems likely that Euripides and the oligarchic
theorists had a special place in their hearts for the peasant. It
is certainly true that the peasant played a key role in their
theoretical programmes. As I pointed out earlier, the *autourgos*
performs a double role for them: on the one hand he is the 'sturdy
yeoman', modestly prosperous, independent, capable of
supplying his own arms, the backbone of the nation; on the other,
he is the poor farmer living far from Athens, coming only rarely
to the assembly, bowed with toil, and respectful of his betters.
The latter type was the peasant the oligarchs were able to overawe
in 411, but it was the former who figured in their theoretical
programmes, and who legitimated their coup.

The portraits of the peasant in Euripides and Aristophanes are
complementary. The latter's reflects his maker's temperament;
he is high-spirited, fiercely independent, lusty and vigorous,
proud of his country ways, his traditions, and festivals, hating
the city; the former is more sober, responsible, serious, hard-
working; both are pillars of traditional values and contrast with
the supposed corruption of city life.

The bond which the oligarchs imagined to exist between the
peasants and themselves could only have been created in
opposition to the democracy. In the time of Solon the rich
landowner had been the peasant's enemy.

The creation of the popular jury courts by which the
democracy achieved its final form seems almost from the start
to have put fear into the hearts of rich Athenians. The claim
to *apragmosynē* with which so many lawcourt speeches are prefaced
gives a vivid picture of a class of Athenian who was not from
a governing tradition and did not aspire to power. Both Plato
and Aristotle in the fourth century juxtapose the money-makers
with those who seek for power. Most of the evidence for the rich
apragmōn comes from the fourth century, but there are scattered
references from the fifth in Aristophanes, and in Antiphon's
Tetralogies. Crito, as portrayed by Plato and Xenophon, would
be one such. There seems to have been a natural antipathy
between these men and those who swarmed upon the benches
of the jury courts. The tone of their speeches is invariably
conciliatory and pleading: to men who make do on half a
drachma a day they will boast of spending thousands on civic

splendour, festivals, processions, ceremonies. The condition of these men, as represented in their speeches, was one particularly congenial to the jurymen: the wealthy citizen lavished his wealth on public events, but adopted at the same time a timid and retiring disposition towards themselves — adopted, in fact, an un-Athenian attitude, for this supplication of the jury was something otherwise to be despised: it was *mikropsychos*, the sort of behaviour acceptable in a metic, an alien living in the city on sufferance. A citizen, as Aristotle defines him, is one who partakes of *timē* — the honours and rewards of the State — and should take a proper and normal pride in the dignity of citizenship.

This fear of the assembly had an inhibiting effect even on those who did aspire to partake of *timē*: in a man like Nicias, *apragmosynē* seemed to sit nervously side by side with a desire to conciliate the crowd with lavish displays — a 'certain vulgar ostentation' or *philotimia* as Plutarch says; in him, even love of prominence and prestige is conditioned by a fear of the crowd. Others such as Lamachus and Laches, who performed duties traditionally assigned to members of the upper class, of leading the people into battle and negotiating on their behalf, have a definite nervousness about the assembly. Aristophanes' portrait of Lamachus is of a rather pitiable character, and Laches was prosecuted for mishandling a command. These prosecutions must have exerted a considerable disincentive to a prospective general; some stayed away from Athens after a campaign for fear of it. Aristophanes' point in his fantasy trial-scene in the *Wasps* is that the qualities which make a good general are not the same as those necessary to defend oneself before an Athenian jury when confronted by a 'watch-dog of the people'. In the fourth century, the functions of general and politician became clearly separated.

I have identified three broad categories of *apragmosynē* in the late fifth century. Of these, two are linked. In 411 and 404, when the oligarchs made their attempts to seize power, it was in the name of the hoplite section of the population. This is never explicitly identified with the *autourgos*, but it included him, and it was his virtues, predominantly *apragmosynē*, which was attractive to the oligarchs in other parts of the hoplite census. The collapse of the oligarchs in both events was in circumstances shameful to themselves though redounding to the credit of the democracy.

The reaction of Plato to these events is of the greatest importance. It was not merely that his closest relatives and friends had failed in their attempt to set up a government which should be distinguished, in contrast to the democracy, by moderation and justice, but that their conduct was itself actually most unjust and immoderate. 404 was a year of anarchy and murder. Ironically, it was the democracy when it was restored which distinguished itself by its moderation and humanity. Plato's disorientation must have been profound.

It was out of this that he set about constructing a new kind of *apragmosynē* that should be proof against the errors and crimes of Critias and his like. This is the origin of the Contemplative Life: Plato's philosopher will come out of the cave, will recognize that city life with its honours and prizes, everything that for Aristotle made man a political being, is a sham, a delusion, a shadow. The philosopher will be a free man, while those in the lawcourts will be 'a slave disputing with another slave'. The philosopher's freedom and the politician's slavery both have reference to *timē*, the honour which, conferred by the city, validates the citizen's existence. In thus raising the philosopher above the honours and prizes of city life, Plato made what I regard as one of the greatest leaps in Greek thought. Man is a political being, said Aristotle, but Plato's philosopher is a new kind of man who is not political.

When he introduced this figure into his work, Plato had encouraged the illusion that his philosopher was merely continuing a tradition that stretched back into the sixth century and that Greece had long known philosophers who were above politics. His philosopher should be dignified by seeming to stand in a venerable tradition stretching back to the 'Seven Wise Men'. In fact, whether Plato knew it or not, earlier philosophers had stood in a different relation to the city — they were 'wise men' who directed their intellects towards the solution of practical problems.

In order to justify his vision of the philosophic life, Plato introduced one of the most fruitful concepts into European thought: the theory of the Forms. This necessitated the introduction of a transcendental element, crudely at first in the *Gorgias* and its underworld judgement, but then infinitely more boldly in the parable of the cave in the *Republic*. The boldness and originality of this concept is a measure of the effort needed to legitimate this new mode of life.

Plato's portrait of the philosopher, though inspired by Socrates, is not Socrates, who was too much of his age: Socrates' wit, his nimble and adroit mind, and his sense of humour, have their counterpart in the varied and colourful throng that made up the Athenian democracy, and in a way reflect it. And although Socrates must figure importantly in a study of *apragmosynē*, yet he does not easily slot into any category; his kind of *apragmosynē* was a thing all of his own; he was, as he said, a 'busybody — in private'.

The Platonic philosopher has had an enormous and distinguished progeny: through the Epicureans and the Stoics he has become Everyman's image of a philosopher, and to this day we habitually picture the philosopher in Plato's terms. He also contributed a significant element to the composition of the Christian life when it came to be formulated. The early Christian was to an important extent the Platonic philosopher, the man for whom the values of this world were subordinated to those of a transcendental vision. This vision the Christians borrowed, then enlarged, deepened, and justified by a complex theology. In this way it is fair to say that the phenomenon of Athenian *apragmosynē* has had an influence and a history down to the present day.

In the last analysis, unfortunately, it is not easy to assess its significance in its own time. Our evidence for *apragmosynē* is almost entirely literary, and to a large extent embodied in works of fiction, whether as comedy, tragedy, or in philosophical dialogues. We cannot even be sure that lawcourt speeches were not revised for publication after they had been delivered, and that Thucydides was not, to an extent, interpreting the intention of his speakers. Again, these writers were almost all in favour of *apragmosynē*, which they saw as a passive reaction against the democracy. (It is a wonder that our general impression of the democracy is so favourable, considering how almost uniformly hostile are our sources.) Thucydides is to my knowledge the only writer who expresses a derogatory opinion — through Pericles — of the *apragmones*.

Nevertheless, the fact that so many of Athens' greatest writers did embrace the *apragmones* must in itself be significant.

Aristophanes and Euripides took up the *autourgos*; Plato dedicated himself to a life of *apragmosynē*; Lysias made a living out of defending *apragmones* in court. These writers came from well-to-do backgrounds, and it might be thought natural that they should seek out and befriend those who were not in sympathy with the radical democracy. Yet Aristophanes was the friend of the *apragmōn* peasant in the 420s when otherwise he was a staunch supporter of the democracy and its war with Sparta. Euripides, who had been strongly for the democracy in the 420s, only became disillusioned in the years after the Sicilian disaster, when he explores the possibilities of an *apragmōn* existence in his last plays. Thucydides himself, who had been such an admirer of Pericles in the 420s, comes to support the *apragmōn* policy of Nicias against Alcibiades. *Apragmosynē*, that is, becomes more attractive to writers when the aggressive policy of the radical democracy had become discredited.

The central importance of a study of *apragmosynē* lies in correcting our overall vision of the democracy. It comes as a shock to be reminded, for instance, that a full meeting of the assembly numbered about 6,000 men, but that the citizen population at the outbreak of the war was around 30,000. The Athenians had *never seen* a full meeting of the citizen body, though the very idea of democracy was predicated on it. From the very start they must have accepted that any meeting of the assembly was bound to be a sample of the citizenship—and not even a random sample: the assembly was inevitably going to reflect the views of the town-dwellers against those living in the outlying villages and hamlets. This is the first tension inherent in the democracy.

The second is that between the *chrēstoi* and the demagogues during the war; the disgruntled, disaffected nobility, who considered themselves ejected from their rightful place at the helm of State, against a new kind of brash, upstart leader. After the war this tension disappears, but the *chrēstoi* re-emerge transmuted by Plato into a philosophic image.

My third tension is that between the money-making class and the poorer citizens who swarmed on the benches of the jury courts. The payment of liturgies was a mechanism within the democracy by which a potentially dangerous tension could be relieved. The tension between *chrēstoi* and demagogues was to be resolved only by bloody conflict; the tension between town and country was never resolved, and even in the late fourth century Aristotle is still grappling with the problem. He recommends emptying the city rabble (as he sees it) out into the countryside and, by means of a division of the city's revenues, securing them to a piece of property; an *apragmōn* existence is for Aristotle the ultimate political solution, as for Plato it was the philosophic one.

Nevertheless, it remains very difficult to go behind these writers, most of them of considerable artistic stature, and assess the significance of *apragmsoynē* in social and political life—what it meant for the ordinary Athenians. In any case, the danger is that *apragmosynē* will, by its nature, seldom make a strong impact in politics. Plato summed up the situation for the peasants: 'Seldom together, but when gather together, all-powerful'. Two such occasions may be 429 BC, when the peasants were crowded into the city and peace overtures were made to Sparta; and again 411 BC, when they were once more a majority in Athens, and offers of peace were again made. Yet the real political significance of the peasant lay not in activity, but in relative inactivity, and in this lay his attraction for the oligarchic theorist.

The significance of that set of frustrated nobles which I discussed under the heading of 'noble youths' was of course profound, since they took the city to the verge of destruction. In the event, it was they themselves whom they destroyed; consumed with hatred for the democracy, their heads filled with ideological and philosophic master-plans, they were yet incapable of offering an alternative form of Government that appealed to anyone outside their own narrow circle.

The significance of my third group—the 'rich quietists'—is perhaps the greatest. The man who dips deeply into his own resources to provide lavish civic celebrations (and we must accept that this was often done voluntarily, willingly), the man who will spend in a year's contribution the equivalent of half a lifetime's earnings for a craftsman, and who at the same time is happy to occupy a relatively modest status in society (politically, at any rate): this tells us something very important about the character of the democracy. The relationship between the rich quietist and the *dēmos* throws a unique light on the democracy.

Appendix:
The Date of Composition of Pericles' Speeches at Th. 2.35 and 2.60

The date of composition of these speeches has been much disputed. The arguments for a late date (after 404 BC) are weak, though accepted by many scholars. The problem is, as de Romilly accepts, that there are no explicit indications in the text itself to allow such an assumption. There are passages in the *History* which are definitely after 404 — 2.65 and 3.82–4 — but it cannot be argued from these passages that their contexts are also of that late date. On the contrary, these passages are clearly separate from their contexts and a reflection on them composed at a later date.

Yet although the speeches carry no overt signs of a late revision, they are most certainly full of evidence to the contrary. In tone, content, and vocabulary they contain many echoes of other literature of the period when they might naturally have been thought to be composed, that is the 420s (or very soon after; at 2.34.7 Thucydides, in talking of the public funeral after the first season's fighting, says that the Athenians carried on this tradition throughout the war, and this may refer to the Archidamian War only).

The exhortation by Pericles to become lovers of Athens (2.43.1) is satirized by Aristophanes in the *Knights* (732). Compare Athenian rule as a tyranny in Th. 2.63.2 and 3.37.2 with Aristophanes, *Knights*, 1111. Or Athens as an island in Th. 1.143.5 with Ps.-Xen. *Ath. Pol.* 2.14, and the profusion of goods flowing into Athens from all parts of the Mediterranean in Th. 2.38.2. with Ps.-Xen. *Ath. Pol.* 2.7. Compare Pericles' remarks on the useless *apragmōn* with Eupolis' fragment 234 (*Cities*, c.431): 'The man who has no enthusiasm (*aspoudos*) for civic affairs is worse than he who is too ambitious for office'. Euripides' plays throughout the 420s abound in echoes from the Funeral Speech. Compare Th. 2. 37. 2–4 on the Athenians' tolerance of each other and their adherence to the unwritten laws (which will include protection of suppliants) with his *Herakleidai* (429–427 BC), lines 182 and 196. At the start of that play, Iolaus makes the general observation that he who pursues his own profit too keenly will be useless to the city—compare Th. 2. 40. 2 on the *apragmones*. The implication that the city's interests should take precedence is stated explicitly in the second speech (Th. 2. 60. 3), and this idea is again clear in the *Erechtheus* (423–422 BC): the tone of high-hearted patriotism and self-sacrifice in the long speech of Praxithea (fr. 360) is closely in keeping with the Funeral Speech. 'The city is the most important thing we have. We are sprung from its very soil [cf. *Herakleidai*, 69]; others may be citizens in word—we are so in fact . . . There is only one city, though many citizens—shall they be destroyed when I have it in my power to give my child? I hate a mother who will not offer her child . . .'. (Cf. Goossens, *Euripide et Athènes*, 468; di Benedetto, *Euripide: Teatro e società*, 146.) Compare too the thought 'Out of striving arise good things for men' (fr. 364) with Th. 2. 62. 3.

Finally, Euripides takes up the themes of Pericles' speeches again in his *Suppliant Women* (*c.* 421). Compare Theseus' speech on the freedom of Athens with Th. 2. 37. 1. The herald says later: 'You and your city are accustomed to achieve much'; Theseus replies: 'We strive well and thrive well' (576 ff.). This is the quality with which Thucydides particularly characterized the Athenians in Book 1. Compare also line 323 (and Goossens, op. cit., 423).

Now if Thucydides is writing a clever pastiche in the very different climate after 404, what does that signify? The ideas expressed are in accordance with those of the 420s and to manipulate the evidence against this compelling conclusion seems to me futile (e.g. to suppose that the *apragmones* who would like to go off and live on their own (Th. 2. 63. 2) is a reference to those oligarchs who went off to Eleusis in 403—de Romilly, *Thucydide et l'impérialisme athénienne*, 133).

Bibliography

ADKINS, A. W. H., *Merit and Responsibility* (Oxford, 1960).
—— 'Honour and Punishment in the Homeric Poems', *BICS* 7 (1960), 23–32.
—— *Moral Values and Political Behaviour in Ancient Greece* (London, 1972).
—— 'Polypragmosyne and 'Minding One's Own Business': a Study in Greek Social and Political Values', *CP* 71 (1976), 301–27.
ALBINI, U., 'Antifonte logografo', *Maia* 10 (1958).
—— ed., Ps.-Herodes Atticus, *Peri Politeias* (Florence, 1968).
ALLISON, J. W., 'Thucydides and Polypragmosyne', *AJAH* 4: 1 (1979), 10–22.
ANDREEV, V. N., 'Some Aspects of Agrarian Conditions in Attica, 5th to 3rd Centuries', *Eirene*, 12 (1974), 5–46.
ANDREWES, A., *The Greek Tyrants* (London, 1956).
—— 'The Opposition to Pericles', *JHS* 98 (1978), 1–8.
BARRETT, W. S., ed. and comm., Euripides' *Hippolytus* (Oxford, 1964).
BENEDETTO, V. di, *Euripide: Teatro e società* (Turin, 1971).
BILINSKI, B., *L'agonistica sportiva nella Grecia antica* (Rome, 1959).
BLAYDES, F. H., ed. and comm., Aristophanes' *Knights* (Halle, 1892).
BOARDMAN, J., *Athenian Black-Figure Vases* (London, 1974).
BOLL, F., *Vita contemplativa* (Heidelberg, 1920).
BOWERSOCK, G. W., intro. and trans., Ps.-Xen. *Ath. Pol.* (LCL, London, 1968).
BOWRA, M., *Pindar* (Oxford, 1964).
BRUNT, P. A., 'Athenian Settlements Abroad in the Fifth Century BC', in *Ancient Society and Institutions: Studies Presented to V. Ehrenberg* (Oxford, 1966).
BUHMANN, H., *Der Sieg in Olympia und in den anderen panhellenischen Spielen* (Munich, 1975).
—— *Lore and Science in Ancient Pythagoreanism* (Harvard, 1972).
CALHOUN, M., *Athenian Clubs* (Rome, 1964).
CEADEL, E. B., 'Resolved Feet in the Trimeters of Euripides and the Chronology of the Plays', *CQ* 35 (1941), 66–89.
CONNOR, W. R., *Theopompus and Fifth Century Athens* (Washington 1968).
—— *The New Politicians in Fifth Century Athens* (Princeton, 1971).
CROISET, M., *Aristophanes and the Political Parties at Athens* (trans. J. Loeb, 1909).

DE STE CROIX, G., *Origins of the Peloponnesian War* (London, 1972).
—— *The Class Struggles in the Ancient World* (London, 1981).
DAVIES, J. K., 'Demosthenes on Liturgies: A Note', *JHS* 87 (1967), 33–40.
—— *Democracy and Classical Greece* (London, 1978).
—— *Wealth and the Power of Wealth in Classical Athens* (Salem, NH, 1981).
DAVISON, J. A., 'Pythagoras, Democritus and Anaxagoras', *CQ* Ns 3 (1953), 33–45.
DECHARME, P., *Euripide et l'esprit de son théatre* (Paris, 1893).
DELATTE, M. A., *Étude sur la littérature Pythagoricienne* (Liège, 1915).
—— *Essai sur la politique Pythagoricienne* Liège and Paris, 1922).
DELEBECQUE, E., *Euripide et la guerre du Péloponnèse* (Paris, 1951).
DENNISTON, J. D., and PAGE, D., ed. and comm., Aeschylus' *Agamemnon* (Oxford, 1957).
DETIENNE, M., *Les Maîtres de vérité dans la Grèce archaïque* (Paris, 1967).
DEUBNER, L., ed., Iamblichus' *De Vita Pythagorica* (Leipzig, 1937).
DIENELT, K., 'Apragmosyne', *Wiener Studien*, 66 (1953), 94–104, reprinted with an addition in *Die Friedenspolitik des Perikles* (Vienna, 1958).
DODDS, E. R., *The Greeks and the Irrational* (Berkeley, California, 1951).
—— ed. and comm., Plato's *Gorgias* (Oxford, 1959).
—— 'Euripides the Irrationalist', *CQ* 43 (1929).
DOVER, K. J., *Lysias and the Corpus Lysiacum* (Berkeley, 1968).
—— ed. and comm., Aristophanes' *Clouds* (Oxford, 1968).
—— *Greek Popular Morality in the Time of Plato and Aristotle* (Oxford, 1975).
—— *Greek Homosexuality* (London, 1978).
EDELSTEIN, L., *Plato's Seventh Letter* (Leiden, 1966).
EDMONDS, J., ed. and trans., *The Fragments of Attic Comedy* (Leiden, 1957).
EHRENBERG, V., 'Polypragmosyne: A Study in Greek Politics', *JHS* 67 (1947), 46–67.
—— *The People of Aristophanes* (Oxford, 1951).
—— *Sophokles and Perikles* (Oxford, 1954).
ELIOT, C. W. J., *Coastal Demes of Attica* (Toronto, 1962).
ERIKSEN, T. B., *Bios Theoretikos* (Oslo, 1976).
FARNELL, L. R., ed. and comm., Pindar (London, 1932).
FESTUGIÈRE, A. J., *Contemplation et vie contemplative selon Platon* (Paris, 1936).
FINLEY, M. I., 'Athenian Demagogues', *Past and Present*, 21 (1962), 3–24, reprinted in *Studies in Ancient Society*, (London and Boston, 1974), from which the page numbers in the text are taken.

—— *Aspects of Antiquity* (London, 1968).

—— 'Sparta', in *Problèmes de la terre en Grèce ancienne* (Paris, 1968).

——'The Alienability of Land in Ancient Greece: a Point of View', *Eirene*, 7 (1968), 25–32.

—— ed., *Problèmes de la terre en Grèce ancienne* (Paris, 1973).

—— *The World of Odysseus* (London, 1977).

—— 'Empire in the Greco-Roman World', *Greece and Rome*², 25 (1978), 1–15.

FINLEY, M. I., and PLEKET, H. W., *The Olympic Games* (London, 1976).

FORNARA, C. W., 'The Athenian Board of Generals from 501 to 404', *Historia Einzelschrift* (Wiesbaden, 1971).

FORREST, W. G., 'Aristophanes and the Empire', in *The Ancient Historian and his Materials: Essays in Honour of C. E. Stevens* (London, 1975).

—— 'The date of the Ps.-Xen. *Ath. Pol.*', *Klio*, 52 (1970), 107–16.

—— 'The Athenian Generation Gap', *YCS* 24 (1975).

FRAENKEL, H., *Dichtung und Philosophie des frühen Griechentums* (Munich, 1962).

GARDINER, E. N., *Greek Athletic Sports and Festivals* (London, 1910).

—— *Athletics in the Ancient World* (Oxford, 1930).

GERNET, L., *Recherches sur le développement de la pensée juridique et morale en Grèce* (Paris, 1917).

GILBERT, G., *Beiträge zur inneren Geschichte Athens im Zeitalter des Peloponnesischen Krieges* (Leipzig, 1887).

GLOTZ, G., *The Ancient World at Work* (London, 1926).

—— and COHEN, R., *Histoire grecque* (Paris, 1931).

GOMME, A. W., 'Aristophanes and Politics', in *More Studies in Greek History and Literature* (Oxford, 1962).

—— *The Population of Athens in the Fifth and Fourth Centuries BC* (Oxford, 1933).

—— 'The Old Oligarch', in *More Studies in Greek History and Literature* (Oxford, 1962).

—— 'The Working of the Athenian Democracy', in *More Studies in Greek History and Literature* (Oxford, 1962).

GOOSSENS, R., *Euripide et Athènes* (Brussels, 1962).

GROTE, G., *History of Greece* (London, 1880); ten volumes: reference by volume and page number.

GUTHRIE, W. K. C., *The Sophists* (Cambridge, 1971). (Taken from vol. III of his *History of Greek Philosophy*.)

HAMMOND, N. G. L., *A History of Greece to 322 BC* (Oxford, 1967).

HANSEN, M. H., 'How Many Athenians Attended the Ecclesia?', *GRBS* 17 (1976), 115–34.

—— 'Perquisites for Magistrates', *Class. et Med.* 32 (1980), 105–25.

HANSEN, M. H., *The Athenian Ecclesia* (Copenhagen, 1983).

HARDING, P., 'In Search of a Polypragmatist', in *Classical Contributions: Studies in Honour of M. F. McGregor*, ed. G. S. Shrimpton and D. J. McCargar (New York, 1981).

HARRISON, A. R. W., *The Law of Athens* (Oxford, 1971).

HIGNETT, C., *A History of the Athenian Constitution* (Oxford, 1952).

HOW, W. W., and WELLS, J., comm., *Herodotus* (Oxford, 1912).

HUMPHREYS, S. C., 'The Nothoi of Kynosarges' *JHS* 94 (1974), 88–95.

—— 'Public and Private Interests', *CJ* 73 (1977–8). 97–104.

—— *Anthropology and the Greeks* (London, 1978).

—— *The Family, Women and Death* (London, 1983).

IMHOF, M., *Euripides Ion: Eine literarische Studie* (Bern and Munich, 1966).

ISAAC, J., *Les Oligarques* (Paris, 1945).

JAEGER, W., 'Über Ursprung und Kreislauf des philosophischen Lebensideal', *Sonderabdruck aus den Sitzungsberichten der Preussischen Akad. der Wissenschaft Phil. Hist. Klasse* (Berlin, 1928).

—— 'Tyrtaios Über die wahre *Arete*' (1932), reprinted in *Die griechische Elegie*, ed. G. Pfohl (Darmstadt 1972).

JOLY, R., 'Le Thème philosophique des genres de vie', *Académie Royale de Belgique: mémoires (lettres)*, 51 (1956–7).

JONES, J. E., SACKETT, L. H. and GRAHAM, A. J., 'The Dema House in Attica', *BSA* 57 (1962), 75–114.

—— 'An Attic Country House below the cave of Pan at Vari', *BSA* 68 (1973), 355–452.

KAIBEL, G., *Epigrammata Graeca ex Lapidibus Conlecta* (Berlin, 1878).

KAMBITSIS, K., ed. and comm., *Euripides' Antiope* (Athens, 1972).

KASTROUMENOS, P., *Die Demen von Attika* (Leipzig, 1886).

KIRK, G. S., and RAVEN, J. E., *The Presocratic Philosophers* (Cambridge, 1957).

KLEVE, K., 'Apragmosyne and Polypragmosyne: Two Slogans in Athenian Politics', *Symbolae Osloenses*, 39 (1964).

KNOX, B., *The Heroic Temper* (Berkeley, California and London, 1964).

LACTOR, *The Athenian Empire* (3rd edn.) (London, 1983).

LANGDON, M. K., 'A Sanctuary of Zeus on Mount Hymettos', *Hesperia*, suppl. 16 (1976).

LANZA, D., *Anassagora* (Florence, 1966).

LAUTER, H., 'Zu Heimstatten und Gutshäusern im klassischen Attika', in *Forschungen und Funde: Festschrift Bernhard Neutsch* (Innsbruck, 1980), 279–85.

LAUTER-BUFFE, H., 'Das "Wehrdorf" Lathouresa bei Vari', *Mitteilungen des Deutschen Archäologischen Instituts, Athenische Abteilung* 94 (1979), 161–92.

LENARDON, R. J., *The Saga of Themistocles* (London, 1978).
LESKY, A., *Griechische Trägodie* (Stuttgart, 1938).
LEVI, P., trans. and comm., Pausanias' *Guide to Greece* (London, 1971).
LEVY, E., *Athènes devant la défait de 404* (Athens, 1976).
LOSADA, A. L., *The Fifth Column in the Peloponnesian War* (Leiden, 1972).
LUCAS, D. W., 'Hippolytus' *CQ* 40 (1946), 65 ff.
MACDOWELL, D. M., ed. and comm., Andocides' *On the Mysteries* (Oxford, 1962).
—— ed. and comm., Aristophanes' *Wasps* (Oxford, 1971).
MANSFIELD, J., 'The Chronology of Anaxagoras' Athenian Period and the Date of His Trial', part 2, *Mnemosyne*[4], 33. 1–2 (1980), 17–9.
MARTINAZZOLI, F., *Euripide* (Rome, 1961).
MASQUERAY, P., *Euripide et ses idées* (Paris, 1908).
MÉAUTIS, G., 'Les Adversaires de Périclès', in *Raccolta di scritti in onore di Felice Ramorino* (Milan, 1927), 212–18.
—— *L'Aristocratie athénienne* (Paris, 1927).
MEIGGS, R., *The Athenian Empire* (Oxford, 1972).
MELAS, E., *Temples and Sanctuaries of Ancient Greece* (London, 1973).
MERITT, B. D., *The Athenian Calendar in the Fifth Century BC* (Harvard, 1928).
MONDOLFO, R., 'L'origine del ideale filosofico della vita' *Rendic. Ac. delle Scienze di Bologna*, (1938).
MOORE, J. M., *Aristotle and Xenophon on Democracy and Oligarchy* (London, 1975).
MORRISON, J. S., 'The Place of Protagoras in Athenian Public Life', *CQ* 35 (1941), 1–16.
MOSLEY, D. J., 'Envoys and Diplomacy in Ancient Greece', *Historia Einzelschrift*, 22 (1973).
MOSSÉ, C., *La Fin de la démocratie athénienne* (Paris, 1962).
—— *The Ancient World at Work* (London, 1969).
—— 'Le Statut des paysans en Attique au IVe siècle', in *Problèmes de la terre en Grèce ancienne* (Paris, 1973).
MURRAY, O., *Early Greece* (London, 1980).
NEIL, R. A., ed. and comm., Aristophanes' *Knights* (Cambridge, 1901).
NESTLE, W., 'Apragmosyne', *Philologus*, 81 (1926), 129–40.
NEUGEBAUER, O., *The Exact Sciences in Antiquity* (Copenhagen, 1957).
NORTH, H., 'A Period of Opposition to Sophrosyne in Greek Thought' *TAPhA* 78 (1947), 1–17.
—— *Sophrosyne* (New York), 1966).
OWEN, A. S., ed. and comm., Euripides' *Ion* (Oxford, 1939).

PAGE, D. L., ed. and comm., Euripides' *Medea* (Oxford, 1938).
—— *Sappho and Alcaeus* (Oxford, 1955).
PATTERSON, C., *Pericles' Citizenship Law of 451–450 BC*, (Salem, NH, 1981).
PECIRKA, J., 'Homestead Farms in Classical and Hellenistic Hellas', in *Problèmes de la terre en Grèce Ancienne* (Paris, 1973).
PEPPLER, C. W., 'The Termination *-kos* as used by Aristophanes for Comic Effect', *AJP* 31 (1910), 428–44.
PLATNAUER, M., ed. and comm., Aristophanes' *Peace* (Oxford, 1964).
PLEKET, H. W., (*see* FINLEY, M. I.).
POHLENZ, M., *Die griechische Tragödie* (Göttingen, 1954).
PRITCHETT, W. K., 'The Attic Stelai', *Hesperia*, 22 (1953), 225–99.
—— *The Greek State at War* (Berkeley, California, and London, 1974).
RAUBITSCHEK, A. E., 'Philinos', *Hesperia*, 23 (1954) 67–71.
RAVEN, J. E., (*see* KIRK, G. S.).
REDFIELD, J. M., *Nature and Culture in the Iliad: The Tragedy of Hector* (Chicago and London, 1975).
RENNIE, W., ed. and comm., Aristophanes' *Acharnians* (London, 1909).
ROBERT, L., 'De Delphes à L'Oxus: inscriptions grecques nouvelles de la Bactriane', *CRAI* (1968), 416–57.
ROBERTS, J. W., *The City of Socrates* (London, 1984).
ROHDICH, H., *Die Euripideische Tragödie* (Heidelberg, 1968).
ROMILLY, J. de, *Thucydide et L'impérialisme athénienne* (Paris, 1947). English trans. (Oxford, 1963).
RUSSELL, D., *Greek Declamation* (London, 1983).
SACKETT, L. H., (*see* JONES, J. E.)
SARTORI, F., *Le Eterie nella vita politica ateniese del VI e V Secoli A.C.* (Rome, 1957).
SCHWARZ, E., *Scholia in Euripidem* (Berlin, 1887).
SEAGER, R., 'Alcibiades and the Charge of Aiming at the Tyranny', *Historia* 16 (1967), 6–18.
SNELL, B., *Theorie und Praxis im Denken des Abendlandes* (Hamburg, 1951).
—— *Poetry and Society* (Bloomington, 1961).
—— *Scenes from Greek Drama* (Berkeley, California, 1964).
SOLMSEN, F., 'Euripides *Ion* im Vergleich mit anderen Tragödien', *Hermes*, 69 (1934).
STANFORD, W. B., ed. and comm., Aristophanes' *Frogs* (London, 1958).
STARR, C. G., *The Economic and Social Growth of Early Greece* (New York, 1977).
SWADDLING, J., *The Ancient Olympic Games* (London, 1980).

TAYLOR, A. E. 'On the Date of the Trial of Anaxagoras', *CQ* 11 (1917), 81–7.

THUMMER, E., *Pindar: Die Isthmischen Gedichte* (Heidelberg, 1969).

TOD, M. N., *Sidelights on Greek History* (Oxford, 1932).

TOMLINSON, R. A., *Greek Sanctuaries* (London, 1976).

TRAILL, J. S., 'The Political Organisation of Attica', *Hesperia*, suppl. 14 (1975).

TUCKEY, T. G., *Plato's Charmides* (Cambridge, 1951).

USSHER, R. G., ed. and comm., Aristophanes' *Ecclesiazousae* (Oxford, 1973).

VERRALL, A. W., ed. and comm., Euripides' *Ion* (Cambridge, 1890).

—— ed. and comm., Euripides' *Medea* (Cambridge, 1892).

WADE-GERY, H. T., 'Thucydides the Son of Melesias', *JHS* 52 (1932), reprinted in *Essays in Greek History* (Oxford, 1958), 239–70.

—— ''Kritias and Herodes', *CQ* 39 (1945), 19–33, reprinted in *Essays in Greek History*, from which the page numbers in the text are taken.

—— 'On Miltiades', in *Essays in Greek History* (Oxford, 1958).

WEBSTER, T. B. L., *Studies in Later Greek Comedy* (London, 1953).

—— *The Tragedies of Euripides* (London, 1967).

—— *Potter and Painter in Classical Athens* (London, 1972).

WELLS, J., (*see* HOW, W. W.).

WEST, M. L., ed., *Iambi et Elegi Graeci*, vol. II (Oxford, 1972).

WHIBLEY, L., *Political Parties in Athens* (Cambridge, 1889).

WHITEHEAD, D., *The Ideology of the Athenian Metic* (Cambridge, 1977).

WILAMOWITZ, U. von, ed. and comm., Euripides' *Ion* (Berlin, 1925).

WOLFF, C., 'Design and Myth in Euripides' *Ion*', *HSCP* 69 (1965), 169 ff.

WOOD, E. M., and N., *Class Ideology and Ancient Political Theory* (Oxford, 1978).

ZUNTZ, G., 'Earliest Attic Prose Style: On Antiphon's Second Tetralogy', *Class. et Med.*[2] (1939).

Index of Passages Quoted or Cited in the Text

AESCHYLUS:
Myrmidons, 73
ANAXAGORAS:
(DK 59A1), 142 n. 40; (DK 59A29–30),
142 n. 43; (DK 59A2), 143
ANDOCIDES:
(1. 22), 67; (1. 32), 35; (1. 47), 57, 67;
(3. 15), 37
ANTIPHON:
Tetralogy (2. 2. 1), 106
ANTIPHON the sophist:
(DK 87B44), 144 n. 51
ARISTOPHANES:
Acharnians (22), 78; (32 ff.), 81; (597 ff.),
116; (646–7), 13; (685–8), 120;
(1071 ff.), 117
Banqueters (fr. 198K), 119
Birds (44), 86; (110), 86; (1432), 58
Clouds (43 ff.), 84; (51 ff.), 84; (102–3),
153; (218–19), 153; (316), 183; (334),
183; (457), 13; (627), 153; (961), 58;
(984 f.), 119; (993 ff.), 102; (1003),
122; (1353 ff.), 119
Ecclesiazousai (379), 78; (817 ff.), 81
Frogs (1498), 183
Georgoi (fr. 100K), 83
Islands (fr. 368K), 86
Knights (116), 115; (166), 31; (259–65),
113; (288), 115; (624 ff.), 83 n. 13;
(805), 83; (877 ff.), 122; (1375–81),
121; (1382–3), 122
Lysistrata (807), 125
Peace (190), 85; (572 ff.), 81, 85; (871),
85; (1297), 58
Thesmophoriazousai (136), 165 n. 34
Wasps (134), 63; (380), 144 n. 47;
(473 ff.), 63; (687 ff.), 122; (924), 118;
(949 ff.), 118; (1087), 73; (1168), 64;
(1196), 65
Wealth (911–22), 87
ARISTOTLE:
Athenaiōn Politeia (25), 105; (29. 5), 93;
(41. 3), 78 n. 2

Eudemian Ethics (1216ᵃ 11), 135; (1232ᵇ
7), 65; (1233ᵃ 28), 126
Nicomachean Ethics (1095ᵇ 22), 18;
(1096ᵃ 11), 135; (1107ᵇ 21), 126;
(1141ᵇ 3), 143 n. 44; (1179ᵃ 13) 143
n. 44
Politics (1278ᵃ 37), 126 n. 14; (1282ᵃ
31), 32; (1289ᵇ 33), 76; (1292ᵇ 25),
94; (1295ᵇ 30), 95; (1318ᵇ 10), 94;
(1319ᵃ 24), 95
Protrepticus (fr. 11), 135

CICERO:
Letter to Atticus (5. 16), (5. 18), (5. 21), 33
CRITIAS:
(DK 88B6), 62; (DK 88B7), 62;
DK 88B47), 62

DEMOCRITUS:
(DK 68B157), 11; (fr. 194), 141
DEMOSTHENES:
(8. 24), 34; (18. 114), 32; (49. 6–8), 32
DIO CHRYSOSTOM:
Oration 59: 28

EUPOLIS:
Demes (fr. 95K), 121
EURIPIDES:
Bacchae (717), 87
Electra (37), 89; (53), 89; (67), 89; (73),
89; (78 ff.), 89; (253 ff.), 89;
(367–90), 89
Hippolytus (986–9), (1013–20), 54
Ion (53), 156 n. 2; (54), 156 n. 3; (112),
156 n. 5; (301), 156 n. 4; (578), 159
n. 11; (595–606), 158; (621 ff.), 159;
(640 ff.), 156 n. 4; (643 ff.), 161;
(646–7), 178
Medea (294 ff.), 146; (807–9), 147
Orestes (902 ff.), 91; (920 schol.), 77;
(930), 161 n. 18; (982), 148

205

Euripides *(cont.)*:
Phoenician Women (499 ff.), 16; (531 ff.), 16
Suppliant Women (12), 45; (245), 88; (321–5), 45; (417–22), 88; (438–42), 13; (88–900), 127
fragments:
Antiope (184N), 164; (185N), 165; (186N), 166; (187N), 164; (188N), 166; (193N), 167; (194N), 169; (196N), 167; (198N), 168; (199N), 168; (200N), 170; (210N), 169; (202N), 170; (219N), 166; (395N), 164; (910N), 148; (1023N), 163
Autolycus (248N), 22
Erechtheus (360N), 10; (369N), 149
1st Hippolytus (434N), 14
Ixion (426N), 11
Likymnios (474N), 11
Melanippe (484N), 148
Phaethon (782N), 148; (783N), 148
Philoctetes (787–9N), 28
Temenos (745N), 11
unidentified (1113N), 162 n. 20

HERACLITUS:
(DK 22A1), (DK 22A2), 138 n. 23
Fragments: (1), (5), (29), (104), 138; (29), (36), 139
Ps-HERODES ATTICUS:
(30), 93 n. 26
HERODOTUS:
(1. 65), 44; (5. 78), 14; (103. 1–3), 23
HOMER:
Iliad (1. 3), 7; (1. 118), 5; (1. 165), 4; (1. 277), 5; (4. 195), 2; (5. 3), 2; (7. 91), 2; (9. 22), 2; (9. 111), 5; (9. 412), 2; (9. 602), 4; (10. 212), 3; (12. 310), 4; (12. 322), 6; (15. 564), 2; (16. 83), 5; (18. 121), 6; (21. 462), 6; (22. 389), 7
Odyssey (1. 338), 3; (4.584), 2; (8. 147), 2; (9. 19), 3; (11. 94), 7; (24. 6), 7; (24. 83), 2

IAMBLICHUS:
de Vita Pythagorica (58–9), 133 n. 7; (254), 136
inscriptions:
decree of Aristoteles (Tod, SGHI II. 123), 36; decree of Kleinias (ML 46), 35; IGi² 1085 (ML 51), 69 n. 38; on

Androtion (Tod, SGHI II. 152), 34; treaty of Athens and Selymbria (ML 87), 36
ISOCRATES:
(12. 145), 104

LYSIAS:
(7. 1), 108; (7. 30), 108; (7. 41), 108; (19. 9), 109; (19. 22), 32; (19. 55), 109; (19. 59), 109; (20. 11), 67; (20. 13), 67; (21. 5), 104; (21. 7), 103; (24. 17), 77; (24. 24), 76; (25. 12), 104; (26. 3), 111; (34 intro.), 93

MENANDER:
Samia (41), 153

PAUSANIAS:
(1. 30. 4), 125
PINDAR:
Isthmian Odes (4. 12), 23; (5. 22), 44; (7. 39), 43
Nemean Odes (3. 31), 23; (4. 39), 24; (11. 48), 43
Olympian Odes (1. 54) 43; (1. 114), 23; (3. 43), 23; (4. 16), 42; (5. 15), 11; (7. 90), 23; (8. 67), 24; (9. 16), 44; (13. 1), 43; (13. 6), 44; (13. 9), 23
Paean (1. 10), 44
Pythian Odes (1. 70), 42; (1. 85), 24; (2. 21), 43; (5. 67), 44; (8. 1), 43; (8. 85), 24; (10. 27), 23; (11. 53), 43; (11. 54), 24; (12. 28), 11
fr. 109, 42
PLATO:
Apology (21 B), 152; (21 D), 140; (26 D), 143 n. 45; (31 C), 185; (32 A), 183
Charmides (154 D), 57 n. 15; (157 E), 57; (158 E), 57; (159 B), 57; (159 D), 58; (161 B), 58; (163 D), 62
Euthydemus (305 B), 65 n. 33
Euthyphro (4), 37
Gorgias (473 E), 184; (484 C), 173; (485 D), 174; (486 B), 174; (486 C), 174; (493), 135; (500 C), 175; (515 E), 55 n. 11; (518 E), 47; (518 E), 175; (526 D), 176
Hippias Major (281 C), 131 n. 1, 142 n. 40; (283 A), 142 n. 39
Laches (178 A), 117; (180 B), 117
Meno (71 E), 60; (93 B), 60
Phaedo (68 B–C), 134 n. 12

Phaedrus (269 E), 142 n. 38
Protagoras (316 B), 20; (319 A), 61; (319 B), 61
Republic (347 B), 179; (496 D), 178; (516 C), 177; (517 B), 177; (519 C), 179; (520 C), 179; (532 A), 134 n. 11; (540 B), 179; (549 C), 19; (557 B), 96; (565 A), 77; (565 B), 125; (580 D), 134
Seventh Letter (324 D), 180; (325 A), 180; (325 D), 180; (326 A), 180; (330 D–331 D), 182
Theaetetus (172 D), 178; (173 D), 178; (174), 131 n. 1.
PLATO (comic dramatist):
(fr. 103K), 65
PLUTARCH:
Aristides (26), 105
Life of Alcibiades (16), 125; (21), 116
Lives of 10 Orators (833 E), 70
Nicias (2), 102; (3), 104; (4), 102, 106; (23), 143
Pericles (4–5), 142 n. 38; (9), 77; (16), 142; (32), 144
Solon (22), 80

SIMONIDES:
(fr. 122), 10
SOPHOCLES:
Electra (678), 58 n. 18

THEOPOMPUS:
FGH (115F73), 137 n. 21
THUCYDIDES:
I (18), 44; (32. 5), 45; (67), 44; (69. 4), 45; (70. 3), 12; (70. 8), 12, 45; (71. 1), 45; (80 ff.), 46; (84. 2), 46
II (14 ff.), 78; (37. 1), 26; (40. 2), 27; (43), 141 n. 34; (43. 2), 10; (60), 38; (63. 1), 99; (64. 4), 39; (65.7), 99
III (27), 35; (37. 3), 66, 124; (82), 35
IV (118. 11), 117
V (16. 1), 99; (43. 2), 117
VI (13. 1), 99; (16), 14; (18. 3), 100; (18. 6), 99, 100; (31. 2), 79, (39), 124; (49. 1), 116
VII (27. 3), 86
VIII (48. 5), 33; (66), 94; (68.1), 65, 70; (68.2), 65; (68. 3), 70; (72. 2), 79; (89. 3), 15; (97), 93
TYRTAEUS:
(fr. 12), 8; (fr. 12. 29), 9; (fr. 12. 31–7), 9

XENOPHANES:
(DK 21B2), 22
XENOPHON:
Cyropaedia (8. 3. 37–8), 88
Hellinica (1. 2. 12), 24; (2. 2. 3), 24; (2. 3. 21), 128; (2. 3. 48), 93; (2. 4. 19), 70
Hiero (7. 3), 20
Memorabilia (1. 2. 48), 184; (1. 6. 15), 184; (2. 9), 112; (3. 4), 32, 116 n. 39; (3. 6), 61; (3. 6. 2), 20; (3. 7), 58; (3. 7. 9), 184; (4. 5. 10), 185
Oeconomica (4. 3), 76; (5. 4), 77
Symposium (1. 4) 66
Ps.-XENOPHON:
Constitution of the Athenians (1. 3), 32; (1. 13), 104; (1. 14), 35, 105; (2. 19), 105 n. 15

General Index

Names which occur in the text only in passing are omitted.

Achilles, 4 ff.
Aeschylus:
on *hēsychia*, 42
Agamemnon, 4 ff.
age:
ages of man, 53, 57 n. 15; age
versus youth, 119 ff.; Nicias' age,
102; respect for age, 130
agora:
in Aristophanes, 82 ff.; evils of, 87
Alcibiades:
his *lamprotēs*, 14; speech before the
Sicilian expedition, 95 ff.; as
synēgoros, 119 ff.; and Timon, 125
Ameinias the Pythagorean, 140
Anaxagoras, 131, 135, 141 ff., 147, 163
and Euripides, 148 ff.
Andocides, 67 ff.
Androtion:
his decree, 34
Antiphon, 65, 70, 74, 129, 188
date of second tetralogy, 106
Apatouria, 85
Archedemus:
and Crito, 112, 120
Archidamian War, 30
Archidamus, 46
aretē, 8, 11, 109, 141
of the Athenian people, 12; in
Aristotle, 18; in the games, 21, 23;
in Pericles' Funeral Speech, 26; in
Pindar, 44; Meno's definition, 60,
109; and *physis*, 165
Arginousai, battle of, 31
Aristophanes:
his *tolma*, 13; his 'Paphlagonian', 31,
56, 83, 113, 115; on Thucydides
son of Melesias, 41; his 'Right
Argument' in the *Clouds*, 60, 72;
his peasants, 82 ff.; sycophants in
the *Birds*, 105; opinion of
Archedemus, 112; his beggars, 150
n. 69

Aristophanes, *On the Property of*, speech
by Lysias, 108
Aristotle:
on *timē*, 18; on the peasants, 94; his
preferred constitution, 95
Artemis:
in the *Hippolytus*, 52 ff.; A.
Brauronia, 85, 97; temple in
Ephesus, 138
atē, 44
of Athens, 100
Athenagoras, 124
autourgos, 77 ff.; 189
in Aristophanes, 82 ff.; in Euripides,
88 ff.; in Eur. *Electra*, 88 ff.; in
Eur. *Orestes*, 89 ff.; his
'intelligence', 91; in Aristotle,
94 ff.; his *apragmosynē* 115

banausos, 76, 97
Bellerophon:
in Pindar, 43
Bias, 131
Bios Theōrētikos, 8, 131 ff., 141, 145,
155 ff.
in Plato's *Republic*, 178 ff.

Callias:
peace of, 47; property of, 110
Callicles:
in Plato's *Gorgias*, 173 ff.
charis, 55
Charmides:
in Plato's dialogue, 57 ff.;
in Xenophon, 58 f.; as oligarch, 70,
71, 180
Chersonese, 113 ff.
chrēstoi, 38, 49, 162, 171, 187, 193
in Pericles' speeches, 27; Odysseus as
chrēstos, 29; in Eur. *Orestes*, 92; in
Eur. *Ion*, 158
Cicero:
in Cappadocia, 33

Cleon, 161
  in Ar. *Wasps*, 63 ff., 118; takes over
    Nicias' command, 102; in Ar.
    Knights, 113 ff., 122; his speech on
    Mitylene, 123
Conon:
  his wealth, 37, 110
Corinthians:
  at the conference of Spartan allies,
    44
Critias, 68, 74, 187
  on *apragmosynē*, 47; in Plato's
    Charmidēs, 56 ff.; his own writings,
    62 ff.; studying with Prodicus, 74;
    one of the Thirty, 180
Crito, 189
  in Xenophon, 111 ff.; friendship with
    Archedemus, 112

Decelian War:
  destruction of property, 86
Delian League, 34
Democritus, 132, 141, 144, 151
dēmos:
  in Tyrtaeus, 9; in Athens, 11, 13,
    18, 116, 118, 159; in control, 27;
    in Mitylene, 35; Plato's *dēmos*, 76;
    Aristophanes' *dēmos*, 83;
    appreciation of Nicias, 102, 105
Demosthenes:
  on extortion, 34
dexios, 121, 123
Dikaiarchus:
  on Pythagoras, 133
dikaiosynē:
  in the Melian dialogue, 101
Dionysia, rural:
  in Aristophanes, 83
Dionysius, of Syracuse, 181

Euboea:
  special relationship with Athens, 37
Eunomia, 43 ff.
Euripides:
  his *Philoctetes*, 28 ff; on the peasant,
    46, 86 ff; a pupil of Anaxagoras,
    141 ff.; his career as a playwright,
    150
euthynai, 30, 31, 114
  of Paches, 114; of Laches, 118
Evandrus:
  Lysias' speech, 111

fame (see *kleos*)
forensic inflation, 110
Forms:
  in Plato, 135, 177, 191

games, 8, 21 ff.
generals:
  the generalship, 31; trial after
    Arginousai, 31; enriching
    themselves, 35; *apragmōn* generals,
    116 ff.; ambition of, 129
geras, 4 ff.

Hades, 7
Heraclides of Pontus:
  on Pythagoras, 133 ff.
Heraclitus, 138 ff., 145, 147
Herms:
  hermokopid inscriptions, 36;
    mutilation of, 66, 68
hēsychia, 42
  of Sparta, 45 ff., 100; in Plato's
    Charmides, 58 ff., 71, 73; in Eur.
    Antiope, 167; *hēsychos*, the moderate
    man, 169
hetaeria (political clubs), 56, 74
Hippias the sophist, 40, 48
Hippocrates:
  in Plato's Protagoras, 61, 74
Hippolytus, 52 ff., 71, 113
  and the games, 59
Homer:
  on fame and honour, 2 ff.
homosexuality, 72 ff.
  in the *palaestra*, 57; in Ar. *Wasps*,
    63 ff.; in Ar. *Knights*, 122
hybris, 43 ff., 71
  not in Euripides' peasant, 90

internationalism, 40, 42, 47 ff., 188

Kleinias, decree of, 35
kleos (fame), 2 ff.
  in the *Philoctetes*, 28, 49
kompsos, 54

Laches:
  as Labes in Ar. *Wasps*, 31, 32,
    118 ff.; as an *apragmōn* general,
    117, 129, 190
lalein (to chatter), 121, 123, 167

Lamachus:
  as a poor general, 30, 116; his
    euthynai, 116; as an *apragmōn*
    general, 117, 190
lamprotēs (prominence in the city), 13 ff.
  of Alcibiades, 14
Last Judgement:
  in Plato's *Gorgias*, 176
law courts, 103 ff.
  pay for jury service, 107; power of
    juries, 107; popular character, 129;
    survival in, 165
leisure:
  its first appearance, in Eur. *Ion*, 159;
    as a requirement of the
    Contemplative Life, 160
Leogoras, father of Andocides, 69
liturgies, 17
  in Lysias' speeches, 103 ff.; of
    Nicias, 104 ff.; threshold for
    service, 110
Lycon, 66
Lysistratus, 66, 69

Marathon:
  Marathōnomachoi, 98
meirakia (striplings), 121
Melian Dialogue, 101
Meno:
  on *aretē*, 60
metics, 126 ff.
  in law, 128; metic sycophants, 128 n.
    56
'middle class':
  in Eur. *Suppliant Women*, 88 ff.
mikropsychos, 126 ff., 190
Miltiades, 115
Mitylene:
  siege of, 35
mochthos:
  extreme form of *ponos*, 11

Nicias, 67, 69, 161, 190
  his wealth, 37; peace of, 99; his
    apragmosynē, 99 ff., 129; his
    philotimia, 102; spending on
    liturgies, 104; and sycophants, 105
nomos:
  and *physis*, 48, 161

Odysseus, 2, 3, 7, 186
  in Eur. *Philoctetes*, 28 ff.; 49; as
    chrēstos, 29; in Plato, 29

Oionias:
  property of, 36
oligarchs, oligarchy, 49
Phrynichus, 67; in 411 BC, 70, 79,
    97; constitutions, 92 ff.
olive stump:
  Lysias' speech in the case of, 107

Paches:
  his death, 31, 114
palaestra:
  in Plato's *Charmides*, 56; in Ar.
    Clouds, 122
Panathenaea, Great, 103
Paphlagonian, *see* Aristophanes
Parmenides, 140, 147
patriotism:
  and Anaxagoras, 145
peasant (*see autourgos*)
Pericles:
  his Funeral Speech, 13, 26; attitude
    to *apragmones*, 27, 40, 172; tyranny
    of Athens, 33; second speech, 38;
    marriage laws, 48; and his sons,
    60; in Alcibiades' speech, 99;
    discussion with Protagoras, 107; in
    tears at Aspasia's trial, 107; pupil
    of Anaxagoras, 141
Phaiax, 121
philotimia:
  in Eur. *Phoenician Women*, 15, 16; in
    Thucydides, 15; of Nicias, 102,
    190; in performance of liturgies,
    111; as 'seeking after' *timē*, 136 n.
    16
Phormisius:
  proposal of, 93
Phrynichus, 33, 67
physikē:
  in Ar. *Clouds*, 151 ff.
physis:
  and *Nomos*, 48, 161; and *aretē*, 165,
    171
Pindar:
  on success in the games, 21 ff.; on
    defeat, 24; friendship with
    Melesias, 42; Pindaric values, 46;
    on homosexuality, 73
Pittacus, 131
Plato:
  his *Gorgias* and *Republic*, 16, 40;
    definition of *apragmosynē*, 19; three
    modes of life, 20, 130; on

Odysseus, 29; imperfect societies, 45; spartan values in, 46; his *dēmos*, 77; his *dēmos* as the 'middle class', 88; transcendental reality in his *Republic*, 177 ff.; political career, 179 ff.
Pnyx:
  in Ar. *Acharnians*, 78; size of, 79
polis, 21
  in Tyrtaeus, 8
pollution:
  legal aspect, 107
polypragmosynē, 117, 118
  in Ar. *Wealth*, 87
ponos (striving):
  in Democritus, 11; of the Athenians, 38, 45
population:
  of Athens, 79 ff.
Potidaea:
  funeral inscription at, 10
pragmata (civic and legal affairs), 19, 41, 87, 108, 122
  of Crito, 112; in Ar. *Knights*, 113; in his *Wasps*, 118; and metics, 127
probouloi, 70, 102
  Sophocles as *proboulos*, 151
Protagoras, 40, 48, 74
psychē, 7
Pythagoras, 133 ff., 164
Pythagoristai, 137, 152 ff.

semnos (proud):
  Hippolytus as, 53; in Ar. *Wasps*, 63
Seven Wise Men, 132, 191
Socrates:
  as *apragmōn*, 40, 183 ff., in Plato's *Charmides*, 56 ff., 73; and Crito, in Xenophon, 112; his *aporia*, 135; on Anaxagoras, 143; in Ar. *Clouds*, 151 ff.; in Old Comedy, 152; and Ion, 160; his *sophrosynē*, 173; in Plato's *Gorgias*, 173 ff.
Solon, 96
sophoi:
  in *Hippolytus*, 55
sophrosynē, 15
  of Hippolytus, 52 ff., 71; in Plato's *Charmides*, 57 ff.; in Critias' writings, 62; of Lysias' cripple, 77; of Euripides' *autourgos*, 90 ff.; in Eur. *Antiope*, 166; and Socrates, 174

Sparta:
  eunomia in, 44; Spartan values, 46, 58, 71 ff.; tastes in Ar. *Wasps*, 63; ravages Attica, 83; embassy to, 97; peace with, in 421 BC, 99
sycophant:
  Phrynichus as, 67; in Aristophanes, 83 ff.; in the *Wealth*, 87; and Nicias, 105; earliest reference, 105; in Ar. *Birds*, 105; in Ar. *Knights*, 114; metic sycophants, 128 n. 56; and generals, 129
synēgoroi, 122 ff.
  in Ar. *Banqueters*, 119.
Syracuse:
  debate in, 124

tamiai (stewards):
  as treasurers, 17, 35, 114, 129
Thales, 131, 142, 145
Thargelia, 103
Themistocles, 24
Theognis, 42
theōria, 134 ff., 142, 145, 163
Theseus:
  in the *Hippolytus*, 53; unification of Attica, 78
Thirty, the:
  seize the metics, 128; and Plato, 180
Thucydides son of Melesias, 40
  and his sons, 60; ostracism, 70; in Aristophanes, 121
timē:
  in Homer, 1 ff.; in Tyrtaeus, 9; of the Athenians, 13, 38; in Aristotle, 18; in Plato, 20; in Xenophon, 20; in Eur. *Philoctetes*, 29; of Nicias, 102; as reward for lavish spending, 104; in performing liturgies, 104; contrasted with 'minding one's own business', 109; in Plato's *Republic*, 177
Timon, 125
tolma (daring), 11, 12, 13
  its impious aspect, 14; of the Athenians, 45
tyranny, 11, 17
  in Ar. *Wasps*, 64 ff., 74; in Eur. *Ion*, 159
Tyrtaeus, 8, 9

Xenophon:
  on *timē*, 20; his Charmides, 58 ff.; on the *kalokagathos*, 76

youth culture, 101

BETHANY
COLLEGE
LIBRARY

DISCARD